PITTSBURGH

Documentary
History
of
American
Cities

Series
Editors:
Tamara K.
Hareven
and
Stephan
Thernstrom

PITTSBURGH

Edited
by
Roy
Lubove

New Viewpoints

A Division of Franklin Watts
New York / London / 1976

For Becky and Seth

Library of Congress Cataloging in Publication Data

Main entry under title:

Pittsburgh.

  (Documentary history of American cities)
  Includes bibliographical references and index.
  1. Pittsburgh—History—Addresses, essays, lectures.
2. Labor and laboring classes—Pittsburgh—History—
Addresses, essays, lectures. I. Lubove, Roy.
F159.P6P49   974.8'86   76–3119
ISBN 0–531–05384–9
ISBN 0–531–05590–6 pbk.

New Viewpoints
A Division of Franklin Watts
730 Fifth Avenue
New York, New York 10019

CONTENTS

PROLOGUE

Introduction

Incorporated as a city in 1816 (population: 6,000), Pittsburgh was a vital link to the South and West. Following the Revolutionary War, and well into the nineteenth century, the community had prospered as a servicing center for emigrants heading toward the Old Northwest or Mississippi Valley. Nestled at the juncture of the Allegheny and Monongahela rivers, which formed the Ohio at the point of the original fortified settlement, Pittsburgh was located at the threshold of a journey that enabled goods and persons to reach New Orleans by continuous water routes. The Allegheny River extended the community's trade area to northern Pennsylvania; the Monongahela tapped northern Virginia and the southern edge of Pennsylvania.

Resources as well as location promoted the economic growth of Pittsburgh. For at least a generation after 1800, the town's economy was diversified—a benign balance of agriculture, commerce, and manufacturing. Surrounding forests and farms supplied the timber and foodstuffs to outfit emigrants and provide for the resident population. The abundant timber resources encouraged development of a thriving boatbuilding industry—flatboats, keelboats—which carried persons and goods down the Ohio and Mississippi rivers. The forests also supplied fuel for the nascent iron and glass industries (until su-

perseded by coking coal, with which the region was well endowed).

When F. A. Michaux visited Pittsburgh in 1802, he observed a largely rural scene and an economy dominated by commerce. At the time of G. W. Ogden's arrival in 1821, manufacturing enterprise was conspicuous enough to conjure up the image of "Birmingham of America." By 1826, the value of manufactured goods in Pittsburgh was estimated at more than $2.5 million, iron production representing more than $1.5 million of the total. The favorable conjunction of resources and markets eventually led to the disruption of a once-balanced regional economy. The "City of Iron" had emerged by the 1860s. By the end of the Civil War, Pittsburgh produced about 40 percent of the nation's iron.

Pittsburgh was also a center of the glass industry. From its small beginnings in the 1790s, when General James O'Hara and Major Isaac Craig established a glassworks along the Monongahela, glass production grew in total value to more than $1 million by the 1830s. Other major industries in the antebellum era included textiles, leather goods, boat building, and wood products.

The Scotch-Irish who conquered the western Pennsylvania frontier took their work and religion seriously. The Presbyterian Calvinist influence remained strong, despite extensive Irish and German immigration to the area (immigrants comprised about one-third of a total population of 50,000 in 1860). The predominantly northern European flavor of the community was increasingly modified by the arrival of southern and eastern European immigrants in the 1880s and 1890s. The 1880s also marked the beginnings of a dramatic expansion of the steel industry. Thus the 1880s witnessed significant changes in the ethnic and economic life of Pittsburgh. The following chapters, focusing on the late-nineteenth and twentieth centuries, describe the evolution of the nation's leading industrial city in its maturity and the labor force upon which it depended.

Pittsburgh in 1802
by François André Michaux

Pittsburgh is situated at the conflux of the rivers Monongahela and Alleghany, the uniting of which forms the Ohio. The even soil upon which it is built is not more than forty or fifty acres in extent. It is in the form of an angle, the three sides of which are enclosed either by the bed of the two rivers or by stupendous mountains. The houses are principally brick, they are computed to be about four hundred, most of which are built upon the Monongahela; that side is considered the most commercial part of the town. As a great number of the houses are separated from each other by large spaces, the whole surface of the angle is completely taken up. On the summit of the angle the French built Fort Duquesne, which is now entirely destroyed, and nothing more is seen than the vestige of the ditches that surrounded it. This spot affords the most pleasing view, produced by the perspective of the rivers, overshadowed with forests, and especially the Ohio, which flows in a straight line, and, to appearance, loses itself in space.

The air is very salubrious at Pittsburgh and its environs; intermittent fevers are unknown there, although so common in the southern states, neither are they tormented in the summer with mosquitoes. A person may subsist there for one-third of what he pays at Philadelphia. Two printing-offices have been long established there, and, for the amusement of the curious, each publish a newspaper weekly.

Pittsburgh has been long considered by the Americans as the key to the western country. Thence the federal forces were marched against the Indians who opposed the former settlement of the Americans in Kentucky, and on the banks of the Ohio. However, now the Indian nations are repulsed to considerable distance, and reduced to the impossibility of hurting the most remote settlers in the interior of the states; besides, the western country has acquired a great mass of population, insomuch that there is nothing now at Pittsburgh but a feeble garrison, barracked in a fort belonging to the town, on the banks of the river Allighany.

However, though this town has lost its importance as a military post, it has acquired a still greater one in respect to commerce. It serves as a staple for the different sorts of merchandise that Philadelphia and Baltimore send, in the beginning of spring and autumn, for supplying the states of Ohio, Kentucky, and the settlement of Natches.

Travels to the west of the Alleghany Mountains, in the states of Ohio, Kentucky, and Tennessea, and back to Charleston, by the upper Carolines. . . . (London, 1805), pp. 58–64.

The conveyance of merchandise from Philadelphia to Pittsburgh is made in large covered waggons, drawn by four horses two a-breast. The price of carrying goods varies according to the season; but in general it does not exceed six piastres the quintal. They reckon it to be three hundred miles from Philadelphia to Pittsburgh, and the carriers generally make it a journey of from twenty to twenty-four days. The price of conveyance would not be so high as it really is, were it not that the waggons frequently return empty; notwithstanding they sometimes bring back, on their return to Philadelphia or Baltimore, fur skins that come from Illinois or Ginseng, which is very common in that part of Pennsylvania.

Pittsburgh is not only the staple of the Philadelphia and Baltimore trade with the western country, but of the numerous settlements that are formed upon the Monongahela and Alleghany. The territorial produce of that part of the country finds an easy and advantageous conveyance by the Ohio and Mississippi. Corn, hams and dried pork are the principal articles sent to New Orleans, whence they are re-exported into the Carribbees. They also export for the consumption of Louisiana, bar-iron, coarse linen, bottles manufactured at Pittsburgh, whiskey, and salt butter. A great part of these provisions come from Redstone, a small commercial town, situated upon the Monongahela, about fifty miles beyond Pittsburgh. All these advantages joined together have, within these ten years, increased tenfold the population and price of articles in the town, and contribute to its improvements, which daily grow more and more rapid.

The major part of the merchants settled at Pittsburgh, or in the environs, are the partners, or else the factors, belonging to the houses at Philadelphia. Their brokers at New Orleans sell, as much as they can, for ready money; or rather, take in exchange cottons, indigo, raw sugar, the produce of Low Louisiana, which they send off by sea to the houses at Philadelphia and Baltimore, and thus cover their first advances. The bargemen return thus by sea to Philadelphia or Baltimore, whence they go by land to Pittsburgh and the environs, where the major part of them generally reside. Although the passage from New Orleans to one of these two ports is twenty or thirty days, and that they have to take a route by land of three hundred miles to return to Pittsburgh, they prefer this way, being not so difficult as the return by land from New Orleans to Pittsburgh, this last distance being fourteen or fifteen hundred miles. However, when the barges are only destined for Limeston, in Kentucky, or for Cincinnati, in the state of Ohio, the bargemen return by land, and by that means take a route of four or five hundred miles.

The navigation of the Ohio and Mississippi is so much improved of late that they can tell almost to a certainty the distance from Pittsburgh to New Orleans, which they compute to be two thousand one hundred miles. The barges in the spring season usually take forty or fifty days to make the passage, which two or three persons in a *pirogue*[1] make in five and-twenty days.

What many, perhaps, are ignorant of in Europe is, that they build large vessels on the Ohio, and at the town of Pittsburgh. One of the principal ship yards is upon the Monongahela, about two hundred fathoms beyond the last houses in the town. The timber they make use of is the white oak, or *quercus alba;* the red oak, or *quercus rubra;* the black oak, or *quercus tinctoria;* a kind of nut tree, or *juglans minima;* the Virginia cherry-tree, or *cerasus Virginia;* and a kind of pine, which they use for masting, as well as for the sides of the vessels which require a slighter wood. The whole of this timber being near at hand, the expense of building is not so great as in the ports of the Atlantic states. The cordage is manufactured at Redstone and Lexinton, where there are two extensive rope-walks, which also supply ships with rigging that are built at Marietta and Louisville. On my journey to Pittsburgh in the month of July 1802, there was a three-mast vessel[2] of two hundred and fifty tons, and a smaller one of ninety, which was on the point of being finished. These ships were to go, in the spring following, to New Orleans, loaded with the produce of the country, after having made a passage of two thousand two hundred miles before they got into the ocean.

Pittsburgh in 1821
by George W. Ogden

I have now arrived at Pittsburgh, a pleasant and flourishing town, where the Alleghany from the north and the Monongahela from the

1. An Indian boat.
2. I have been informed since my return, that this ship, named the *Pittsburgh*, was arrived at Philadelphia.

east, unite and form the beautiful river Ohio, one of the handsomest streams of water in the known world, as allowed by all travellers, both European and American. Pittsburgh stands on the point of land formed by the junction of these two rivers, and is very eligibly situated in a commercial point of view, and bids fair to become the emporium of almost the whole western world. It carries on a very considerable trade with Philadelphia, Baltimore and New-Orleans; and likewise some little with New-York, by way of the Hudson and Mohawk rivers, the lakes, &c. In this place, there is scarcely any mechanical art but what is carried on to the greatest perfection. Ship building was, until lately, but owing to the great labor and hazard of getting them down the river, it is not so much attended to now as formerly. Boat building is, however, carried on to a very considerable extent at Pittsburgh;—very few of the boats, built here, ever return up the river again so far as this place; and there is of course, a constant demand for new ones. Movers from every part of the eastern sea-board, generally take this place in their way to the west. Emigrants from all the New-England States, and from many other adjacent States, are constantly arriving here, and stand in need of boats, of various sizes, to transport their goods and their families. A great many foreign emigrants arrive, particularly those of them who are mechanics, from New-York, Philadelphia, and Baltimore, to Pittsburgh;—and, from the latter place, some of them pass on to the manufacturing establishments further west. But the most considerable manufactories of this place, are those in Iron-works, which are carried on in all their various branches and to a great extent. Furnaces and forges are numerous, and the production of them supply a large portion of the western country with the very useful and necessary articles of Ironmongry. This place may, with propriety, be called the Birmingham of America. Here we may see the surprising progress that our country is making in every branch of mechanism, both as it respects invention and workmanship. Indeed the body politic of this country are in a most healthful state, and we are rapidly approaching to a vigorous and glorious manhood.—In our progress however, we have to guard against two evils—an inordinate attachment to money, and too little regard for sound morals and solid learning. But if the one is kept within proper bounds,

Letters from the West; comprising a tour through the western Country and a residence of two summers in the states of Ohio and Kentucky: originally written in letters to a brother. (New Bedford, Mass.: Melcher and Rogers, 1823), pp. 6—11.

and the other is supported and encouraged throughout the nation, we must become a happy, virtuous and prosperous people.

As many have conceived this place to be in the State of Ohio, I would advertise you that it is within the limits of Pennsylvania; and at the head of the navigation of the Ohio river. The town, viewed from the confluence of the two rivers, presents rather a disagreeable and unfavourable appearance; but from other situations, it wears quite a different aspect. Its scite is low and very level; and during the rise of the rivers, the waters flow for a considerable distance into the streets. The town is large; the greater part of its buildings are of brick, and of a large size. The streets cross each other at right angles, but are very disagreeable, on account of their being so narrow. Owing to almost the exclusive use of coal, the town presents rather an unpleasant and smoky appearance; and even the complexions of the people are affected by this cause.

The business of Pittsburgh is great, and it is generally believed to be increasing.—This town is engaged in trade with the whole western world, and may be considered the metropolis of this vast extent of country. It procures its foreign goods, in a great measure, from Philadelphia and Baltimore; which goods are brought in wagons across the Alleghany mountains. The distance from these places, to Pittsburgh, is about three hundred and fifty miles; and the price of carrying goods thither is from four to six dollars for one hundred weight. Owing to the expense of getting foreign goods to this place, they are necessarily very high. In this town, is a Fort which constitutes a link in that great chain of Forts, which extend from Cincinnati to the Lakes, and even beyond them. Fort Pitt occupies the scite of the old Ford Du Quesne; but even the former is now in ruins. There is another Fort about two miles up the Alleghany; and here some soldiers are stationed: its situation is very retired and pleasant, but as no attention is taken to preserve it from decay, it is very rapidly deteriorating. Opposite to Pittsburgh, on the Alleghany, is a considerable village, and preparations are making to erect a bridge across this part of the river. There is likewise a considerable number of buildings on the opposite side of the Monongahela. Back of these buildings there are ridges of very high hills, which contain inexhaustible coal mines; and, in fact, it exists in abundance in ten or twelve of the surrounding counties. The strata of coal is about six inches thick, and appears unlimited in its duration through the mountain. The usual price of this article, at Pittsburgh, is from 4 to 6 cents per bushel.

On the back part of Pittsburgh is a rise of ground, called Grant's Hill. Here the curious traveller, who wishes to view the city in every way in which it can be presented, may have a prospect from the top of the hill; and its appearance is, from this situation, much in its favour.

About nine miles up the Monongahela, is a place called Braddock's Fields. It is much celebrated as being the place where the General of that name was defeated in 1755. It will here be recollected that the immortal Washington, then a youth, acted as volunteer aid to General Braddock, and by his intrepidity, and matchless military skill, preserved the English troops from an almost total defeat and destruction. Many vestiges of this bloody engagement are still visible. Here too our young Washington, it is said, had two horses shot under him, and four balls through his coat.[1]

As to the character and manners of the people of Pittsburgh, they are peculiar to themselves. They are extremely jealous of the yankees, and from the character of some of them, ungenerously and uncharitably, condemn the whole. This is more or less the case throughout the western and southern states. But so far as I became acquainted with them, I found them humane and hospitable, kind and attentive to strangers; and for so large a place, very free from those demoralizing vices which are to be found in other cities.

I REMAIN YOUR
AFFECTIONATE BROTHER.

Pittsburgh in 1866
by James Parton

It is chiefly at Pittsburg that the products of the Pennsylvania hills and mountains are converted into wealth and distributed over the world. The wonder is, not that Pittsburg is an assemblage of flour-

---

1. I would wish to advertise my readers that, although I may have occasion, in the subsequent pages of this work, to mention military men, and military exploits, yet I am far from wishing to aid or abet in a cause which (I am sorry to say) has already too many advocates. But we think the time is rapidly approaching when the prediction will be fulfilled "that the nations will learn war no more?" When the idols set up by ambitious man will be worshipped no more.

ishing towns of 230,000 inhabitants, but that, placed at such a com-
manding point, it is not the *most* flourishing and the *most* populous
city in America.

This it might have been, perhaps, if the site had been ten level
square miles, instead of two, and those two surrounded by steep hills
four hundred feet high, and by rivers a third of a mile wide. It is curiously hemmed in,—that small triangle of low land upon which the
city was originally built. A stranger walking about the streets on a
summer afternoon is haunted by the idea that a terrific thunder-
storm is hanging over the place. Every street appears to end in a
huge black cloud, and there is everywhere the ominous darkness
that creeps over the scene when a storm is approaching. When the
traveller has satisfied himself that the black clouds are only the
smoke-covered hills that rise from each of the three rivers, still he
catches himself occasionally quickening his steps, so as to get back
to his umbrella before the storm bursts. During our first stroll about
the town, some years ago, we remained under this delusion for half
an hour; and only recovered from it after observing that the old ladies who sat knitting about the markets never stirred to get their
small stock of small wares under cover.

Pittsburg announces its peculiar character from afar off. Those
who approach it in the night see before them, first of all, a black hill,
in the side of which are six round flaming fires, in a row, like six
fiery eyes. Then other black hills loom dimly up, with other rows of
fires half-way up their sides; and there are similar fiery dots in the
gloom as far as the eye can reach. This is wonderfully picturesque,
and excites the curiosity of the traveller to the highest point. He
thinks that Pittsburg must be at work behind those fires, naked to
the waist, with hairy chest and brawny arms, doing tremendous
things with molten iron, or forging huge masses white-hot, amid
showers of sparks. No such thing. These rows of fires, of which
scores can be counted from a favorable point, are merely the
chimneys of coke-ovens, quietly doing their duty during the night,
unattended. That duty is to convert the waste coal-dust at the
mouths of the mines, where it has been accumulating for a century,
into serviceable coke. These are almost the only fires about Pittsburgh that are always burning, night and day, Sundays and holidays. . . .

"Pittsburg," *Atlantic Monthly,* 21 (January, 1868), pp. 17–18, 21–22, 25–26, 28,
30–32, 34–35.

There is one evening scene in Pittsburg which no visitor should miss. Owing to the abruptness of the hill behind the town, there is a street along the edge of a bluff, from which you can look directly down upon all that part of the city which lies low, near the level of the rivers. On the evening of this dark day, we were conducted to the edge of the abyss, and looked over the iron railing upon the most striking spectacle we ever beheld. The entire space lying between the hills was filled with blackest smoke, from out of which the hidden chimneys sent forth tongues of flame, while from the depths of the abyss came up the noise of hundreds of steam-hammers. There would be moments when no flames were visible; but soon the wind would force the smoky curtains aside, and the whole black expanse would be dimly lighted with dull wreaths of fire. It is an unprofitable business, view-hunting; but if any one would enjoy a spectacle as striking as Niagara, he may do so by simply walking up a long hill to Cliff Street in Pittsburg, and looking over into—hell with the lid taken off.

Such is the kind of day of which Pittsburg boasts. The first feeling of the stranger is one of compassion for the people who are compelled to live in such an atmosphere. When hard pressed, a son of Pittsburg will not deny that the smoke *has* its inconveniences. He admits that it does prevent some inconsiderate people from living there, who, but for the prejudice against smoke in which they have been educated, would become residents of the place. He insists, however, that the smoke of bituminous coal kills malaria, and saves the eyesight. The smoke, he informs you, is a perpetual public sun-shade and color-subduer. There is no glare in Pittsburg, except from fire and red-hot iron; no object meets the eye that demands much of that organ, and consequently diseases of the eyes are remarkably rare. It is interesting to hear a Pittsburgher discourse on this subject; and it much relieves the mind of a visitor to be told, and to have the assertion proved, that the smoke, so far from being an evil, is a blessing. The really pernicious atmospheres, say the Pittsburg philosophers, convey to man no intimation of the poison with which they are laden, and we inhale death while enjoying every breath we draw; but this smoke is an evil only to the imagination, and it destroys every property of the atmosphere which is hostile to life. In proof of which the traveller is referred to the tables of mortality, which show that Pittsburg is the most favorable city in the world to longevity. All this is comforting to the benevolent mind. Still more so is the fact, that the fashion of living a few miles out of the smoke is beginning to prevail among the people of Pittsburg. Villages are springing up as far as twenty miles away, to which the business men repair, when, in consequence of having inhaled the smoke all day, they feel able to bear the common country atmosphere through the night. It is probable that, in coming years, the smoky abyss of Pittsburg will be occupied only by factories and "works," and that nearly the whole population will deny themselves the privilege of living in the smoke. With three rivers and half a dozen railroads, the people have ready means of access to places of almost unequalled beauty and pleasantness.

The "great fact" of Pittsburg is coal. Iron and copper can better afford to come to coal to be melted, than send for coal to come and melt them. All those hills that frown down upon Pittsburg, and those that rise from the rivers back of Pittsburg, have a stratum of coal in them from four to twelve feet thick. This stratum is about three hundred feet above the water's edge, and about one hundred feet from the average summit of the hills. It is simply a great cake of coal, lying flat in the hills, uniform, compact, as though this region had once been a lake of liquid coal, upon which mountains had been tossed, pressing it solid. The higher the hill rises above the coal cake, the better is the coal. It has had more pressure, is more compact and less impure. What this black stuff really is that we have named coal, how it got laid away so evenly in these hills, why the stratum of coal is always found just so high up the hill, why coal is found here and not everywhere, and why it is better here than elsewhere, are questions to which answers have often been attempted. We have read some of these answers, and remain up to the present moment perfectly ignorant of the whole matter. The mere quantity of coal in this region is sufficiently staggering. All the foundries and ironworks on earth could find ample room in this region, at the edge of a navigable stream, and have a coal mine at their back doors. The coal that is used in the foundries along the Monongahela is only shovelled twice. Deep in the heart of the hill that rises behind the foundry, the coal is mined, and thrown upon a car, by which it is conveyed to the mouth of the mine, and thence down an inclined plane to the foundry, where it is dumped at the door of the furnace which is to consume it. And, it seems, there are fifteen thousand square miles of "this sort of thing." The "great Pittsburg coal seam," as it is called, which consists of bituminous coal only, is put down in the books as covering eight and a half million of acres. . . .

There are in the congregation of towns which the outside world knows only by the name of Pittsburg, five hundred manufactories and "works." Fifty of these are glass-works, in which one half of all our glass-ware is made, and which employ three thousand persons. . . .

Oil Creek is a branch of the Alleghany River, and empties into it one hundred miles above Pittsburg. Pittsburg is, consequently, the great petroleum mart of the world. It is but five years ago that this material became important; and yet there were received at Pittsburg during the year 1866 more than sixteen hundred thousand barrels of it. The Alleghany River is one of the swiftest of navigable streams; but there is never a moment when its surface at Pittsburg is not streaked with petroleum. It would not require remarkable talent in an inhabitant of this place to "set the river on fire." The crude oil is floated down this impetuous river in the slightest-built barges,—mere oblong boxes made of common boards,—into which the oil is poured as into an enormous trough. Petroleum is lighter than water, and would float very well without being boxed in; only it would be difficult to keep each proprietor's lot separate. It needs but a slight accident to knock a hole in one of these thin barges. When such an accident has occurred, the fact is revealed by the rising of the petroleum in the barge; and the vessel gets fuller and fuller, until it overflows. In a few minutes, the petroleum lies all spread out upon the swift river, making its way toward Pittsburg, while the barge is filled with water and sunk. . . .

Down by the swift and turbid Alleghany, close to the river, as all the great foundries are, we discovered with difficulty, on a very dark morning, the celebrated Fort Pitt Foundry, where twenty-five hundred of the great guns were cast that blew the late "So-Called" out of water. In this establishment may be seen the sublime of the mechanic arts. Only here, on the continent of America, have there ever been cast those monsters of artillery which are called by the ridiculous diminutive of "the twenty-inch gun." A twenty-inch gun is one of those corpulent pieces of ordnance that we see mounted on forts about our harbors, which weigh sixty tons, cost fifty thousand dollars each, and send a ball of a thousand pounds three miles. To be exact, the ball weighs one thousand and eighty pounds, and it costs one hundred and sixty-five dollars. To discharge a twenty-inch gun, loaded with one of these balls, requires one hundred and twenty-five pounds of powder, worth forty cents a pound; so that every time one of the guns is fired it costs a hundred and ninety-five dollars, without counting the wear and tear of the gun and its carriage, and the pay of the men. . . .

From seeing one of these enormous guns cast, the visitor at Pittsburg may go, if he chooses, to an establishment where they make tacks so minute that it takes a thousand of them to weigh an ounce. We went thither, having long had an imbecile curiosity to know how nails and tacks are made. How startling the contrast between the slow movements, and tranquil, gloomy vastness of the cannon foundry, and the animation of the great rattling, roaring, crowded nail-works of Chess, Smyth, & Co., all glaring and flashing with light, with many tall chimneys pouring out black smoke and red blaze into the December evening! Noise? There is only one place in this world as noisy as a large nail-factory in full operation, and that is under the sheet at Niagara Falls. How should it be otherwise, when the factory is making many thousand nails a minute, and when every single nail, spike, brad, and tack is *cut* from a strip of cold iron, and headed by a blow upon cold iron? We saw one machine there pouring out shoemakers' brads at the rate of three thousand a minute, and it required the attendance of only one boy. They came rattling down a tin gutter as fast as meal comes from a mill. But to see this wonderful machine astonishes the stranger less than to see a girl in the packing-room who *weighs* and packs two thousand papers of tacks in nine hours. . . .

The crowning glory of Pittsburg is the "American Iron-Works" of Messrs. Jones and Laughlins. This establishment, which employs twenty-five hundred men, which has a coal mine at its back door and an iron mine on Lake Superior, which makes almost every large and difficult iron thing the country requires, which usually has "on hand" seven hundred thousand dollars' worth of finished work, is such a world of wonder that this whole magazine would not contain an adequate account of it. Here are machines ponderous and exact; here are a thousand ingenuities; here is the net result of all that man has done in iron masses during the whole period of his residence upon earth. What should there be here, too, but a specimen of what man can *undo* in iron, in the form of a great heap of rusty twisted rails from Georgia, so completely spoiled by General Sherman's troops that there was nothing to be done with them but sell them for old iron! It is at these works alone that iron is subjected to the new process called "cold-rolling." Every reader has stood by a steam-engine, and admired the perfect roundness, the silvery brightness, and the irresistible thrust of the piston-rod. A piston-rod is usually made thus. A huge, jagged mass of white-hot iron, just on the point of fusion, is fished out of the furnace, and is swung across the foundry to the rolling-machine, which rolls it into a long round roll, a little thicker than the piston-rod is to be. It is next put into a turning lathe, where it is turned and polished to the size required,—a long and costly process. That is the usual way. The "cold-rolling" process is this: the long round roll, a little thicker than the piston-rod is to be, is passed *cold* through another rolling-mill of immense power, and simply *squeezed* to the size required. Advantages: 1. The process is quicker and cheaper; 2. The rod issues from the mill as brilliantly polished as the plate on a queen's table; 3. The pressure so increases the density of the iron, that the rod is about two and a half times stronger than those made in the old way. Iron plates and bars are made on the same principle.

We cannot linger among these wondrous "works" of the strong men of Pittsburg. The men themselves have claims upon our notice.

The masters of Pittsburg are mostly of the Scotch-Irish race, Presbyterians, keen and steady in the prosecution of their affairs, indifferent to pleasure, singularly devoid of the usual vanities and ostentations, proud to possess a solid and spacious factory, and to live in an insignificant house. There are no men of leisure in the town. Mr. George H. Thurston, President of the Pacific and Atlantic Telegraph Company,—who, from having superintended the preparation of the Directory for many years, as well as from his very great interest in all that relates to the prosperity and glory of Pittsburg, knows the town better than any other person that ever lived in it—assured us positively that there were not, in all the region which we call Pittsburg, three persons out of business who were physically capable of conducting business. The old men never think of "retiring," nor is there anything for them to retire to. The family tie being powerful in this race, the great firms are usually composed of near relatives, and generally survive the generation that founded them. Thus, the Fort Pitt Foundry, founded in 1803, has cast cannon for every war in which the United States has been engaged, and is now conducted by the worthy and talented nephews of the Charles Knap who made the establishment what it is. In the American Iron-Works, we find six partners, namely, the two chiefs, Messrs. Jones and Laughlin, two sons of one of these chiefs, and two brothers of the other,—a nice family party. Hence, there are few hired clerks in Pittsburg. These mighty "works" are managed with the minimum of expense. The visitor generally finds "the old man" bustling about the "works" in his cap and fustian jacket; while perhaps his eldest son is keeping the books, a son-in-law or nephew is making up the wages accounts, and a younger son is in the warehouse.

The conservative elements here are powerful, as they are in all communities in which families *endure*. Until very recently, in Pittsburg, it would have boded ill for a man to build a handsome house a few miles out of the smoke; and to this day it is said that a Pittsburg man of business who should publish a poem would find his "paper" doubted at the bank. "A good man, sir, but not practical." These excellent and strenuous men accuse themselves vehemently of a want of public spirit, and it is evident the charge is just. For the last few years, business has rushed in upon them like a torrent; and all their force having been expended in doing this business, they now awake to the fact, that a GREAT CITY is upon their hands, to be consolidated, organized, paved, policed, parked, purified, and adorned. They now feel that some of those iron kings, those great men of glass, oil, coal, salt, and clay, must leave business to their sons and nephews, and take hold of Pittsburg. . . .

Nothing in the life of Pittsburg is more striking to a visitor than the completeness of the cessation from labor at the close of the week. The Scotch-Irish race are strict Sabbatarians, and nothing goes on in Pittsburg on Sundays which it is possible to stop. Of all those five hundred tall chimneys, there will not usually be more than two that smoke on Sundays. During the week the town gets under such a headway of industry, that it takes all Saturday afternoon for it to come to a stand. The regular work ceases at noon, but the afternoon is spent in paying wages, grinding tools, cleaning up, making repairs, and getting ready for a fair start on Monday morning. By seven in the evening, the principal streets of Pittsburg are densely filled with washed men. They stroll about; they stand conversing in groups; they gather, in thick semicircles, about every shop-window that has a picture in it, or any bright or curious object; especially do they haunt the news-stands, which provide a free picture-gallery for them of Illustrated News, Comic Monthlies, and Funny Fellows. The men are so numerous, that the whole width of some of the streets is filled with them; and there is not a woman to be seen! Not a single petticoat among thousands of other coats! Yet no crowd could be more orderly and quiet. These men, after a week of intense monotony,—gazing at dull objects and doing the same dull act ten hours a day,—how hungry they seemed for some brightness to flash into their lives! How we longed to usher them all into some gorgeous scene, and give them a banquet of splendors! Mere brilliancy of color and light is transport, we should suppose, to a man who has been making nails or digging coal from Monday morning until Saturday noon.

PART ONE

The Age of Steel, 1880-1914

Introduction

Pittsburgh in the 1880s, portrayed by Willard Glazier in the opening selection, was already a symbol of American industrial growth. Like most other visitors, Glazier responded to the scene with a combination of awe and revulsion. The topography and fiery industrial panorama were spectacular; production statistics evoked pride in the nation's technological achievements. Yet the visitor to Pittsburgh could not avoid a sense of unease and even despair. It was not only the miasma of smoke that enveloped the community or the environmental desecration. It seemed that the price of progress was exorbitant. The civic and social amenities that made urban life tolerable elsewhere did not exist in Pittsburgh, because work had become an end in itself. The mill-master lived for work, and the laborer worked merely to survive.

If Glazier had returned to Pittsburgh three decades later (around 1910), he would have discovered several significant changes. Steel had superseded iron as the master industry. The labor force was now comprised of immigrants from southern and eastern Europe. The regional economy and community system had reached a mature state. The Aliquippa works of Jones and Laughlin, and the Midland works of Crucible Steel (1909–1911) ended the era of major plant construction. Mining had produced a scattering of desolate villages and wreaked havoc upon the landscape through acid discharge and alterations in topography. The mill towns, strung along the Monongahela, Allegheny, and Ohio rivers, were dominated by one or more large plants, whose transportation and water needs resulted in a usurpation of the flatlands. The region's population, dispersed by employment opportunity and the hilly terrain, was further fragmented by ethnic allegiances following the influx of unskilled southern and eastern European labor after 1880.

If steel was the master industry, it was also the center of resistance to unionization. The violent, protracted Homestead strike of 1892 forced the nation to confront basic issues of capital-labor relations: the right to organize; the nature of contract in a corporate economy; limits to the traditional prerogatives of capital. The issues, from the perspective of labor, are explored in the article by T. V. Powderly.

The next two selections are studies of the immigrant wage earner by Margaret Byington and Peter Roberts. The research was done in connection with the monumental Pittsburgh Survey, conducted in 1907–1908, and published in six summary volumes, 1909–1914. The most detailed study ever made of an American community, the Survey was distinctive for its emphasis upon the effects of the industrial process upon human life—the family and home, health and welfare. The problem, as described by Byington, was that "the mill, which demands strong, cheap labor, concerns itself but little whether that labor is provided with living conditions that will maintain its efficiency or secure the efficiency of the next generation."

The recurrent theme of the Pittsburgh Survey was the disparity between the industrial and civic sectors of the community. The industrial sector was a model of centralized, rational management and coordination; the civic sector was fragmented, archaic, neglected. The consequences were vividly delineated by Edward T. Devine, secretary of the New York Charity Organization Society. No community had ever possessed such a surplus, yet "never before has a great community applied what it had so meagerly to the rational purposes of human life." The work ethic had run amuck: Sunday work, night work, the twelve-hour shift in the mills. The life of the district was keyed to the twelve-hour day: "foremen and superintendents, and ultimately directors and financiers, are subject to its law." But for all the work, wages were too low to maintain a "normal standard of living," especially for women. Immigrant workers and families coped by "abnormally low expenditures for food and shelter, and inadequate provision for sickness, accident and death."

The Pittsburgh way of life and work destroyed the family in the most literal way: "by the demands of the day's work, and by the very demonstrable and material method of typhoid fever, and industrial accidents, both preventable. . . ." Civic agencies were too inept to prevent or salvage; the community suffered from "archaic social institutions such as the aldermanic court, the ward school district, the family garbage disposal, and the unregenerate charitable institution, still surviving after the conditions to which they were adapted have disappeared."

The black migrant occupied the least enviable niche on the socioeconomic ladder. His condition is described in the selection by Abraham Epstein. Although, as Epstein points out, the black was motivated by a quest for economic and social opportunity, he was kept in the "ranks of unskilled labor and in the field of personal service." If effective labor organization was blocked by conflicts between native American and immigrant, skilled and unskilled, it suffered also from discrimination against the black worker.

The selection by John Fitch describes the working conditions that prevailed in the absence of unionism. It formed part of his authoritative study of the steel industry for the Pittsburgh Survey. In essence, labor relations in early-twentieth-century Pittsburgh were governed by a combination of managerial autocracy tempered by paternalism. Margaret Byington, in her Homestead study, captured the irony of the situation: "Mr. Carnegie has given a library, Mr. Schwab a manual training school, and Mr. Frick a charming little park in the centre of the hill section." The population appreciated these gifts, to be sure, "but they resent the philanthropy which provides opportunities for intellectual and social advancement while it withholds conditions which make it possible to take advantage of them."

Pittsburgh in the early twentieth century can be understood best as a cohesive industrial organism. Economic disciplines and imperatives, first and foremost, shaped every aspect of the region's life. All the "progressiveness and invention," Paul Kellogg complained on behalf of the Survey, had gone into the creation of the economic en-

terprise and very little into "Pittsburgh, the community." The demand for unskilled labor had directed the immigrant flow and determined the nature of the population mix. Criteria of profit maximization led to the repression of unionism and insured that wage rates and working conditions would remain the exclusive prerogative of management. Economic criteria shaped the physical environment as well. Heavy industry usurped the flatlands along the rivers, which became polluted with waste discharges; and industrial locational criteria determined the regional system of mill and mining town.

The authors of the Pittsburgh Survey had stressed that Pittsburgh was representative rather than unique in the extent to which a dynamic, progressive industrial sector contrasted sharply with inept civic and social institutions. In the latter case, authority was as diffuse and fragmented as the topography and the political jurisdictions of the region. This problem was rooted in the nature of the nineteenth-century urbanization process and social system. It was difficult to achieve consensus on civic and social values, on the purpose of government, in a context of ethnic, class, and religious heterogeneity. The most pervasive shared commitment among Americans was to increase the material wealth of the society. In effect, an ideology of material growth, of the primacy of business enterprise, filled the ideological vacuum. It was difficult to define the role of government, its welfare and service functions in particular, where no cohesive sense of community existed. Equally important, the government role had to be adapted to reality of a corporate power structure.

In the early twentieth century, the business, managerial, and professional elite of Pittsburgh were becoming concerned about the flaccid social machinery of the community. Inefficient and fragmented civic or governmental institutions were, to be sure, a source of corporate authority. But this advantage was compromised by the fact that they could not cope with the serious environmental and social problems that plagued the community and affected business enterprise adversely. Reform was increasingly defined as a business proposition. As the selection by John Holdsworth suggests, the "smoke nuisance" was viewed as the "greatest hindrance to Pittsburgh's economic progress." It may have been the symbol of material prosperity, but it was also a symbol of waste, a source of dirt and deterioration, and a hindrance to the community's image as an attractive place to settle. Business leaders also viewed health and housing reform as a business proposition. The Pittsburgh Chamber of Commerce was notably active in confronting health and housing problems. Disease and bad health adversely affected the efficiency and productivity of the labor force. Each life unnecessarily lost represented a sales deterrent. The consequences of long neglect are delineated in the selection by F. Elisabeth Crowell.

The development of recreational agencies is surveyed in the selection by Beulah Kennard. She complains that in work-oriented Pittsburgh, children "literally did not know how to play." Reformers, on the other hand, were distressed by adult play in the form of commercialized vice, a significant business enterprise in an economy dominated by industrial towns containing "an unnatural proportion of single men." The selection by James Forbes examines this phenomenon.

These and other reform movements represented no threat to business hegemony. Business and professional leaders, not the mass of the population, initiated or financed many of the reform movements and institutions. The objective was a degree of environmental and social melioration that would enhance the efficiency of the worker, but which did not significantly challenge the distribution of wealth and power in the community. Although reform rhetoric was often phrased in terms of expanded democracy or restoring government to the people, the real issue was class power. A great deal of power remained vested in the wards of Pittsburgh in the early twentieth century, and political "reform" was synonymous with the aspiration to transfer authority from the wards to a city government dominated by the managerial and professional elite.

The authors of the Pittsburgh Survey had cited the business corporation as the model for the centralized efficiency and coordination that was needed in the civic sector. As it happened, the reform crusade of the early twentieth century can be interpreted as a quest for bureaucratic rationalization of the community's civic and political institutions, enhancing the decision-making authority of the business and professional elite. In the process, governmental authority would be increased, but limited to largely negative, regulatory functions.

The Great Furnace of America
by Willard Glazier

By all means make your first approach to Pittsburg in the night time, and you will behold a spectacle which has not a parallel on this continent. Darkness gives the city and its surroundings a picturesqueness which they wholly lack by daylight. It lies low down in a hollow of encompassing hills, gleaming with a thousand points of light, which are reflected from the rivers, whose waters glimmer, it may be, in the faint moonlight, and catch and reflect the shadows as well. Around the city's edge, and on the sides of the hills which encircle it like a gloomy amphitheatre, their outlines rising dark against the sky, through numberless apertures, fiery lights stream forth, looking angrily and fiercely up toward the heavens, while over all these settles a heavy pall of smoke. It is as though one had reached the outer edge of the infernal regions, and saw before him the great furnace of Pandemonium with all the lids lifted. The scene is so strange and weird that it will live in the memory forever. One pictures, as he beholds it, the tortured spirits writhing in agony, their sinewy limbs convulsed, and the very air oppressive with pain and rage.

But the scene is illusive. This is the domain of Vulcan, not of Pluto. Here, in this gigantic workshop, in the midst of the materials of his labor, the god of fire, having left his ancient home on Olympus, and established himself in this newer world, stretches himself beside his forge, and sleeps the peaceful sleep which is the reward of honest industry. Right at his doorway are mountains of coal to keep a perpetual fire upon his altar; within the reach of his outstretched grasp are rivers of coal oil; and a little further away great stores of iron for him to forge and weld, and shape into a thousand forms; and at his feet is the shining river, an impetuous Mercury, ever ready to do his bidding. Grecian mythology never conceived of an abode so fitting for the son of Zeus as that which he has selected for himself on this western hemisphere. And his ancient tasks were child's play compared with the mighty ones he has undertaken today.

Peculiarities of American Cities (Philadelphia: Hubbard Brothers, 1883), pp. 332–342.

Failing a night approach, the traveler should reach the Iron City on a dismal day in autumn, when the air is heavy with moisture, and the very atmosphere looks dark. All romance has disappeared. In this nineteenth century the gods of mythology find no place in daylight. There is only a very busy city shrouded in gloom. The buildings, whatever their original material and color, are smoked to a uniform, dirty drab; the smoke sinks, and mingling with the moisture in the air, becomes of a consistency which may almost be felt as well as seen. Under a drab sky a drab twilight hangs over the town, and the gas-lights, which are left burning at mid-day, shine out of the murkiness with a dull, reddish glare. Then is Pittsburg herself. Such days as these are her especial boast, and in their frequency and dismalness, in all the world she has no rival.

In truth, Pittsburg is a smoky, dismal city, at her best. At her worst, nothing darker, dingier or more dispiriting can be imagined. The city is in the heart of the soft coal region; and the smoke from her dwellings, stores, factories, foundries and steamboats, uniting, settles in a cloud over the narrow valley in which she is built, until the very sun looks coppery through the sooty haze. According to a circular of the Pittsburg Board of Trade, about twenty per cent., or one-fifth, of all the coal used in the factories and dwellings of the city escapes into the air in the form of smoke, being the finer and lighter particles of carbon of the coal, which, set free by fire, escapes unconsumed with the gases. The consequences of several thousand bushels of coal in the air at one and the same time may be imagined. But her inhabitants do not seem to mind it; and the doctors hold that this smoke, from the carbon, sulphur and iodine contained in it, is highly favorable to lung and cutaneous diseases, and is the sure death of malaria and its attendant fevers. And certainly, whatever the cause may be, Pittsburg is one of the healthiest cities in the United States. Her inhabitants are all too busy to reflect upon the inconvenience or uncomeliness of this smoke. Work is the object of life with them. It occupies them from morning until night, from the cradle to the grave, only on Sundays, when, for the most part, the furnaces are idle, and the forges are silent. For Pittsburg, settled by Irish-Scotch Presbyterians, is a great Sunday-keeping day. Save on this day her business men do not stop for rest or recreation, nor do they "retire" from business. They die with the harness on, and die, perhaps, all the sooner for having worn it so continuously and so long.

Pittsburg is not a beautiful city. That stands to reason, with the heavy pall of smoke which constantly overhangs her. But she lacks beauty in other respects. She is substantially and compactly built, and contains some handsome edifices; but she lacks the architectural magnificence of some of her sister cities; while her suburbs present all that is unsightly and forbidding in appearance, the original beauties of nature having been ruthlessly sacrificed to utility.

Pittsburg is situated in western Pennsylvania, in a narrow valley at the confluence of the Allegheny and Monongahela rivers, and at the head of the Ohio, and is surrounded by hills rising to the height of four or five hundred feet. These hills once possessed rounded outlines, with sufficient exceptional abruptness to lend them variety and picturesqueness. But they have been leveled down, cut into, sliced off, and ruthlessly marred and mutilated, until not a trace of their original outlines remain. Great black coal cars crawl up and down their sides, and plunge into unexpected and mysterious openings, their sudden disappearance lending, even in daylight, an air of mystery and diablerie to the region. Railroad tracks gridiron the ground everywhere, debris of all sorts lies in heaps, and is scattered over the earth, and huts and hovels are perched here and there, in every available spot. There is no verdure—nothing but mud and coal, the one yellow the other black. And on the edge of the city are the unpicturesque outlines of factories and foundries, their tall chimneys belching forth columns of inky blackness, which roll and whirl in fantastic shapes, and finally lose themselves in the general murkiness above.

The tranquil Monongahela comes up from the south, alive with barges and tug boats; while the swifter current of the Allegheny bears from the oil regions, at the north, slight-built barges with their freights of crude petroleum. Oil is not infrequently poured upon the troubled waters, when one of these barges sinks, and its freight, liberated from the open tanks, refuses to sink with it, and spreads itself out on the surface of the stream.

The oil fever was sorely felt in Pittsburg, and it was a form of malaria against which the smoke-laden atmosphere was no protection. During the early years of the great oil speculation the city was in a perpetual state of excitement. Men talked oil upon the streets, in the cars and counting-houses, and no doubt thought of oil in church. Wells and barrels of petroleum, and shares of oil stock were the things most often mentioned. And though that was nearly twenty years ago, and the oil speculation has settled into a safe and legitimate pursuit, Pittsburg is still the greatest oil mart in the world. By the means of Oil Creek and the Allegheny, the oil which is to supply all markets is first shipped to Pittsburg, passes through the refineries there, and is then exported.

The Ohio River makes its beginning here, and in all but the season of low water the wharves of the city are lined with boats, barges and tugs, destined for every mentionable point on the Ohio and Mississippi rivers. The Ohio River is here, as all along its course, an uncertain and capricious stream. Sometimes, in spring or early summer, it creeps up its banks and looks menacingly at the city. At other times it seems to become weary of bearing the boats, heavily laden with merchandise, to their destined ports, and so takes a nap, as it were. The last time we beheld this water-course its bed was lying nearly bare and dry, while a small, sluggish creek, a few feet, or at most, a few yards wide, crept along the bottom, small barges being towed down stream by horses, which waded in the water. The giant was resting.

The public buildings and churches of Pittsburg are, some of them, of fine appearance, while the Mercantile Library is an institution to be proud of, being both handsome and spacious, and containing a fine library and well-supplied reading room. The city boasts of universities, colleges, hospitals, and asylums, and the Convent of the Sisters of Mercy is the oldest house of the order in America. There are also two theatres, an Opera House, an Academy of Music, and several public halls.

But it is not any of these which has made the city what she is, or to which she will point with the greatest pride. The crowning glory of Pittsburg is her monster iron and glass works. One-half the glass produced in all the United States comes from Pittsburg. This important business was first established here in 1787, by Albert Gallatin, and it has increased since then to giant proportions. Probably, not less than one hundred millions of bottles and vials are annually produced here, besides large quantities of window glass. The best wine bottles in America are made here, though they are inferior to those of French manufacture. A great number of flint-glass works turn out the best flint glass produced in the country.

In addition to these glass works—which, though they employ thousands of workmen, represent but a fraction of the city's industries—there are rolling mills, foundries, potteries, oil refineries, and factories of machinery. All these works are rendered possible by the coal which abounds in measureless quantities in the immediate neighborhood of the city. All the hills which rise from the river back of Pittsburg have a thick stratum of bituminous coal running through them, which can be mined without shafts, or any of the usual accessories of mining. All that is to be done is to shovel the coal out of the hill-side, convey it in cars or by means of an inclined plane to the factory or foundry door, and dump it, ready for use. In fact, these hills are but immense coal cellars, ready filled for the convenience of the Pittsburg manufacturers. True, in shoveling the coal out of the hill-side, the excavations finally become galleries, running one, two or three miles directly into the earth. But there is neither ascent nor descent; no lowering of miners or mules in great buckets down a deep and narrow shaft, no elevating of coal through the same means. It is all like a great cellar, divided into rooms, the ceilings supported by arches of the coal itself. Each miner works a separate room, and when the room is finished, and that part of the mine exhausted the arches are knocked away, pillars of large upright logs substituted, the coal removed, and the hill left to settle gradually down, until the logs are crushed and flattened.

The "Great Pittsburg Coal Seam" is from four to twelve feet thick, about three hundred feet above the water's edge, and about one hundred feet from the average summit of the hills. It is bituminous coal which has been pressed solid by the great mass of earth above it. The thicker the mass and the greater the pressure, the better the coal. It has been estimated as covering eight and a half millions of acres, and that it would take the entire product of the gold mines of California for one thousand years to buy this one seam. When we remember the numerous other coal mines, anthracite as well as bituminous, found within the limits of the State of Pennsylvania, we are fairly stupefied in trying to comprehend the mineral wealth of that State.

The coal mined in the rooms in these long galleries is conveyed in a mule-drawn car to the mouth of the gallery, and if to be used by the foundries at the foot of the hill, is simply sent to its destination down an inclined plane. Probably not less than ten thousand men are employed in these coal mines in and near Pittsburg, adding a population not far from fifty thousand to that region. Pittsburg herself consumes one-third of the coal produced, and a large proportion of the rest is shipped down the Ohio and Mississippi rivers, some of it as far as New Orleans.

The monster iron works of Pittsburg consume large quantities of this coal, and it is the abundance and convenience of the latter material which have made the former possible. No other city begins to compare with Pittsburg in the number and variety of her factories. Down by the banks of the swift-flowing Allegheny most of the great foundries are to be discovered. The Fort Pitt Works are on a gigantic scale. Here are cast those monsters of artillery known as the twenty-inch gun. Not by any means a gun twenty inches in length, but a gun with a bore twenty inches in diameter, so accurate that it does not vary one-hundredth part of an inch from the true line in its whole length. The ball for this gun weighs one thousand and eighty pounds, and costs a hundred and sixty-five dollars. The gun itself weighs sixty tons, and costs fifty thousand dollars, and yet one of these giants is cast every day, and the operation is performed with the utmost composure and absence of confusion. The mould is an enormous structure of iron and sand, weighing forty tons, and to adjust this properly is the most difficult and delicate work in the foundry. When it is all ready, three streams of molten iron, from as many furnaces, flow through curved troughs and pour their fiery cataracts into the mould. These streams run for twenty minutes, and then, the mould being full, the furnaces from which they flow are closed with a piece of clay. Left to itself, the gun would be thirty days in cooling, but this process is expedited to eighteen days, by means of cold water constantly flowing in and out of the bore. While it is still hot, the great gun is lifted out of the pit, swung across the foundry to the turning shop, the end shaven off, the outside turned smooth, and the inside hollowed out, with an almost miraculous precision. The weight of the gun is thus reduced twenty tons.

The American Iron Works employ two thousand five hundred hands, and cover seventeen acres. They have a coal mine at their back door, and an iron mine on Lake Superior, and they make any and every difficult iron thing the country requires. Nothing is too ponderous, nothing too delicate and exact, to be produced. The nail works of the city are well worth seeing. In them a thousand nails a minute are manufactured, each nail being headed by a blow on cold iron. The noise arising from this work can only be described as deafening. In one nail factory two hundred different kinds of nails,

tacks and brads are manufactured. The productions of these different factories and foundries amount in the aggregate to an almost incredible number and value, and embrace everything made of iron
which can be used by man.

George F. Thurston, writing of Pittsburg, says, it has "thirty-
five miles of factories in daily operation, twisted up into a compact
tangle; all belching forth smoke; all glowing with fire; all swarming
with workmen; all echoing with the clank of machinery." Actual
measurement shows that there are, in the limits of what is known as
Pittsburg, nearly thirty-five miles of manufactories of iron, of steel,
of cotton, and of brass alone, not mentioning manufactories of
other materials. In a distance of thirty-five and one-half miles
of streets, there are four hundred and seventy-eight manufactories
of iron, steel, cotton, brass, oil, glass, copper and wood, occupying
less than four hundred feet each; for a measurement of the ground
shows that these factories are so contiguous in their positions upon
the various streets of the city, that if placed in a continuous row,
they would reach thirty-five miles, and each factory have less than
the average front stated. This is "manufacturing Pittsburg." In four
years the sale and consumption of pig iron alone was one-fourth the
whole immense production of the United States; and through the
Ohio and Mississippi rivers and their tributaries, its people control
the shipment of goods, without breaking bulk, over twelve thousand
miles of water transportation, and are thus enabled to deliver the
products of their thrift in nearly four hundred counties in the territory of fifteen States. There is no city of its size in the country which
has so large a banking capital as Pittsburg. The bank of Pittsburg, it is said, is the only bank in the Union that never suspended
specie payments.

Pittsburg is a city of workers. From the proprietors of these extensive works, down to the youngest apprentices, all are busy; and
perhaps the higher up in the scale the harder the work and the
greater the worry. A man who carries upon his shoulders the responsibility of an establishment whose business amounts to millions of
dollars in a year; who must oversee all departments of labor; accurately adjust the buying of the crude materials and the scale of
wages on the one hand, with the price of the manufactured article on
the other, so that the profit shall be on the right side; and who at the
same time shall keep himself posted as to all which bears any rela-

tion to his business, has no time for leisure or social pleasures, and must even stint his hours of necessary rest.

The Homestead Strike
by T. V. Powderly

The principle involved in the Homestead trouble is the same as that by which the founders of this republic were governed in rebelling against the British government. To have accepted decisions, decrees, and laws without question, and without a voice in their making, would have stamped the colonists as slaves. To accept, without inquiring the why or wherefore, such terms and wages as the Carnegie Steel Company saw fit to offer would stamp the brand of inferiority upon the workmen of Homestead. Independence is worth as much to the workingman as it can be to the employer. The right to sell his labor in the highest market is as dear to the workman as the right of the manufacturer to sell the product of that labor can possibly be to the latter. It is folly to assert that the workman has no right to a voice in determining what the minimum rate of compensation shall be. If the manufacturer is permitted to invade the market place and undersell competitors a reduction in the wages of his employees must inevitably follow. It was to protect the manufacturer as well as the workman that the Amalgamated Association insisted on a minimum rate of pay. The fixing of that rate imposed no hardship on the manufacturer; it gave no competitor the advantage over him, for the majority of mills were operated under the Amalgamated scale, and this of itself fixed a rate below which manufacturers would not sell. The minimum rate was therefore as advantageous to the manufacturer as to the workman in the steel trade. The question at issue between the Carnegie Steel Company and the steel workers does not so much concern the price as the right to a voice in fixing that price.

Individual employers no longer exist; the day no longer dawns on the employer taking his place in the shop among the men. When

"The Homestead Strike: A Knight of Labor's View," *North American Review,* 155 (September, 1892), pp. 370–375.

that condition of workshop life existed employer and employee experienced a feeling of lasting friendship for each other; the interests of each were faithfully guarded by the other. Now the employer of them may be three thousand miles away from the workshop; he may be a part of a syndicate or corporation which deals with the employees through a special agent or superintendent, whose desire to secure the confidence and good will of the corporation may cause him to create friction in order to demonstrate that he is vigilant in looking after the interests of those to whom he looks for favors. The corporation, composed of many men, is an association of capital which delegates its authority to an agent whose duty it is to deal with the workmen and make terms with them. The Amalgamated Association, and all other bodies of organized workmen, stand in the same relation to the men as the corporation does to the capitalists whose money is invested. One invests money, that is, his capital; the other invests his labor, which to him is not only his capital but his all. That the workman should have the same right to be heard through his legitimately appointed agent, the officer of the labor organization, that the corporation has to be heard through the superintendent or agent, is but equity. This is the bone of contention at Homestead, and in fact everywhere else where a labor organization attempts to guard the rights of its members.

Every law, every right, every concession which the workingmen now enjoy has come to them through the labor organization. Philanthropists have spoken honeyed words for the laboring man, but he has always been forced to knock, and knock hard, with his organization in order to take what equity would have accorded him without a struggle if greed had not entered its protest. Equality of rights is what the workmen are contesting for, and because of its immense wealth the Carnegie Steel Company denies that right. It is argued that this trouble is between the employer and the employed and that no other has the right to interfere. That is a doubtful position to take. In a store, in a small shop, or where but a few persons are interested, a strike or lockout may be said to affect only those directly engaged in it, but in the present instance the case presents a different aspect to the thoughtful person. If the great steel plant were not just where it is the town of Homestead would not be the flourishing place that it is. The establishment of that plant attracted workmen to the spot; they built homes, raised their families, and invested every dollar of their earnings there. Business men, professional men, and clergymen followed them, and a community of well-behaved, respectable citizens surrounds the steel works. The workmen by their labor made the steel works prosperous and great; on the other hand they made Homestead what it is. The men depend for their support on steady work, and the community back of them depends on their steady employment. Three parties are interested in this struggle, the Carnegie Steel Company, the employees of that concern, and the community. By community I mean the whole people. Other towns have grown up as Homestead grew, by the labor of workmen, and each one is to a certain extent interested in the welfare of the other. The articles manufactured in one place are sold in another, and a mutuality of interests exists to-day which did not, and could not, exist years ago when men required but few things to serve the everyday needs of life. The manager of the Carnegie Steel Company in asserting that he has the right to turn the makers of a prosperous town out of employment and out of the town,—for that naturally follows,—stands upon treacherous ground, for the makers of towns have equally as good a right to be heard as have the investors of money. If we go to a higher law than that of the land, the moral law, there will be no disputing the assertion that flesh and blood should receive more consideration than dollars and cents.

The Carnegie Steel Company and like concerns owe their prosperity to the protective laws of the United States. These laws were passed in the interest of labor. During discussion on the tariff laws it was never advanced as a reason why they should be passed, that capital would be protected,—the argument was always that labor would be protected. The workman has not been protected from foreign competition by the government. He has had to fight the battle for himself through the labor organization. Not only has he had to fight against foreign competition, largely attracted by our delusive tariff laws, but he has had to wage war with the employer for a share of that protection which his government decreed by law that he should have. Our government has enacted protective legislation in the interest of labor, if we read congressional speeches aright, but it quiescently allows the manufacturer to absorb the bulk of protection, and then throws its armies around the establishment at the slightest provocation when the workmen ask for what their government admitted that they had a right to enjoy.

What would have averted this trouble at Homestead, is asked? Industries which are protected by tariff laws should be open to inspection by government officials. When the managers of such concerns seek to absorb all of the protection the government should interfere on behalf of the workingmen. If we must have protection let us see to it that it protects the man who works.

At the hands of the law-making power of State and nation the Knights of Labor demand "the enactment of laws providing for arbitration between employers and employed, and to enforce the decision of the arbitrators." It should be a law in every State that in disputed cases the employer should be obliged to select two arbitrators and the employees two, these four to select the fifth; this arbitration commission to have access to all books, papers, and facts bearing on the question at issue from both sides. It goes without saying that the commission should be made up of reasonable, well-disposed men, and that publicity would not be given to such information as they might become possessed of.

An established board of arbitration, appointed by a governor or other authority, is simply no board of arbitration at all, for the reason that the workmen would have no voice in its selection, and the other side, having all the money and influence, would be tempted to "fix" such a board preparatory to engaging in a controversy with workingmen. For either side to refuse to appoint its arbitrators should be held to be cause for their appointment by the Governor of the State. No strike or lockout should be entered upon before the decision of the board of arbitrators. Provisions for appeal from the decision of the arbitrators should be made in order to prevent intimidation or money from influencing the board.

In no case should the introduction of an armed force, such as the Pinkerton detective agency arms and equips, be tolerated. The system which makes one man a millionaire makes tramps and paupers of thousands. The thousands go down to the brothels and slums, where they sprout the germs of anarchy and stand ready for any deed of desperation. The millionaire becomes more arrogant and unreasonable as his millions accumulate. Victimizing and blacklisting are the concomitants of the rule of industrial establishments by our millionaire "lords of industry," and these measures furnish recruits for the army of greed when organized labor enters its protest against such acts of injustice as has made tramps of other men under like circumstances. The employer who is satisfied with a reasonable profit will not fear to intrust his case to such a board of arbitrators as I have described. The employer who refuses arbitration fears for the justice of his case. He who would acquire legitimately need not fear investigation; he who would steal must do it in the dark in order to be successful.

Those who harshly criticise the workmen of Homestead should put themselves in the place of these workmen for a few brief moments of thought. Picture the skill required to turn out faultless work, the loss of eyesight which follows a few years of toil before the seething furnace, the devotion to duty which must be shown in order to succeed. Then step outside of the mill and witness the erection of a high fence and its armament. Consider what it means and that it is being erected before a threat has been made or a disagreement considered among the possibilities. Think of the stigma which the erection of that fence casts on the man who works, the builder of the town; and then reflect that it is being built to serve as a prison-pen for those who must work so cheap that they will not be able to erect homes or maintain families in respectability. Ponder over the fact that when cheap men take the places of well-paid men, they do not buy carpets, organs, pianos, decent, respectable furniture or raiment, and that the makers of these articles elsewhere will be thrown out of employment, and that other manufacturers will be driven to bankruptcy because of a falling off in the demand for their product. Then read what Mr. Carnegie said six short years ago in speaking of the question of employing non-union, cheap men:

"To expect that one dependent upon his daily wage for the necessaries of life will stand by peaceably and see a man employed in his stead is to expect much. This poor man may have a wife and children dependent upon his labor. Whether medicine for a sick child, or even nourishing food for a delicate wife, is procurable, depends upon his steady employment. In all but a very few departments of labor it is unnecessary, and, I think, improper, to subject men to such an ordeal. In the case of railways and a few other employments it is, of course, essential for the public wants that no interruption occur, and in such case substitutes must be employed; but the employer of labor will find it much more to his interest, wherever possible, to allow his works to remain idle and await the result of a dispute than to employ the class of men that can be induced to take the place of other men who have stopped work. Neither the best men, nor the best men as workers, are thus to be obtained. There is an unwritten law among the best workmen: 'Thou shalt not take they neighbor's job.' No wise employer will lightly lose his old employees. Length of service counts for much in many ways. Calling upon strange men should be the last resort."

The introduction of an armed body of men at the outset was an
indication that some man would be expected to "take his neighbor's
job," and at once. The arbitrament of the sword was the first
thought with the Carnegie Steel Company. The laws of Pennsylvania were disregarded in arming citizens of other States and assigning them to duty at Homestead. In that awful spectacle to which the
eyes of humanity turned on the 6th of July could be seen the final
abolition of brute force in the settlement of strikes and lockouts.
What the law will not do for men they must do themselves, and
by the light of the blazing guns at Homestead it was written that arbitration must take the place of "Pinkertonism."

Family and Milltown: Homestead
by Margaret F. Byington

The effect of our industrial system on family life is in most cities
rendered indefinite by the pressure of complicating factors. In a
small community, however, which is dependent on a single industry,
the factors of the problem are simplified, and therefore the relation
is clearer and the conclusions more obvious.

For this reason I venture to offer a very simple and concrete description of the type of family and the conditions of family life in a
steel-mill town, believing that it may serve at least as an illustration
for this afternoon's discussion. The facts offered are the result of a
six months' investigation as to the cost of living in Homestead, and
are, I believe, true in the main of the steel towns of the Pittsburg
district.

When, in 1881, Klomans started to build a small steel mill, he located it in a little village seven miles from Pittsburg, appropriately
enough called Homestead. The industrial development of the city
had seemed too remote to affect it. But the mill became a part of
the United States Steel Corporation and is now the largest steel
plant in the world, while the village, which has grown with it, now
has a population of about 25,000. Not only did the initial impulse

"The Family in a Typical Mill Town," *American Journal of Sociology,* 14
(March, 1909), pp. 648–659.

of the town's growth come from the mill, but throughout the industry has, for two reasons, definitely determined Homestead's development—one, that, as there is no other considerable industry in
the town, the men are dependent for occupation on the mill; the
other, that, since the strike of 1892, when the power of the Amalgamated Association came to an end, the corporation has, by its decisions as to wage and hours of labor, determined practically without
hindrance the conditions under which the men live. Because of these
two factors we may consider that the social and economic institutions of Homestead are typical of those which a powerful organized industry is likely to develop, a statement limited by the fact
that conditions would be very different in a community where the
prevailing industry was of another type.

The conditions to be discussed are simplified by a marked homo-
geneity of type in the families of Homestead, in itself a result of the
industrial situation. Marked distinctions of wealth are totally absent. Two groups do indeed exist with different standards and no
common interests; the Slavs and the English-speaking workers; but
this distinction is of race rather than of wealth. The Slavs are usually day laborers, while the majority of the English-speaking men
are skilled or semi-skilled, but in spite of these differences both
groups are wage-earners. Even the number of professional men is
not as large as in a town farther from a city, while the owners of the
mill—the stockholders—scattered throughout the country, knowing
their property only as a source of dividends, have no part or interest
in the town's development. As a result, this town of working-men
has not the lack of mutual understanding resulting from great differences in wealth and standards, but neither has it the stimulus
which comes from the presence and leadership of men of education
with leisure. What the town offers is what the working-people have
created for themselves under the conditions imposed by the industry.

From the standpoint of family development probably the most
significant fact about the town is that it offers work for men only.
Aside from the steel mill and one machine shop, the only work in
the town is in providing for the needs of the workers, with but
chance work for women. As Pittsburg is a 45 minutes' car ride distant the work it offers is not easily available. The wage in the mill,
moreover, though by no means abundant, is fair and steady. The

laborer earns at a minimum rate of 16½ cents an hour, $1.65 a day, while the semi-skilled or skilled workers earn from $2.00 to $4.00, and occasionally as high as $5.00 or $6.00 a day.

The work is in addition regular. From the panic of 1893 to that of 1907, I am told that the mill was not shut down for a single day. The day men, therefore, who are paid their full wage unless the mill actually closes, have a steady income the year round, except in periods of industrial depression. The tonnage men, who are paid according to output, do feel even a temporary cutting-down of orders, but as they are the ones who ordinarily receive the highest pay, the occasional lessening of their wage is not so disastrous.

As a result of these factors the town in general seems to have adopted the position that the women should stay at home, and, by good housekeeping, make the money go a long way, rather than go out to work and earn a little more. This is shown concretely in the incomes of those families whose budgets were secured for the investigation. Among the English-speaking people the husbands and sons contributed 92.8 per cent. among the native whites—practically the entire income, and 94.6 per cent. among the English-speaking Europeans. There was no income from the work of women unless one would so consider what was received from lodgers. This constituted 4.6 per cent. of the total income in the European group, and 2.7 per cent. among the native white.

We find, then, that as a result of the kind of work offered the town consists of a group of working-men's families; the man is the breadwinner. The effect of the industrial situation is further shown in the work of the children. The girls show little more tendency than their mothers to become wage-earners. In the thirty-eight English-speaking families there were fifteen girls over fourteen, not one of whom was at work. Four were in the high school, the remainder at home helping with the housework. While this is probably an extreme figure, as some girls in Homestead do go to work in stores or offices, it reveals a general feeling in the town that "the home is woman's sphere." While one may question whether from the standpoint of the present the additional income from the girl's wages would not add more to the comfort of the family than her help in the household, from my acquaintance with housekeepers of all sorts I am convinced that good home training is invaluable in preparing girls for their own homes later. The four champion housekeepers of my acquaintance were the daughters of Pennsylvania farmers. One of them, when I expressed my surprise at how much more she had accomplished than others with the same income, gave as the reason for her success, that girls who had been in stores or factories had no training in management and were quite helpless when they faced a housekeeper's problems.

The situation as far as the sons are concerned is somewhat different. Fifteen of the seventeen boys over fourteen were at work contributing among the whites 9.6 per cent., and among the English-speaking Europeans 18 per cent. of the total income. Though the other two boys were still in the high school we find on the whole a marked absence of interest in academic or even in technical training for these sons. As the daughters, instead of learning trades are at home becoming practical housekeepers under their mothers' direction, so the sons following in their fathers' footsteps, are entering directly into the practical work of the mill to get there the training for future success. That the best-paid men in the mill, such as rollers and heaters, have secured their jobs through experience in the mill rather than through outside training has doubtless much to do with this attitude. Through the influence of the fathers, the boys sometimes get what are known as pencil jobs, or other places where the work is light and apparently more gentlemanly, but where the pay is seldom so high. Usually, however, they begin in the regular boy's work, as messenger-boys in the yards, or door-openers. Though these give no special training for the future, as the line of promotion is usually open a boy has a good chance of becoming at least a semi-skilled workman on fair pay. Promotion is sometimes unduly rapid, however, so that boys of 16 or 18 are earning men's wages, with little chance of further promotion. One woman who regretted that her son had not learned a trade, said that he was unwilling to go through a long apprenticeship when in the mill he could earn good pay at once. In spite of the fact that because of long hours and the danger from accident, women often wish their sons to take some other work, they usually do go into the mill. This means that as for some years they stay at home and contribute their share to the family income, they create a period of economic prosperity. The family is at this time often able to make extra provision for the future, as, for instance, buying a house.

We find then that the industry has by its very nature helped to create a type of family life. But in those factors where it has a choice open to it such as wages and hours, has it by its decisions, made possible for these families a genuine home life, a carrying out of their ideals for themselves? For two facts must be considered in any study of standards of living, one the limitations or opportunities from without, which the family cannot affect, the other those family ideals, sometimes limited in themselves, sometimes hampered by outside forces, which are continually struggling toward realization. How far are Homestead's ideals realizable on the pay the mill offers?

It is impossible in the limits of this discussion to consider at all in detail the results of the budget investigation in Homestead. Figures are too complicated without elaborate explanations. A few facts however may be used in this general discussion.

To my mind, the fundamental fact brought out by the investigation was, that, the question of expenditure is always one of choices, of doing without some things in order to get others. This may seem axiomatic, but when applied to a wage of less than $12 a week it expresses pretty much the whole problem of life. Do we find that in order to carry out ideals of home life, such as having an attractive house, making due provision for the future, or buying a house, certain absolute essentials must be gone without? Any study of the budgets of families receiving less than $12 a week, or even those earning from $12 to $15 demonstrates very clearly that this is the case. As the unskilled men, who earn $10 and $12 a week, compose 58 per cent. of the employees, it is worth while to consider briefly the problem which this large percentage of Homestead's population is facing.

To indicate its extent I will give the average expenses of 40 families with an income of less than $12 a week. Of a total expenditure of $530 a year, $241 goes for food; $103 for rent; $50 for clothing; $18 for furniture; $25 for fuel; $11 for medical care, and $13 for tobacco and liquor. In addition an average of $38 was spent annually for insurance, leaving but $31 a year for amusements of all sorts, church expenses, savings, and the necessary sundries. Now obviously no one of these items is adequate, to say nothing of being superabundant. Rent, for example, at $2 a week provides only a two-room tenement, and that without water or toilet in the house. Food at $4.64 a week would mean for a family of five, only 20 cents a day, two cents a day less than Prof. Chittenden estimates as absolutely essential in New York. Fifty dollars for clothing is just one-half the sum Mr. Chapin gives as necessary. The tobacco and liquor item which is especially large among the Slavs, could, of course, be cut with profit, but in no other way can that pitably small sum of $31 be increased. Yet from that sum savings must come if there are to be any.

The different nationalities meet this problem in varying ways according to their ideals. Among the native white families a comfortable home is an essential proof of respectability. Consequently we find that they spend for rent 21.2 per cent. as against 16.4 per cent. among the Slavs. On the other hand, the Slav spends 54.3 per cent. for food, while the native whites spend but 44.7 per cent. That is, the Slavic family will have enough food anyway, while the American demands a big enough house. Inadequate food or bad housing alike endanger physical efficiency, while with overcrowding any semblance of home life becomes impossible. In neither group is there any margin for amusements.

It is not a question of good management. The cleverest housekeeper I know was doing marvelously on $14 a week, and the following statement of her average expenditure for 8 weeks, shows how she did it: Food $7.05; clothing .57; household expenses .59; rent $2.50; insurance and lodge dues .65; church and charity .09; recreation and spending money .03; doctor $1.46; sundries .35. Though, as you may see, she was keeping the unessential elements of expenditure at their lowest point, her food-supply was still quite inadequate. I found by a rough estimate that it was deficient about 20 per cent. in both proteida and calories. The budget revealed a wise choice of foods aside from a possibly extravagant expenditure for fresh fruit and vegetables. If a skilful woman of Pennsylvania Dutch stock cannot manage on this wage, what can be expected of the average housekeeper?

The necessity of facing these problems three times a day has its effect on the overtaxed mother. One woman, who on an income of from $2 to $3 a day was providing for five children, had bought a small farm and was carrying heavy insurance. In order to accomplish this, she told me, she must not spend even five cents for a visit to the nickelodeon. When she described to me her hunts for bargains and her long hours of sewing to make her girls presentable, I did not wonder that she had the reputation of being a cranky person.

These two women were Americans, but by far the largest majority of the laborers are Slavs, and it is among them that we find the worst results of the low wage.

The mill has sent out a call for young vigorous men who will do its heavy work for a small wage. In answer to this has come a great number of Slavic immigrants. As is often true of a new group most of these men are either single or with families in the old country. Of the 3,602 Slavs in the mill, 1,099 or 30.5 per cent. were single men. This has had a disastrous effect on the family life of the Slavs, for these men usually board in families of their own nationality who live in the wretched courts in the Second Ward of Homestead. A study made of 21 of these courts revealed appalling conditions. Among the 239 families living there, the 102 who took lodgers had on an average four persons to a room. Fifty-one of these families—more than one-fifth—lived in one room. The two-room tenements were not infrequently occupied by a man, his wife, two children, and two or three boarders. Under these conditions any genuine family life becomes impossible.

The death-rate among the children is high, twice as high as in the other wards of Homestead. Moreover, training children under these conditions is difficult and a terrible knowledge of evil results from the close mingling of the children with this group of careless, drinking men.

Aside from the presence of these single men and a growth of population with which the number of houses has not kept pace, the overcrowding is due to the dominant ambition of the Slav to own a bit of property here or in the old country, or to have a bank account. As we have seen, strenuous economies are necessary if their desires are to be attained. That it is ambition rather than a permanently low standard which is responsible for the bad conditions is shown by the comfort and even good taste displayed by some who have succeeded in buying their own homes.

These people do need, however, to have impressed upon their minds the value of education. As there is no effective school enumeration, and the responsibility is divided between the public and parochial schools, it is easy enough, where the parents are indifferent, for the children to drift away from regular attendance. As the steel mill with its heavy work and enormous machinery cannot utilize the work of children there is almost no labor problem in Homestead, but usually as soon as the children are fourteen they start in to work.

Between ignorance and ambition these newcomers are failing to secure for themselves or their children a real home life, that would result either in the physical or moral efficiency of the next generation.

The mill which demands strong, cheap labor concerns itself but little whether that labor is provided with living conditions that will maintain its efficiency or secure the efficiency of the next generation. The housing situation is in the hands of men actuated only by a desire for the largest possible profit. More intelligent members of the community, on the other hand, though realizing the situation do not take their responsibility for the aliens in their midst with sufficient seriousness to limit the power of these landlords. The Slavs, moreover, people used to the limitations of country life, are ignorant of the evil physical and moral effect of transferring the small rooms, the overcrowding, the insufficient sanitary provisions which may be endurable in country life with all outdoors about them, to these crowded courts under the shadow of the mill.

Summing up the results of indifference on one side and ignorance on the other, we find a high infant death-rate, a knowledge of evil among little children, intolerable sanitary conditions, a low standard of living, a failure of the community to assimilate this new race in its midst.

As we waited in one of the little railroad stations in Homestead, a Slavak came in and sat down next to a woman and her two-year-old child. He began making shy advances to the baby, and coaxing her in a voice of heart-breaking loneliness. But she would not come to him, and finally the two left the room. As they went he turned to the rest of the company, and in a tone of sadness, taking us all into his confidence said simply, "Me wife, me babe Hungar." But were they here it would mean death for one baby in three, it would mean hard work in a dirty, unsanitary house for the wife, it would mean sickness and much evil. With them away, it means for him isolation and loneliness and the abnormal life of the crowded lodging-house.

While this low wage, either among Slavs or Americans, is insufficient to maintain a standard of physical efficiency, the industry adds further that element of uncertainty for the future so destructive to ambitions and plans. Accidents are frequent. Even though they are not often fatal, one that lays a man up even for two weeks has a disastrous effect on a slender surplus. One family had saved $300 to buy a house, but when the man was injured by a weight falling on his feet, and was laid up for six weeks, $80 went from the surplus. Soon after, when last winter's hard times came, practically all the savings had to go for food. Now the family wonders whether, with all these possibilities of disaster, it will ever dare to put all its savings into a house.

In addition, cuts in wages are made periodically. As these most frequently affect the better-paid men, even they cannot start out on any plan involving any number of years without realizing that before the end of the time conditions may have changed so as to make its carrying out impossible.

By the 12-hour shift as well as by the low wage the mill is affecting the lives of these families. Though the long hours and hard work may seem to be hardships that only the man would feel, they do react on family life. Not only do his weariness and his irregular hours make him less inclined to enter into the family pleasures, but he also fails to change, through political or other action, the conditions under which they live. Because of this weariness-induced apathy, a man usually stays at home and smokes his pipe instead of troubling himself with outside affairs. This tendency is doubtless intensified by conditions within the industry. As since the strike of 1892 there have been no labor organizations in the town, the men do not meet to discuss the conditions under which they work, and accept passively whatever is offered. This same indifference seems to affect their attitude toward politics, so that instead of taking an active part they allow the wholesale liquor interests to dominate. Yet, through schools and through sanitation, the political situation does bear a close relation to family problems. In Homestead, for instance, the drinking water comes, only partly filtered, from a river which has already received the sewage of a number of towns and cities. The man continues to go three times a day for water from a neighbor's well and pay him 50 cents a month for the privilege instead of insisting that the borough provide a decent supply. There are no ordinances requiring landlords to place water or toilets in the houses, though the family are longing for the day when they can move to a house with these conveniences. An industrial situation which creates an attitude so passive that men accept, without protest, perfectly remediable evils that immediately affect the family, is a serious one.

These long hours have a further harm in their tendency to lessen the demand for amusement. Aside from roller-skating rinks and the five-cent variety shows known as nickelodeons, there is, outside of the home, no real chance for amusement save the ever present light and refreshment offered by the fifty or more saloons which Homestead licenses. The mothers, who realize that the rinks are a source of danger to the girls, and the saloons an ever-present menace to family happiness, make a heroic and often pathetic effort to keep the home attractive enough to offset these temptations. While the results are perhaps not undesirable when the mother succeeds, every woman is not a genius, and when she fails there is little wholesome amusement to compensate for her failure. The people do not want this provided for them by philanthropy. When speaking of the Carnegie library, men often said to me "We didn't want him to build a library for us, we would rather have had higher wages and spent the money for ourselves." Aside from the money, and the margin for amusements, as we have seen, is painfully small, they need the leisure to plan and enjoy. The town offers to its inhabitants the chance to work but it gives them little chance to play. And yet play is essential if even physical efficiency is to be maintained.

To sum up the situation then, we find that the mill by the nature of the work offered helps to develop a normal family type, but because of low wages, long hours, and opposition to industrial organization, it has done much to hamper the family in carrying out its ideals.

May I in conclusion state briefly what facts as to the relation of family to industrial life were clarified in my own mind by this investigation? In the first place, in a town dominated by one industry the type of family is largely determined by the nature of that industry. Theoretical discussions as to the normal family have little effect, even the ideals of individual families must often be modified to meet this situation. In a cotton-mill town, for example, we are almost sure to find the women at work, while in a steel town it is the man's place to earn and the woman's to spend. This relation, obscured in commercial or large manufacturing centers, stands out clearly in Homestead with its one industry.

In the second place, the industry limits the development of the family life by the effect of long hours and overwork, and the absence of the stimulus which trades unions might supply. These react on the family, not only in the man's personal attitude toward them, but through his failure by political or other united action, to improve the conditions under which they live.

The most obvious and fundamental relation of industry and family is the economic one. Without the background of a sufficient wage, even such distinct domestic virtues as thrift become not only impossible but harmful. If to buy a house means to underfeed the children; if to have a bank account means to take lodgers till there is no possibility of home life, we are certainly foolish to laud the man who realizes these ambitions, and class as extravagant and thriftless those who do not. Our preaching must have a closer relation to the economic situation of the families.

In years gone by the family was the industrial unit, the work was done in the house, was close to the problem of the home, and the two developed together. The family ties were strong and the industrial conditions strengthened them. Now the situation is changed, and the industry is dominant. More and more the very nature of the family, its ideals, and its every-day existence are alike molded by the opportunities for work. If we are to keep any abstract ideals of what family life should be, and are to translate these into actualities, our primary query must be whether our industrial system makes them possible. Without the development of the personal virtues economic prosperity might be futile, but the converse is also true. In Homestead at least, I believe, there are more ideals than the industrial situation allows to become realities.

The Immigrant Worker
by Peter Roberts

The day laborer of a generation ago is gone—a change which has been swifter and more complete in Pittsburgh than in many other of our industrial centers. "Where are your Irish? your Welsh? your Germans? your Americans?" I asked an old mill hand. "Go to the city hall and the police station," he said. "Some of them are still in the better paid jobs in the mills; but mostly you'll have to look for them among the doctors and lawyers, office holders, clerks, accountants, salesmen. You'll find them there."

"Immigrant Wage-Earners," *Wage-Earning Pittsburgh* (New York: Survey Associates, Russell Sage Foundation, 1911), pp. 33–49.

The day laborer in the mills today is a Slav. The foreign born of the steel district include, it is true, representatives of every European nation, but I shall deal here only with the races from southeastern Europe, which for twenty-five years have been steadily displacing the Teutonic and Keltic peoples in the rough work of the industries. The tendency of the Italians is to go into construction, railroad work, and the mines, rather than into the plants and yards; and my group narrows itself down to the dominant Magyar, Slav, and Lithuanian. What I have to say of them in Pittsburgh and Allegheny City is in the main true of them in the manufacturing towns of the whole District.

Roughly speaking, one-quarter of the population of Pittsburgh is foreign born.[1] The foreigner is nowhere more at home than here, and nowhere has he been more actively welcomed by employers. The conflict of customs and habits, varying standards of living, prejudices, antipathies, all due to the confluence of representatives of different races of men, may be witnessed here. The whole territory is thrown into a stern struggle for subsistence and wage standards by the displacements due to these resistless accretions to the ranks of the workers. The moral and religious life of the city is equally affected by this inflow of peoples. The most backward of them are superstitious and ignorant, victims of cunning knaves and unscrupulous parasites. Their religious training differs widely from that of peoples of Protestant antecedents, and institutions that were dear to the founders of the city are fast being undermined by the customs of immigrants from southeastern Europe. Yet as a whole, they bring with them physical and cultural resources which as yet, in any large sense, the English-speaking community fails to elicit or thoughtlessly wastes.

An exhaustive study of the immigrant population of the steel district is outside the limits of this chapter. I shall set down only what a month brought me as I visited lodging houses, courts, and the mills of Greater Pittsburgh; as I talked with priest and leader, policeman and doctor, banker and labor boss; but I shall present the facts in the light of many years' residence in the anthracite coal communities, where, in another section of Pennsylvania, at Mahanoy City and Wilkesbarre and Scranton, I have known the Slav and the Lett

1. In 1910 foreign-born whites comprised 26 per cent of the population and Negroes about 5 per cent.

and their efforts to gain a foothold in America. I shall deal with the situation not as it appeared on visits during the hard times of 1907—08, when the immigrants returned home by the thousands, nor in the recurrent depression of 1914; but as I came to know it in the heyday of prosperity, the early fall of 1907. This is the situation with which the intervening years have had much in common and with which we must reckon in a permanent way.

In 1880 Slavs, Lithuanians, Hungarians, and Italians formed less than 1 per cent of the population in Pittsburgh [including Allegheny]. By 1890 these peoples, with the other immigrant elements from Austria, Hungary, Italy, and Russia, had reached 3 per cent; by 1900, 6 per cent; by 1910, 13 per cent. By 1900 over one-fourth of the foreign-born population of the two cities combined came from the four countries named. The movement of the Teutonic and Keltic races had practically ceased. The 1910 census[2] shows an actual decrease of 1,514 (from 33,839 to 32,325) in the number of foreign-born whites from Great Britain and Ireland, while the number of whites born in Austria, Hungary, Italy, and Russia had increased from 29,875 in 1900 to 68,487 in 1910. They constituted practically one-half of the foreign born—49 per cent—a proportion all but twice as great as in 1900.

Polish, Italian, and Jewish immigrants lead the list from these countries. Lithuanians, Croatians, Servians, Slovaks, and Ruthenians are numbered by the thousands, and Magyars, Greeks, Bohemians, and Roumanians are here in lesser groups.

Detailed figures for immigrants from Austria, Hungary, Italy, and Russia follow in tabular form.

The representatives of these nations touch elbows in the streets, so that the languages heard on Saturday night when the people are marketing in the foreign quarters are as numerous as those in a seaport town. Twenty dialects are spoken. Yet the polyglot mass that confuses the visitor and induces pessimistic impressions as to the future of the city is each morning marshalled to work without tumult. The discipline of the industrial establishments converts this babel of tongues into one of the chief forces of production. Therein lies an

2. The foreign-born whites in 1910 numbered 140,436, an increase in ten years of 25,591, or 22.2 per cent. In the same decade the total population of Greater Pittsburgh increased only 18 per cent (from 451,512 to 533,905). It should be noted that the increase in the total population of the entire county was over 30 per cent.

TABLE 1—POPULATION OF AUSTRIAN, HUNGARIAN, ITALIAN, AND RUSSIAN NATIVITY. PITTSBURGH, 1900 AND 1910 [a]

Country of Birth	Persons of Each Specified Nativity in		Per Cent Increase
	1900	1910	
Austria [b]	9,411	21,400	127.4
Hungary	2,684	6,576	145.0
Italy	6,495	14,120	117.4
Russia [c]	11,285	26,391	133.9
Total	29,875	68,487	129.2
Persons born as specified as a percentage of the entire foreign-born white population of Pittsburgh.	26	49	..

a. United States Census, 1900 and 1910.
b. Including Austrian Poland and Bohemia.
c. Including Russian Poland.

It must not, however, be forgotten that Jews and Germans form a large proportion of the foreign born from Austria, Hungary, and Russia.

The "mother tongue statistics" gathered in the last census are interesting in this connection. In Pittsburgh out of the total of foreign-born whites 27.9 per cent spoke "Slavic and Lettic" tongues, and of these more than half were Poles. Immigrants speaking "English and Celtic" tongues formed 25.2 per cent; German-speaking immigrants, 21.6 per cent; Italian-speaking immigrants, 10.1 per cent; and immigrants who spoke Yiddish or Hebrew, 9.1 per cent.

appraisal not only of the American *entrepreneur,* but also of the adaptability of these men coming from nations of low efficiency, who are able so quickly to fall into line and keep step in an industrial army of remarkable discipline and output.

In normal times every day brings its quota of immigrants; occasionally they come by carloads. The records of the ports of entry show that in 1907, 187,618 persons gave Pittsburgh as their destination, but many of these scattered to the neighboring Pennsylvania towns and many undoubtedly went to the mills and mines of eastern Ohio. The city is a distributing point and owing to this shifting of the newcomers the outflow may often equal the inflow. Conditions in local industries determine which of these two currents runs the swifter.

Before taking up the living conditions in Pittsburgh as they especially affect these immigrant laborers, let us consider for a moment certain of their characteristics and their relation to the general economic situation. First, it is the wages that bring them here.[3] The workers on the hills of Galicia, in the vineyards of Italy, and the factories of Kiev, earn from 25 to 50 cents in a day. When the American immigrant writes home that he earns from \$1.50 to \$2.00, the ablebodied wage-earner in the fatherland who hears this will not be satisfied until he also stands where the higher wages govern. It is these homegoing letters more than all else which recruit the labor force. They are efficient promoters of immigration. Said Big Sam to me, in his broken English, "There are no ablebodied men between the ages of sixteen and fifty years left in my native town in Servia; they have all come to America."

When prosperity is at flood, the men in charge of furnaces, foundries, forges, and mills in the Pittsburgh District cannot get the help they need. The cry everywhere is: "Give us men." A foreman, therefore, will assure Pietro and Melukas that if brothers or cousins or friends are sent for, they will get work as soon as they arrive. More than that, the Slav and Italian are no longer dependent upon the English boss in the matter of finding work for their countrymen. The inflow from southeastern Europe has assumed such proportions in the industries of the cities that superintendents have, in some instances, appointed Italian and Polish and Lithuanian foremen; and with these, as with German and Irish, blood is thicker than water. They employ their fellow-countrymen. They know the condition of the labor market and can by suggestion stimulate or retard immigration.

The tonnage industries of Pittsburgh have expanded tremendously in the last two decades. Such industries need strong manual

3. The Federal Immigration Commission, on the basis of its nation-wide inquiry in 1907, reached the same generalization as Dr. Roberts and Mr. Koukol (p. 80) as to the economic motive in present day immigration:

"While social conditions affect the situation in some countries, the present immigration from Europe to the United States is in the largest measure due to economic causes. It should be stated, however, that emigration from Europe is not now an absolute economic necessity, and as a rule those who emigrate to the United States are impelled by a desire for betterment rather than by the necessity for escaping intolerable conditions." Abstracts of Reports of the Immigration Commission, p. 25. Washington, 1911.

laborers as do no others. The Slavs have brawn for sale. Herein, at bottom, is the drawing force which accounts for such a moving in of peoples and the readiness with which they find their places in the specialized industries of the District. Pittsburgh has clamorous need for these men. Take the average Lithuanian, Croatian, Ruthenian, or Slovak, and his physique compares favorably with that of any people. Most of the immigrants are from agricultural communities. Their food in the fatherland is coarse, their habits are simple, their cares few. They have an abundance of vegetable diet, pure water, pure air, and sunshine, and they develop strong physical organisms. Taking them as a whole, we get the best of the agricultural population. The day has not yet come when the weak emigrate and the strong stay at home. No ship agents, however active, can reverse the natural order of the tide of immigration, and natural selection supplemented by federal scrutiny gives us a body of men physically most fit for the heaviest demands made by our industries. Nowhere has this been better illustrated than in Pittsburgh.

These men come to be "the hewers of wood and drawers of water." There are representatives of each race far removed from the lowest industrial stratum; but taking these people as a whole, the bulk of the unskilled labor in the city—the digging and carrying in the street, the heavy labor in the mill, the loading and unloading of raw material on railroad and river, the rough work at forge and foundry, the coarse work around the factory, and the lifting necessary in the machine shop—is performed by them.

This is the level at which they enter the economic order. What trade equipment do they bring into the work with them? Their industrial efficiency is low and I should estimate that 95 per cent have no knowledge of modern machinery or methods of modern production; they are children in factory training. Further, those who have trades find themselves in an industrial environment where their previous training is of little value. They are ignorant of the English language, and the few mechanics and tradesmen among them because of this ignorance can do no better than join the ranks of the common laborers. We must bear in mind, however, that those who know how to use tools, once they are put to work that requires some skill adapt themselves quickly to it. Hence we meet not a few Slavs and Lithuanians who do work of a semi-skilled nature; nor does the exceptional man stop there. Sons, also, of men of these nationalities who settled in the city a generation ago have risen to positions of standing in the industries. It is not unusual to hear of this man or that who has become a foreman in the mills or taken a place in business or in the professions.

But on several counts the average Slav, Lithuanian, and Italian is not as acceptable a day laborer as was the immigrant from northwestern Europe. The common opinion of American employers is that the newer immigrants are stupid and that the supervisory force must be much larger than that required for English-speaking help. Many employers would no doubt prefer the latter; but for the wages they offer they must take the Slav or run short-handed. The United States immigration agent in Pittsburgh is constantly besieged by employers of labor who need help. Many stories are told of one firm stealing a group of laborers marshalled at the port of entry for another.

The influence which letters and money sent home have in recruiting immigrant workmen has been spoken of. These people make little or no use of labor agencies, unless the saloon and the small bank may be so denominated. In each nationality there are acknowledged leaders who play the part of intermediaries between superintendents and their people. But such investigations as I have made at Ellis Island do not lead me to believe that the employers of labor in Pittsburgh violate the contract labor law.[4] Labor agencies in New York City make a specialty of distributing Slavs, Lithuanians, and Italians to firms in need of hands. The leader who supplies men to a mill or mining concern gets so much for each man supplied. Whatever contract there may be is executed this side of the water. For instance, I found a leading Croatian who had a specific understanding with one of the mills of Pittsburgh that all men he brought would find employment. No contract was executed and in the opinion of the local immigration agent there was in the proceeding no violation of the contract labor law.

The drawbacks to the new day laborer as such have been stated. On the other hand, it is a common opinion in the District that some employers of labor give the Slavs and Italians preference over

4. In the western district of Pennsylvania, there have been instituted by the United States attorney within ten years 23 suits for violation of the contract labor law, of which one was pending in June, 1913. Of the remaining 22, 21 were discontinued under direction of the attorney general and one was carried through with the result that a verdict of $2,000 and costs was secured.

English-speaking applicants because of their docility, their habit of silent submission, their amenability to discipline, and their willingness to work long hours and overtime without a murmur. These foreigners as a rule earn the lowest wages and work the full stint of hours; in the machine shops they work sixty hours a week; at the blast furnaces twelve hours a day for seven days in the week with a twenty-four-hour turn every fortnight. The common laborer in and around the mills works nominally a ten-hour day, but overtime is the rule rather than the exception when trade is good. The unit of wages is an hour rate for day labor, and a Slav is willing to take the longer hours (twelve hours a day for men who may have worked fourteen and sixteen on the farms in the fatherland). In 1907 possibly 60 to 70 per cent of the laborers in the mills came out Sundays for the purpose of clearing the yards and repairing.[5] In one mill I found Russians (Greek Orthodox) in favor for the reason that they gladly worked on Sundays.

My belief is that certain employers of labor have reaped advantage from racial antipathies. For instance, the Pole and the Lithuanian have nothing in common and each of them despises the Slovak. Superintendents know this and use their knowledge when foreigners are likely to reach a common understanding upon wages or conditions of labor. These considerations have helped make it less difficult for factory operators to keep open shop and non-union shop in Pittsburgh. The constant influx of raw material from backward nations into the industries of the city has had somewhat the same effect as the flow of water in an estuary when the tide is rising. All is commotion. This condition will exist as long as the inflow of Slavs and Italians continues as it has in the last decade. But when they have become permanently placed and their workaday intelligence and grasp of American conditions rise, racial prejudices will give way to common interests. When this time comes, accustomed as they are to association for protection and to following directions, Pittsburgh will witness the rise of stronger labor organizations than ever were effected by Teuton and Kelt.

We have seen, then, the Slavic day laborers coming into the steel district in vast numbers. Of their strength and their lack of skill at the outset there is no doubt. We have noted some of the snap judg-

5. It was not until 1910 that the Steel Corporation began to enforce its rule against unnecessary Sunday work.

ments that are current about them; such as, that they are stupid and submissive. And we have noted also some of their potentialities which must be reckoned with en masse in the future. All this puts us in position to get the bearings of my first statement that it is the wages that bring them to Pittsburgh, and to see what advances they are able to make once they have gained a foothold. The Slav enters the field at a rate of pay for day labor which is higher than that which brought the Germans and the Kelts. The lowest wage I found Slavs working for was 13 ½ cents an hour. The wage of common labor in a majority of the steel mills in 1907 was 15 or 16 ½ cents for a ten- or a twelve-hour day.[6]

But the newcomers know nothing of a standard wage, and when work is scarce they will offer to work for less than is paid for common labor. Such was the case with a band of Croatians who offered their services to a firm in Pittsburgh for $1.20 a day. When the superintendent heard it he said, "My God, what is the country coming to? How can a man live in Pittsburgh on $1.20 a day?" The foreman replied, "Give them rye bread, a herring, and beer, and they are all right." (I have known a coal operator in the anthracite fields to pay Italians and Slovaks 90 cents a day, and ask neither what was the country coming to nor how they could subsist.)

More, the Slavs will consciously cut wages in order to get work. A man who knows something about blacksmithing or carpentering will work at a trade for little more than half the standard wage of the District. They count their money in the denominations of the fatherland and estimate its value according to old country standards. Some foremen take advantage of this. Again, skilled men will at the command of the boss render menial services without a murmur. "These fellows have no pride," said an American craftsman to me; "they are not ruled by custom. When the foreman demands it they will throw down the saw or hammer and take the wheelbarrow."

So the Slav gains his foothold in the Pittsburgh industries, and while gaining it he undermines the income of the next higher industrial group and incurs the enmity of the Americans. Shrewd superintendents are known not only to take advantage of the influx of unskilled labor to keep down day wages, but to reduce the pay of skilled men by a gradually enforced system of promoting the Slavs. In the place of six men at $10 a day, one will be employed at $15, with five others at half, or less than half, the old rate, who will work

6. For present rates, see Commons, John R.: Wage-earners of Pittsburgh.

under the high-priced man. Inventions, changes in processes, new machines, a hundred elements tend to complicate the situation and render it difficult to disentangle the influence of any one element. But this much is clear: the new immigration is a factor which is influencing the economic status of the whole wage-earning population in Pittsburgh; it is bound to be a permanent factor; and its influence will be more and not less.

It is a mistake to imagine that the Slav or Lithuanian cannot adapt himself to modern industrial conditions. Possibly 20 per cent of these laborers from southeastern Europe now work at machines, the skill needed to operate which requires a week or two weeks to acquire. To be sure, they are machines "so simple that a child could operate them, and so strong that a fool cannot break them." Many Slovaks work for the Pressed Steel Car Company in Allegheny, as riveters, punchers, and pressmen, while others are fitters, carpenters, and blacksmiths. Some Croatians and Servians are rising and are found in the steel mills as roughers and catchers. I saw Ruthenians feeding machines with bars of white-hot steel. It was simple, mechanical work, but of a higher grade than that of scrap-carrier. The Poles who during recent years have emigrated from Russia and Austria-Hungary are as industrially efficient as any group of immigrants and work in both mills and foundries.

A foreigner who has a chance to become a machine operator generally goes into piece work and in 1907 his earnings were likely to average from $2.00 to $2.50 a day. But all men at the machines are not on piece work. A foreman explained this to me as follows: "If the machine depends upon the man for speed, we put him on piece work; if the machine drives the man, we pay him by the day." The man operating a machine by the day got from $1.75 to $2.00. Many boys and young women of Slavic parentage work in the spike, nut and bolt, and steel wire factories. They sat before machines and pickling urns for ten hours and received from 75 cents to $1.00 a day.

The Slovak riveters, punchers, shearsmen, and pressmen in the Pressed Steel Car Company's plant were paid by the piece and for the most part made from $35 to $50 in two weeks.[7] Fitters, carpenters, blacksmiths, and painters were getting from $2.00 to $2.50 by

7. A pooling system, accompanied by rate cuts, which was put in effect in 1909, led to a prolonged strike in which Slavs and Americans joined forces. See *The Survey*, XXII: 656–665 (August 7, 1909).

the day. A Slavic banker told me of Croatians and Servians who made as high as $70 in two weeks, and others who made between $3.00 and $4.00 a day—many of them in positions which once paid English-speaking workmen twice those sums. High and low are relative terms and they signify very different standards to a Slav and to an American.

There is much that inspires to prophecy in the sight of the thousands of Slavs already doing efficient work in the mills. The sooner the English-speaking workers recognize this and make friends of these workers, the better. No class of work is now monopolized by Teuton and Kelt, and the service rendered by the Slav and Lithuanian will before many years equal that of the former in market value.

With this rapid statement of the economic position of the Slavs, we can more intelligently approach the problem of their living conditions. But first let us bear sharply in mind that their work is often cast among dangers; is often inimical to health. Many work in intense heat, the din of machinery, and the noise of escaping steam. The congested condition of most of the plants in Pittsburgh adds to the physical discomforts for an out-of-doors people, while their ignorance of the language and of modern machinery increases the risk. How many of the Slavs, Lithuanians, and Italians were injured in Pittsburgh in one year no one could tell me in 1907. No reliable statistics were compiled. In their absence people guessed and the mischief wrought by contradictory and biased statements was met with on all hands. When I mentioned to a priest a plant that had a bad reputation he said, "Oh, that is the slaughter house; they kill them there every day." I quote him not for his accuracy, but to show how rumors circulate and are real to the people themselves. Exaggerated though such hearsay was, the waste in life and limb has for years been great—and so continues—and if it had all fallen upon the native born a cry would have gone up long since which would have stayed the slaughter.[8]

8. Of the 500 industrial fatalities in one year in Allegheny County (July 1, 1906, to June 30, 1907), gathered by the Pittsburgh Survey from the coroner's office, the employer, and the family, 293 were foreign born. See, in this volume [*Wage-Earning Pittsburgh*], Kellogg, Paul U.; Community and Workshop, p. 24; Porter, op. cit. [Industrial Hygiene of the Pittsburgh District], page 245; and Appendix XX, Bureau of Safety, Relief, Sanitation, and Welfare, U. S. Steel Corporation. See also Eastman, Crystal: Work-Accidents and the Law. (The Pittsburgh Survey.) An appendix

In the matter of compensation for injuries, the American workman has been and remains at sore disadvantage under Pennsylvania
laws, but the foreign speaking has been subjected to additional
injustice.[9]

Up to 1911, if the widow of a man killed in a mine or mill of
Pennsylvania lived in Europe she could not recover any damages,[10]
even though the accident were entirely due to the neglect of the company. Because of this ruling, certain strong companies in the Pittsburgh District seldom paid a cent to the relatives of the deceased if
they dwelt beyond the seas. I asked a leader among the Italians,
"Why do you settle the serious cases for a few hundred dollars?" He
replied: "We find it best after much bitter experience. The courts
are against us; a jury will not mulct a corporation to send money to
Europe; the relatives are not here to bewail their loss in court; the
average American cares nothing for the foreigner. Every step of the
way we meet with prejudices and find positive contempt, from those
in highest authority in the courts down to the tipstaff. When I settle
for $200, I can do nothing better."

The influence of the industries reaches still further into the lives of
the immigrants. Each people has a tendency to colonize in one section of the city and to work in some one mill. The Bohemians are
strong in Allegheny City, but few of them are found in Pittsburgh.
The Slovaks predominate in McKees Rocks and Allegheny City,
and many of them are found in the Soho district of Pittsburgh. The
Poles are numerous in many parts of the Greater City. The Lithuanians live in large numbers on the South Side and near the National
Tube Works and the American Steel and Wire Company. Many
Ruthenians work in the Oliver Steel Works, while the Croatians and
Servians have worked for the most part in the Jones and Laughlin
plants. My information is that other things being equal, foremen try

therein presents the accident prevention work carried on by the constituent companies of the Steel Corporation—the largest employer of the District—under a central safety committee appointed April, 1908. Certain progressive employers, as the
Pittsburgh Steel Company, had earlier addressed themselves to some phases of the
problem; more have done so since. But there is no local or state compilation of accident statistics that amounts to anything, and the public remains in ignorance as to the
current human loss in industry.

9. See p. 24, this volume [*Wage-Earning Pittsburgh*].

10. This law of 1911 provides that when an alien dies from injuries the husband,
widow, parents, or children of such alien, although residing abroad at the time of the
injury, can recover damages.

to get one nationality in assigning work to a group of laborers, for they know that a homogeneous group will give them the best results. National pride also enters into selection. In talking to a Lithuanian of the serious loss of life which had occurred when a furnace blew up, I asked, "Were any of your people killed in that accident?" He answered quickly, "No; catch our people doing such work as that! There you find the Slovak." Of the grades of unskilled labor, the Slovak, Croatian, Servian, and Russian (Greek Orthodox) may be said to perform tasks the roughest and most risky, and the most injurious to health. There is, then, a more or less natural selection of peoples in the neighborhood of the different great mills.

The geographical contour of the region has also had its influence in keeping the foreign population within certain limited districts. The two rivers, the Allegheny and the Monongahela, have cut their beds into the Allegheny range, leaving a narrow strip of land on either side of their banks which offers limited sites for dwellings, mills, and factories. The lowlands were preempted long ago, and the contest for parts of them between the mills and the homes has been intense. There is an advantage to the employer, however, in having his crude labor force within easy call, and night work and the cost of carfare help keep the mass of men employed in common labor near the mills and on the congested lowlands. I visited homes of Slavs and Lithuanians which were clean, well furnished, and equal in comfort to those of Americans of the same economic level. These foreigners had been in the country many years and their children had become thoroughly assimilated.

But our first concern is with the recent comers, who too often live in lodgings that are filthy; whose peasant habits seem to us uncouth; and whose practices are fatal to decency and morality in a thickly settled district.

Yet the foreigner pays a higher rent than does the "white man." In Bass Street, Allegheny City, English-speaking tenants were paying $15 a month for four rooms, but Slavs were charged $20; others paid $10 and $12 a month for houses for which Slavs were charged $17 and $18. On Penn Avenue a Slav paid $17 for three rear rooms, while an English-speaking family renting eight rooms in the front of the building paid but $33. One family paid $9.50 for one large room in an old residence on the South Side; another paid $10 for two rooms, another $16 for three; and on Brandt Street a man was found who paid $22 a month for four.

The rent is not always fixed by the landlord. Where lodgers are taken it is sometimes regulated by the number the "boarding boss" can crowd in, the landlord getting $1.00 a month extra for each boarder. Many houses of from eight to twelve rooms had in them anywhere from three to six families. They were built for one family, and until such time as the owners might be forced by the bureau of health to install sanitary appliances, there was every prospect that they would have equipment for but one. Too many landlords when they deal with foreigners have apparently one dominating passion—rent. They make no repairs, and with the crowded condition above described, the houses soon bear marks of ill usage. Whenever foreigners invade a neighborhood occupied by English-speaking tenants, property depreciates. The former occupants get out, the invaders multiply, and often the properties pass into the hands of speculators. Houses once occupied by Slavs can seldom be rented again to Anglo-Saxons.

It is in the immigrant lodging houses that conditions are the worst, though not always so with the choice of the men. The Croatians, Servians, Roumanians, and Greeks have only from 5 to 10 per cent of women among them; hence the men of these nationalities have but few boarding houses conducted by their own people to go to, and crowding is inevitable. English-speaking and German families will not open their doors to them. Single men in groups of from six to twenty go into one house in charge of a boarding boss and his wife. Each man pays from 75 cents to $1.00 a week for a place to sleep and the little cooking and washing that are to be done. Accounts of food for the company are kept in one book, and every two weeks the sum total is divided equally among the boarders, each man paying his *pro rata* share. The bill for two weeks will hardly amount to $3.00 a man, so that the average boarder will spend perhaps $10 a month on room rent and maintenance. When men pay $3.50 for room rent, soup is included in the contract.[11] The mania for saving results in many cases in skimping on the necessaries of life. A priest told me of a Lithuanian who spent 10 cents a day for food and by helping the landlady in her housework saved his room rent. A number of Russians on Tustine Street were paying $3.00 a month for room rent; they bought bread made by Russian Jews, got

11. For a more extended presentation of the boarding boss system, see Byington, Margaret F.: Homestead: The Households of a Mill Town, pp. 138—140. (The Pittsburgh Survey.)

a herring and a pot of beer, and lived—not always—in peace.

Domestic tragedies sometimes invade these communal house-holds, such as a case of assault and battery which came up in an al-derman's office. The complainant was a single man who appeared with a ghastly scalp wound. When his boarding boss had presented his bill at the end of two weeks, the charges were $5.00 more than the boarder thought they should be. He protested and the boarding boss took a hatchet to silence him.

In these boarding establishments the kitchen is commonly used as a bedroom. When the boarding boss rents two rooms, he and his wife sleep in the kitchen, and the boarders take the other room. It is not altogether unusual for a boarding boss to rent but one room. He and his wife put their bed in one corner, the stove in another, and the boarders take the remaining corners. Sometimes the rooms are so crowded that the boss and his wife sleep on the floor; and cases were repeatedly to be found where beds were being worked double shift—night and day. The city bureau of health in 1907 endeavored to reduce the number of beds in a room, but it did not follow that the people occupying that room got out—they slept on the floor minus the bed. The problem is one of the hardest that sanitary inspectors have to cope with.

Sometimes four or six men rent a house and run it themselves, doing their own cooking and washing and occasionally bringing in a woman to clean a little. They may stand this for about six months and then leave when the rooms are past cleaning. Such crowding is very prevalent in the low-lying parts of the South Side, in the neigh-borhood of Penn Avenue in the city proper, and in sections of Alle-gheny. On Tustine Street I found 33 Russians, composing three families, living in one house of six rooms and an attic. The Croa-tians also crowd badly. A milk dealer told me of 28 who lived in a small house in Carey Alley. When I asked, "How do they live?" his reply was, "I don't know and don't care if I get my money for my milk." His reply summed up the attitude of many of the English-speaking people who have dealings with them. In Pork House Row and near Eckert Street in Allegheny, things were no better, and con-ditions in some blocks of houses under the California Avenue bridge were as bad as any seen. The Italians are close livers; but possibly the worst conditions I saw were among the Armenians in the neigh-borhood of Basin Alley.

Before we condemn immigrants, however, for the filth of their lodgings, we must remember that they are largely rural people unused to such city barracks, and that they are frequent sufferers from our own municipal neglect. This fact is illustrated especially by their own ignorance of the danger of typhoid fever. Dr. Leon Sadowski estimated that as high as 50 per cent of all young foreigners who had come to Pittsburgh up to 1907, contracted typhoid within two years of their coming.[12] Dr. Maracovick told me that in four years no less than 100 Croatians in the neighborhood of Smallman Street had come down with the fever, and that most of them had died. "You cannot make the foreigner believe that Pittsburgh water is unwholesome," said another physician. "He comes from rural communities where contamination of water is unknown." Other physicians told of men who had been warned, deliberately going to the river to quench their thirst.

Where so many single men are huddled together the laws of decency and morality are hard to observe. The boarding boss seldom has a family and, in going the round of these houses, the absence of children is conspicuous. A physician who works among them said, "The average boarding boss's wife cannot have any—the moral conditions make it a physical impossibility." She stands in striking contrast to the average Slavic woman who in her natural environment is the mother of children. These mid-European peoples are not so passionate as the Italians, but many of the single men, as is the case in all barracks life, will fall into vice. A physician told me that gonorrhea is very prevalent among the Croatians and Servians; another said of the Slavs in general, "They frequent cheap bawdy houses and come out diseased and robbed." Many brothels hereabouts are known as "Johnny Houses," for the reason that they are frequented by foreigners whose proper names are unpronounceable and who go by the name of "John." These were houses of the cheapest kind given over to prostitutes in the last stages.[13] The number entering them on a "wide-awake" (pay) Saturday night was large. A man who knew this section fairly well, said, "Sometimes these men have to wait their turn."

12. The municipal filtration plant which has overcome this situation was first operated in 1908. See Wing, Frank E.: Thirty-five Years of Typhoid. The Pittsburgh District, p. 63.
13. See Forbes, James: The Reverse Side [pp. 104–106, this volume].

The presence of young immigrant women in the lodging houses adds to the seriousness of the situation. Here again it is a question of wages that brings them to this country. They do the drudgery in the hotels and restaurants which English-speaking girls will not do; and they are to be found in factories working under conditions which their English-speaking sisters would resent.[14] If any persons need protection, these young women do. There was no adequate inspection of the labor employment agencies in Pittsburgh, which solicit patronage among them, often to wrong them. Not only did some of these agencies make a practice of taking their money but they sent girls to houses unfit for them. An innocent girl may learn the character of the house only when it is too late. And even if sent to the average immigrant lodging house her lot is a hard one, especially when the men of the place are on a carouse.

The Negro Migrant
by Abraham Epstein

The Negro population of the Pittsburgh Districts in Allegheny County was 27,753 in the year 1900 and had increased to 34,217 by the year 1910, according to the latest United States Census figures available.[1] The increase during this period was 23.3 percent. Assuming the continuation of this rate of increase, the total Negro population in 1915 would be about 38,000.

From a canvas of twenty typical industries in the Pittsburgh district, it was found that there were 2,550 Negroes employed in 1915, and 8,325 in 1917, an increase of 5,775 or 227%. It was impossible to obtain labor data from more than approximately 60 percent of the Negro employing concerns, but it is fair to assume that the same ratio of increase holds true of the remaining 40 percent. On this

The Negro Migrant in Pittsburgh (University of Pittsburgh, School of Economics, 1918), pp. 7, 9, 30–34, 38–39.

14. See Butler, Elizabeth B.: Women and the Trades, pp. 24–25. (The Pittsburgh Survey.)

1. 13th U. S. Census, Penna. Bulletin, Table I, page 12; 1910.

basis the number of Negroes now employed in the district may be placed at 14,000. This means that there are about 9,750 more Negroes working in the district today than there were in 1915, an addition due to the migration from the South.

A schedule study of over five hundred Negro migrants indicates that 30 percent of the newcomers have their families with them, and that the average family consists of three persons, excluding the father.[2] Adding to the total number of new workers (9,750), the product obtained by multiplying 30 percent by three (average family), we find a probable total new Negro population of 18,550 in 1917.

This sudden and abnormal increase in the Negro population within so short a time, of necessity, involves a tremendous change, and creates a new situation, which merits the attention of the whole community. Before this great influx of Negroes from the South, the Negro population, which constituted only 3.4 percent of the total city population, lived in a half dozen sections of the city. Although not absolutely segregated, these districts were distinct. . . .

A questionnaire concerning kinds of labor in which Negro migrants engaged, and wages paid them both in Pittsburgh and in their native South, was prepared; and answers to it from over five hundred individuals were obtained during the months of July and August, 1917. Information relating to housing, rents, health and social conditions was elicited in a similar manner. An effort was made to visit and study every Negro quarter in Pittsburgh. Data was secured from the Negro sections in the Hill District and upper Wylie and Bedford Avenues; the Lawrenceville district, about Penn Avenue, between Thirty-fourth and Twenty-eighth Streets; the Northside Negro quarter around Beaver Avenue and Fulton Street; the East Liberty section in the vicinity of Mignonette and Shakespeare Streets, and the new downtown Negro section on Second Avenue, Ross and Water Streets. . . .

The great majority of the Negro migrants come north because of the better economic and social opportunities here. But even here they are not permitted to enter industry freely. They are kept in the ranks of unskilled labor and in the field of personal service. Until the present demand for unskilled labor arose, the Negroes in the North were for the most part servants. There were very few Negroes

2. This average was obtained by dividing the total number of women and children of the families investigated by the number of families.

occupied otherwise than as porters, chauffeurs, janitors and the like. The Negro at present has entered the productive industries, but he is kept still on the lowest rung of the economic ladder. . . .

From a study of colored employees in twenty of the largest industrial plants, in the Pittsburgh district, arbitrarily selected, we find that most of the concerns have employed colored labor only since May or June of 1916. Very few of the Pittsburgh industries have used colored labor in capacities other than as janitors and window cleaners. A few of the plants visited had not begun to employ colored people until in the spring of 1917, while a few others had not yet come to employ Negroes, either because they believed the Negro workers to be inferior and inefficient, or because they feared that their white labor force would refuse to work with the blacks. The Superintendent of one big steel plant which has not employed colored labor during the past few years admitted that he faced a decided shortage of labor, and that he was in need of men; but he said he would employ Negroes only as a last resort, and that the situation was as yet not sufficiently acute to warrant their employment. In a big glass plant, the company attempted to use Negro labor last winter, but the white workers "ran them out" by swearing at them, calling them "Nigger" and making conditions so unpleasant for them that they were forced to quit. This company has therefore given up any further attempts at employing colored labor. It may be interesting to note, however, that one young Negro boy who pays no attention to such persecution persistently stays there.

About 95 percent of the colored workers in the steel mills visited in our survey were doing unskilled labor. In the bigger plants, where many hundreds of Negroes are employed, almost 100 percent are doing common labor, while in the smaller plants, a few might be found doing labor which required some skill. The reasons alleged by the manufacturers are; first, that the migrants are inefficient and unstable, and second, that the opposition to them on the part of white labor prohibits their use on skilled jobs. The latter objection is illustrated by the case of the white bargemen of a big steel company who wanted to walk out because black workers were introduced among them, and who were only appeased by the provision of separate quarters for the Negroes. While there is an undeniable hostility to Negroes on the part of a few white workers, the objection is frequently exaggerated by prejudiced gang bosses.

That this idea is often due to the prejudice of the heads of departments and other labor employers, was the opinion of a sympathetic superintendent of one of the largest steel plants, who said that in many instances it was the superintendents and managers themselves, who are not alive to their own advantage and so oppose the Negro's doing the better classes of work. The same superintendent said that he had employed Negroes for many years; that a number of them have been connected with his company for several years; that they are just as efficient as the white people. More than half of the twenty-five Negroes in his plant were doing semi-skilled and even skilled work. He had one or two colored foremen over colored gangs, and cited an instance of a colored man drawing a hundred and fourteen dollars in his last two weeks' pay. This claim was supported by a very intelligent Negro who was stopped a few blocks away from the plant and questioned as to conditions in the plant. While admitting everything that the Superintendent said, and stating that there is now absolute free opportunity for colored people in that plant, the man claimed that these conditions have come into being only within the last year. The same superintendent told of an episode illustrating the amicable relations existing in his shop between the white and black workers. He related that a gang of workers had come to him with certain complaints and the threat of a walk-out. When their grievances had been satisfactorily adjusted, they pointed to the lonely black man in their group and said that they were not ready to go back unless their Negro fellow worker was satisfied.

From our survey of the situation it must be evident that the southern migrants are not as well established in the Pittsburgh industries as is the white laborer. They are as yet unadapted to the heavy and pace-set labor in our steel mills. Accustomed to the comparatively easy-going plantation and farm work of the South, it will take some time until these migrants have found themselves. The roar and clangor of our mills make these newcomers a little dazed and confused at first. They do not stay long in one place, being birds of passage; they are continually searching for better wages and accommodations. They cannot even be persuaded to wait until pay day, and they like to get money in advance, following the habit they have acquired from the southern economic system. It is often secured on very flimsy pretexts and spent immediately in the saloons and similar places. It is admitted, however, by all employers of labor, that the Negro who was born in the North or has been in the North for some time, although not as subservient to bad treatment, is as efficient as the white; that because of his knowledge of the language and the ways of this country, he is often much better than the foreign laborer who understands neither.

Paradoxical as it may seem, the labor movement in America—which it is claimed was begun and organized primarily to improve the conditions of all workers, and protect their interests from the designs of heartless and cruel industrial captains—has not only made no effort to relieve and help the oppressed black workers who have suffered even more than the whites from exploitation and serfdom, but in many instances has remained indifferent to the economic interests and even served as an obstacle to the free development of the colored people.

Since the East St. Louis race riots in July of this year, and later on the Chester and other race clashes, the press has been full of controversy concerning the colored labor problem in the North. Employers as well as many prominent persons openly laid the blame for the spilling of the blood of women and little children at the door of the labor unions. On the other hand, the labor men almost as a unit have charged the responsibility for these riots to the Northern industrial leaders who are bringing these laborers to be used as a tool to break up the labor movement in the North. . . .

The typical attitude of the complacent trade unionist is illustrated by a letter which was written by a very prominent local labor leader, a member of the "Alliance for Labor and Democracy" in answer to certain questions asked him. This official refused to state anything orally, and asked that the questions be put to him in writing. His answers, we may presume, have been carefully worded after considerable contemplation of the problem.

The letter begins: "While I do not wish to appear evasive, I do not think some of the questions should have been asked me at this time." Questions and answers follow:

Q. Number of white members in the Union?

A. Our Union has had a growth of 100 percent in the past six months in the Pittsburgh district.

Q. Number of colored people in the Union?

A. None.

Q. Has there been an increase in the colored labor in your trade within the last year? If so, state approximately the proportion.

A. Yes, estimates can be made only by the employer, as we do not control all shops.

Q. Has there been an increase in the colored union membership within the last year or two?

A. Yes, statistics can be gotten from Mr. Frank Morrison, Secretary, American Federation of Labor, Washington, D. C.

Q. What efforts does your Union make to organize the colored people in your trade?

A. Same effort as all others, as the A. F. of L. does not bar any worker on account of race or creed.

Q. Has any colored person applied for membership in your Union within the last year?

A. Yes.

Q. Have the colored people in your trade asked for a separate charter?

A. Not that I know of.

Q. Do you personally know of any complaint by a person of color against your Union as regards race discrimination?

A. Yes.

The official admits that there are colored workers in his trade, that some have applied for membership, and that there have been complaints of race discrimination. His statement concerning efforts to organize Negro laborers would seem to have little meaning in view of his assertion that the growth of white membership during the past year was 100 percent, while that of Negro membership was zero.

Steel Industry and Steel Worker
by John Andrews Fitch

The Twelve-Hour Day
The eight-hour day does not flourish in the steel mills. After ten months' residence in the Pittsburgh District, and careful search throughout that time for the facts of the industrial situation, I can

"The Steel Industry and the Labor Problem," *Charities and the Commons*, 21 (March 6, 1909), pp. 1079 – 1082, 1086 – 1092.

state with assurance that with exception of the sheet mills, the eight-hour day is to be found only in the Bessemer departments. There are exceptions to this rule, as in the case of the forty-five rail straight-eners at the Edgar Thomson plant at Braddock, who work in three shifts, with fifteen men in each shift, but generally speaking the eight-hour day is confined to the one department where the Besse-mer converters are operated.

Here the men who are exposed to the greatest heat usually work in three shifts; but their number is not large. After careful inquiry, in which I talked with all grades of workmen and with men in author-ity, I could find only about 120 eight-hour men in 1907 among the 17,000 employes in the three largest plants of the Carnegie Steel Company in Allegheny county, a trifle less than three-fourths of one per cent. This was when the mills were running full, before the finan-cial depression. [My statements throughout this article deal with the normal conditions in the industry.]

The prevailing working day is twelve hours for steel workers, that is, for the men who are actually engaged in the processes of manu-facturing and working steel, skilled and unskilled workmen alike. The yard laborers and machinists are the apparent exceptions. The former are supposed to do day work and to do it on a ten-hour basis, but their hours vary with the demands of the season. A night shift is put on when orders are heavy, and the working day is extended. It is probably that with them overtime is the rule rather than the ex-ception in prosperous times when all departments are crowded; and such conditions governed generally in the mills for the four years previous to November, 1907. To illustrate, in October of that year, as I learned from an authoritative source, the yard men in a blast furnace plant earned about two dollars a day. They are paid at the rate of sixteen and one-half cents an hour, and to earn that amount they must have worked about twelve hours a day.

Molders and machinists have a regular ten-hour day in theory, but the machinists, being also repair men, are sometimes obliged to work much longer. A repairing job has to be finished before the men can leave it, and this quite frequently necessitates a continuous twenty-four-hour period, while sometimes the men work thirty-six hours or longer, without rest.

Seven-Day Week
It is not enough, however, to state the prevailing length of the work-

ing day. Before we can understand what a day exacts of a steel worker we must know the number he works in a week and whether he is employed six, seven or eight days from Sunday to Sunday. In this connection I use the word "day" in two senses. The operating day, from the standpoint of the mill, is twenty-four hours long and there are seven in a week. The working day of the steel worker is twelve hours in length and there are fourteen of them from Sunday morning to Sunday morning.

The work of the rolling mills, shaping and working the steel bars and billets, goes on for six operating days in the week, shutting down Saturday nights at six o'clock and beginning at the same time on Sunday night. Accordingly, each of the two shifts of men who work in the rolling mills has a week of six working days, and a weekly period of rest which is modified by the change of shifts from day to night. The shift that goes on at 6 P.M. Sunday is composed of the day men of the previous week, who have been off duty twenty-four hours. The former night shift, that finished its work Saturday morning, is the day shift of Monday. In this way each shift has twenty-four hours of continuous rest one week, and forty-eight hours the next. But this is a schedule, the exceptions to which in the rolling mills, will be brought out later.

The manner of operating the open-hearth furnaces is such that it is hard to generalize for their department. The furnaces are usually operated from Sunday morning to Saturday night, thirteen working days. Sunday morning the full heat is first turned on the furnaces after twelve hours of low heat. One or two men can do the necessary work, and the full crew does not report until noon or later. The time schedule is correspondingly irregular. I refer here to the plants where the ordinary stationary open-hearth furnaces are found, with capacity varying from thirty to sixty tons. The Talbot open-hearth furnace is a different proposition. It is very much larger than the ordinary furnace. There were five Talbot furnaces in the Jones and Laughlin plant in 1907, each with a capacity of 200 tons, and four more were in process of construction to have 250 tons capacity each. A feature of the Talbot furnace is that the molten steel is poured into the ladle by tilting the furnace. These furnaces are operated continuously seven days in the week.

The only department in the industry similar in this respect to the Talbot furnaces is the blast furnace. This is at the beginning of the whole process, where the red iron ore goes in at the top of a hundred foot stack, and comes out at the foot, molten pig iron. There are forty-four blast furnaces in Allegheny county and every one is operated three hundred and sixty-five days in the year unless a suspension is caused by some extraordinary or unforeseen occurrence. Furnaces may be operated with a fair degree of success even when they are banked occasionally; indeed, there have been furnaces, both in this country and in England, that have been operated successfully although they were banked every Saturday night and blown in on Monday morning. These furnaces were operated before the day of large outputs, however, and it is hardly likely that the large furnaces of the present day could be subjected to that treatment without much loss. In a typical blast furnace plant where the number of men employed was given me from the payroll, I found that about forty per cent of the men worked on the day turn only, and that the other sixty per cent were divided into two shifts. So that thirty per cent of the total force were on duty at night and seventy per cent during the day. With the forty per cent force there were seven full working days in every week. On account of changing the shift, the sixty per cent force alternates between a week of six days and one of eight. Every Sunday the shifts change about. The men in the night shift of the previous week give place on Sunday morning to the former day shift, and these work a period of twenty-four hours instead of twelve, taking a day and a night shift together, so as to get in line for the regular night shift of the week. This is what the men call the "long turn," and it comes every alternate week to each man in blast furnaces and in the Talbot open-hearth furnaces.

It is much easier to indicate the departments where the seven-day week prevails, than it is to give the number of men in the departments. But it is possible to make estimates, and in the two departments where seven-day work is most regular, it is possible to come very close to the true state of affairs. Investigation and information from authoritative sources, covering about half of the open-hearth furnaces in Allegheny county, show that in an open-hearth plant about twenty-five men are employed to a furnace. There were 132 open-hearth furnaces in the county in 1907 and there must have been twenty-five times that number of employes, or 3,300. These are hard to classify on account of the varying periods of Sunday work as described above. In the Talbot furnaces, as we have seen, the crews alternate between six days and eight days a week, just as in the blast furnaces; but in the other style of furnaces one crew works six days and the other from three hours to a full day more, in a given week. In some of the plants they have the long turn. This involves twenty-four hours for the charger and second helper, and shades down to about fifteen hours for a part of the crew.

In the same way it was ascertained that about 200 men are employed at an average blast furnace. There are forty-four blast furnaces in Allegheny county, with a total working force, we may assume, of 8,800 men.

In the 132 open-hearth furnaces, we have, then, 3,300 men whom we may regard as seven-day men each alternate week, or, 1,650 every week. It is true that part of them do not go to work until three o'clock Sunday afternoon, but the rest-day is broken up, and we must call them "seven-day men." Of the 8,800 men in blast furnaces, all are seven-day men if we balance one week against another; and sixty per cent of them, or 5,280, work the long turn every alternate week.

For other departments it is harder to make estimates, but we have by no means set forth the situation as regards Sunday work when we have discussed blast furnaces and open-hearth plants. In a normal year the steel mills are crowded with work. The finishing departments,—the shearmen's crews, the crane men, the yard labor,—all are frequently, if not regularly, obliged to work Sundays in order to catch up with the rolling mills. On Sundays the rollers with their full crews spend several hours changing rolls. Sunday is the day for the repair men. Machinists have already been mentioned in this connection; there is also a large force of men called millwrights, who do repair work, and whose hours are like those at the blast furnace,—twelve hours six days in the week, and on each alternate Sunday, twenty-four. New construction is always pushed to the limit on Sunday. I walked through a steel plant employing about ten thousand men one Sunday in September, 1907. The rolling mills were idle, but hundreds of men were engaged in repairing and in construction, and in piling stock.

I have already shown that there are 8,800 seven-day men in blast furnaces and 1,650 in the open-hearth furnaces of Allegheny county, a total of 10,450 men, or about fourteen per cent of the mill workers of the county. Sunday workmen are seven-day workmen, when the mills are running full, and it is evident that the number would be

very much larger if we were to add those named in my last paragraph. Two hundred such men to each of the five largest steel plants
in the county would be a very conservative estimate. That is five per
cent of the employes in those plants. If we apply that percentage to
the 70,000 mill workers in the county it would give us 3,500; adding
that to the number already secured, we have about 14,000 as the total number of Sunday and seven-day workmen in the mills and furnaces of the county. This is my minimum estimate.

Physical and Nervous Strain

The question of hours is important in itself, but its great importance
comes in the bearing of long hours upon the general conditions of
factory or mill, and the degree of physical or nervous strain demanded. It is well to bear in mind here that there is a difference in
the physical requirements in the different positions. A few of the
most extremely hot jobs are on an eight-hour basis. In the hardest of
the twelve-hour positions spell-hands are provided, so that no one
man works a full twelve hours. In the open-hearth departments and
the blast furnaces, where the twenty-four hour shift prevails, the
work is not continuous. In the blast furnaces, for example, casts are
made about every four hours. While making a cast the men work
very hard, but there are periods of an hour or more of idleness between times, and I have been told that when on the night shift the
men sleep during these periods. On the other hand, the men who fill
the cars that carry the ore and fuel to the furnace top have no period
of rest. Their work is continuous.

When all allowances are made for such respites, however, they do
not in any large way minimize the sense of tension which characterizes much of the work of the steel mills, and much of the twelve-
hour, seven-day work of the 14,000 men of my estimate. Nervous
strain in connection with a workingman's life is not a thing always
remembered or easily calculated. But did you ever sit in the front of
a trolley car where you could see down the track ahead, and notice
the chances people take in crossing the street? You were glad that
you were not the motorman,—and since then hasn't it been easier to
understand the sudden, frantic ringing of the gong, and the quick
grinding of the brakes? Imagine yourself then up in a little cage on a
traveling crane, guiding with a lever the course of a ladle of hot
steel, where a jar may spill the liquid over the edge on some work-

man below, or carrying over the heads of men a section of steel plate, caught up with hooks gripped to the edges. Suppose the crane does not run smoothly and one of the hooks jars loose;—but the fear of injuring someone is not the only thing that keeps a workman keyed up to a high pitch. In the last fifteen years great changes have been made in steel mill practice. Machines have been substituted for human skill wherever possible and where a dozen or so years ago a crew of twenty men worked, to-day two or three men stand and operate intricate machinery with levers. A single false move on the part of these men would mean the wrecking of valuable machinery, the spoiling of a heat of steel, and the interrupting of the operation of the mill, such as would work hardship on a large crew of men whose pay stops when steel ceases to be produced. All in all one cannot be surprised that sometimes a man of thirty-five is gray, or that occasionally a skilled steel worker breaks down, his nerves almost shattered.

The physical strain of the mills may not be any easier to measure than the nervous strain, but it is more readily apparent. It should be remembered, too, that physical strain involves more than muscular exertion. There is the intense heat to be reckoned with. In the Bessemer department men work constantly close beside a ladle containing ten to fifteen tons of liquid steel. In the open-hearth department the labor is not so continuous, but the men are obliged to remain in an atmosphere heated by radiations from rows of immense furnaces, each containing from thirty to sixty tons of boiling metal. The blooming-mills roll down huge ingots sometimes weighing as much as ten tons. These are brought from the furnaces to the rolls, white to the core and throwing out a vicious circle of withering heat. One blooming-mill roller told me that he had substituted wooden handles for the usual steel grips on his levers because the steel got too hot for his bare hands. Until you have visited the mills you can hardly conceive of the heat. "It's hell," is what steel workers usually say of it, and on a July day it is hell concentrated. But no amount of visiting a mill and watching the processes, and guessing at the temperature, will ever convey to one's mind what it really means to the men who work through the twelve hours of the working day. The men to whom this is a daily experience, who must resolutely face the incredible heat of summer as well as the more trying situation of January, when the change from the overheated mill to the icy out-

doors come as a daily shock,—these are the men who understand. . . .

Trade Unionism

Whatever one may think of trade unionism in principle, it must be
recognized that had there been a strong organization of steel workers during the last fifteen years, the sum total of industrial conditions could hardly have developed to the point that has been described. It is necessary to recur, briefly, to the period of union
influence in the steel mills, in order to explain that development. At
the beginning of 1892 the Amalgamated Association of Iron and
Steel Workers controlled the skilled workmen in nearly all the small
mills in Allegheny county and in the two largest steel plants, those
of Jones and Laughlin in Pittsburgh and of the Carnegie Steel Company at Homestead. The other large mills were for the most part
non-union, but conditions approximating those in the union plants
were maintained. It was in the summer of 1892 that the famous
Homestead strike occurred, which resulted in the permanent elimination of union influence in the Carnegie mills of Allegheny county,
and eventually in the absolute overthrow of the union in all the steel
mills of the country.

It is impossible, at this time, to discuss fully the causes of the destruction of unionism in the steel mills. The old question of control,
which made unionism a chaos from the standpoint of the employers,
and the lack of it despotism from the standpoint of the workmen,
was sufficient to precipitate a struggle whenever there was hope, on
either side, of getting the whip hand. Certain elements entered into
the situation, however, that may be considered as influential in
bringing matters to a head. There were policies and customs of the
Amalgamated Association that were more than ordinarily irksome
to the steel manufacturers, and there were customs that grew up
among the members of the locals, entirely apart from the avowed
policies of the national union, that undoubtedly aided in creating a
breach between the employers and the men. One point where the
union was clearly at fault was its insistence upon very high wages for
some of its highly skilled members while it made small effort to better the condition of the others who worked in positions requiring
greater exertion. Another point that concerned the membership of
the locals, and that was in no way connected with the policy of the

national union, was the habit of petty interference with the management of a plant. A feature in the union policy most obnoxious to the employers was the custom of arbitrarily limiting the working day. The union had a limit both on time and on output. That is, it fixed the number of heats that should be worked in a day and also provided that no more heats were to be charged after nine hours and fifteen minutes from the time of commencing to charge. This was the rule in iron mills, which were not equipped for continuous operation, and the effect of it was to make an average of about ten hours to the turn. When this iron mill custom was forced on the steel mills it created dissatisfaction, for they are intended to be operated twenty-four hours in the day. In the sheet mills, the employers, over the opposition of the men, succeeded in introducing a three-turn system, thus providing for continuous operation with a working day of eight hours. This attempt was made with less success in other mills. In 1892, the year of the Homestead strike, Jones and Laughlin tried to change to the three turn system on two of their guide-mills, which were then rolling iron. President Weihe and the other national officers of the Amalgamated Association strongly favored the change, but the men working in these particular mills refused to submit to it. Their objections seem to have been based on a fear that a reduction in hours would mean a corresponding reduction in wages. This is an example of the shortsightedness which characterized the rank and file of the organization. It shows, too, how the association was handicapped, as it has been many times, by an ineffective discipline which has not permitted the exceptionally capable and broadminded leaders, who have held the national offices of the association almost constantly since its organization in 1876, to take the action that their better judgment has dictated.

The leaders of the strike of 1892, many of whom are still working in steel mills in the Pittsburgh District, name these very features as the weak points in the union armor, and they unhesitatingly condemn them to-day on the grounds both of policy and of ethics. But they insist that the thing they fought for in 1892 was their right to organize,—not the right to arbitrary power. On account of such events as these just mentioned, the employers found it difficult to make such a distinction.

However, it is sufficient to note here that with the elimination of organized labor from the Carnegie mills there began a movement in the same direction in the other union plants. The remainder of the decade was marked by a steady decline in union strength. The panic of 1893 weakened its effectiveness. Jones and Laughlin became non-union in 1897. The smaller mills were swept into the non-union movement with the Carnegie Company in 1892, or followed its lead in later years. The final act was played in 1901 in the last frantic struggle of the Amalgamated Association against the rising power of the United States Steel Corporation. The result was the total destruction of unionism in all the steel mills, large and small, in Allegheny county and, with the exception of a few of the sheet mills, its overthrow in all the mills of the corporation throughout the country.

The Employer in Control

It has been since the overthrow of unionism that the work conditions which I have described have crystallized. It is true that before the union had begun to decline, the twelve-hour day was recognized as the standard in a majority of positions. But the eight-hour positions were increasing in the steel mills and at least three departments at Homestead were being operated on the three turn basis. In the Jones and Laughlin plant the eight-hour day made greater headway than elsewhere but in all the Pittsburgh mills it had a foot-hold. The Homestead strike came to an end in November, 1892, and by the end of December all of the rolling mills in that Carnegie plant were operating with two crews of men. The eight-hour day had been abandoned everywhere except in the Bessemer department, where there were still to be found in 1907 nine eight-hour men.

The Jones and Laughlin Company did not abandon the eight-hour policy as rapidly as did the Carnegie Company. Since their break with the union, there has been a slow and steady elimination of the three shift system. It is probably true that in 1897 there were more eight-hour positions in the Jones and Laughlin plant than in any other steel works in Allegheny county. The same held true in 1907; the rollers on the three blooming-mills, the Bessemer converter men, and the men on the narrow gauge engines who handled the hot ingots, all had an eight-hour day. But in the latter part of 1907 some of these positions were changed to twelve hours. In January, 1908, there was a general move in the direction of an extension of hours. The bridge workers and the men in the cold roll shafting department were changed from nine hours to ten, and in all other positions, including the Bessemer department, where the eight-hour system still persisted, the change was made to twelve hours. I made a careful study of this plant, talking with employes and officials of the company, and I was unable to find any eight-hour positions left in 1908. The officials of the company explained the twelve-hour day in the Bessemer department on the ground that this department was not running at its full capacity on account of the greater demand for open-hearth steel.

Another marked tendency in all of the steel mills in the last fifteen years is the extension of Sunday work. Blast furnaces, with a few minor exceptions, have always been operated seven days in the week in this country, but before the elimination of unionism, the rolling mills used to be idle from Saturday evening until Monday morning of each week. The union stoutly opposed all Sunday work and succeeded in reducing it to a minimum in all plants where it had influence. With the decline in union strength, Sunday work began to increase. Like the extension of hours it did not come all at once, but here and there in different mills, the hour for beginning operations was pushed backwards. Instead of starting to roll steel at six on Monday morning the men were first set to work at midnight, Sunday night, and this made it necessary for the heaters to go to work Sunday evening. Now the general rule is for all departments of the mills to begin operations on Sunday evening at six o'clock and in consequence the heaters and many others are obliged to go to work in mid-afternoon Sunday. As has already been pointed out, the open-hearth department must be in operation from Sunday morning so as to have steel to pour on Sunday evening.

A few years ago one of the last mills to adopt Sunday night work induced the men to come out on account of being behind in their orders. Once established in this way the custom has continued, and in this plant men are discharged if they refuse to work on Sunday evenings. Beginning as a favor it is now a fixed policy, and competitive conditions tend to hold it as such. That, and the necessity of retaining the discipline of the organization, led the steel companies during the panic of 1907 and 1908 to take action which brought upon them considerable criticism. The mills were operated only one-fourth time or less, but men were called out to work on an order on Sunday evening, when it was well known that the order would be finished in two or three days at the most, and the mill would have to shut down for the remainder of the week.

Repressive Measures

Again, without regard to any opinions as to labor organization, one is compelled to wonder why the workmen have remained passive while these things were going on, why they have not revived their union and fought these moves, which could not have failed to be distasteful to them. The reason is that the steel companies knew long ago that their reorganization of conditions in the industry would be opposed, and like good generals they prepared to forestall any uprising. They realized from the beginning that eternal vigilance was the price of their control. Consequently, the Steel Corporation pursues very effective methods to prevent an outbreak of unionism or independent action on the part of the men. What the employes call a "spy system" keeps, they believe, the corporation officials informed as to what is going on. At any rate the officials seem to have little difficulty in finding out anything about which they wish information. Either this or something else has made the corporation employes the most suspicious of men. They are careful about what they say to a stranger and even fear to talk freely among themselves. They seem to feel that they are living always in the presence of a hostile critic, though, on occasion, they are capable of throwing off this spirit of suspicion and reticence. They are a generous, open hearted and intelligent sort of men, upon the whole, and are able to discuss a variety of subjects. They will talk with you if you meet them on the street corner either about Hans Wagner's batting average or of the prospects of a war with Japan, or if you wish they will discuss higher criticism in theology. But they will not talk about the steel works and will eye you suspiciously if you so much as mention the works. If you press the discussion, they manifest the most astonishing ignorance concerning the most patent and generally known facts.

I had this experience repeatedly when I was going about in the mill towns. When I tested men whom I met in a casual way, it was almost always with the same result. It was easier to talk with the men in their homes, but here, too, there was suspicion to be broken down. Sometimes I could not get an opportunity to see the man whom I was seeking. Business engagements would suddenly be remembered which prevented an interview. Several whom I saw at their homes refused to talk about mill work. A highly paid employe of the Steel Corporation refused even to see me. I had been at his house, and finding that he was out, I left word that I would return at a specified hour. Returning at the time named, my ring brought his wife to the door, who told me that her husband was at home; but that he would not see me nor talk to me because the company had forbidden its employes to talk with strangers about mill work! Repeatedly I interviewed men who answered my questions guardedly, evidently in great perturbation of spirit, as if they feared that my visit boded them no good. Sometimes when meeting a workingman, after explaining to him my desire to talk over industrial conditions, he would say protestingly, "But I haven't anything to say against the company," although I had not mentioned the company. On several occasions at the close of an interview in which only the most careful statements had been made, my canny informant chuckled in evident relief, "There, I haven't told you anything against the company, have I?" One man of long experience as a steel worker, who gave me a better insight into mill conditions than any other one person, remarked, "I used to write for labor papers a great deal, and sometimes I fairly burn to do it now,—to declare before the world, over my own signature the facts about working conditions in the steel industry. But I can't. It wouldn't be safe."

But in spite of all this fear, whenever I got an opportunity for a quiet talk with the men so that I could show them my letters of introduction and explain my mission, I usually found them sympathetic and helpful, for they said, "We cannot tell about those things ourselves; we cannot write for the papers about our long hours and the unjust restrictions; but we want the public to know, and we are glad to tell you,—but *never mention our names*. We must not lose our jobs, for that is all we have." I remember one man who had evidently been waging a battle, during all of our conversation, between his caution and his desire to tell his true feelings. He went with me to the door as I left and followed me out on the porch into the night, closing the door behind him. Then, certain that no one, not even his family, would hear him, he said anxiously, "Now you won't mention my name in connection with this, will you?" I promised him faithfully that I would not, and gave him my hand on it.

This self-repression, this evident fear of a free expression of personality, manifests itself in other ways than in a hesitancy to talk with strangers. The men do not talk much with one another in the mill itself about conditions that are disliked, except furtively when the foreman is not near. There is little discussion of politics,—that, too, could easily bring one into dangerous waters. There is considerable socialistic sentiment in all of the mill towns. One encounters it not infrequently in going about among the steel workers. I met more socialists in Homestead and Munhall than elsewhere, —numerous enough so that I expected to find a local organization there, but in the four more important steel centers, McKeesport, Duquesne, Braddock and Homestead, there was not in 1907 a trace of a socialistic local. This puzzled me a little until a Homestead steel worker told me that they had not dared have a local within the borough. To be known as a socialist, the men thought, would be to court discharge, and most of the Homestead socialists held membership in a Pittsburgh local. I have since learned that during the campaign of 1908 a local was organized in Homestead.

These skilled steel workers are very much like other Americans. They are neither less nor more intelligent, courageous, and self-reliant than the average citizen. Their extreme caution, the constant state of apprehension in which they live, can have but one explanation. It is the burnt child that fears the fire. It could hardly be expected that after the disastrous strikes of 1892, attempts would not be made to revive unionism. It has been through a series of such attempts that the men have learned to respect the vigilance and power of their employers, and they have learned the cost of defiance.

In 1895 men were discharged at Homestead, so it was alleged, for attending a meeting where officials of the Amalgamated Association spoke. A lodge of the association was formed in the 119-inch mill and the officers of the lodge were immediately discharged. In 1899 another attempt was made at organization which was frustrated by discharging those involved. Again in 1901 there was a move toward organization at Homestead which resulted in the discharge of a large number of men. In the other Carnegie mills there has been less activity than at Homestead, but wherever it has occurred it has been as sternly repressed.

The other corporation mills have fought the union in the same way. The National Tube Company especially has used the weapons of lockout and discharge for twenty-five years. Nor are the independents far behind. In the summer of 1906 the employes of the Jones and Laughlin Company planned a meeting to protest against Sunday work. The management discovered the movement and threatened the men with discharge if they held a meeting. This action is in line with the policy of the United States Steel Corporation, which has refused to recognize or reply to petitions asking for a change in working conditions.

The officials of the steel companies make no secret of their hostility to unionism, and I have been told by two leading employers that they would not tolerate it. Any movement toward organization, they assured me, would mean discharge.

Steel Corporations and Politics

Not only is there repression manifested among the steel workers such as to choke personal initiative in directions the companies may consider inimical; there are indications of coercion to act in support of the companies' interests.

It would not be a complete statement of the control exercised by the employers of the steel districts if we were to omit the political situation. It is commonly understood that the United States Steel Corporation is the dominant force in politics in the mill towns. Repeated allegations have been made to me that workmen have been discharged at Duquesne for refusing to vote the company ticket. If there is coercion it is quite probable that the effect of it extends far beyond the persons actually involved. I was told by one employe that he had been called into the office of the superintendent and remonstrated with for working against the company ticket, and an indirect threat was made of discharge. I was told by men of unimpeachable standing in Braddock, not steel works employes, that, in the spring of 1908 preceding the May primaries, men were induced to vote for the candidates favored by the steel company, by promises of a resumption in industry if the right candidates were nominated. I have it also on good authority that before the same primaries of May, 1908, orders came from the New York office of the United States Steel Corporation, to the general superintendent of the Edgar Thomson plant at Braddock directing him to order the department superintendents to line up their employes for the Penrose candidates for the Legislature. The general superintendent called a meeting of the department superintendents and delivered the orders. This created some dismay, for local option was an issue in the primaries and the Penrose candidates were opposed to local option. Some of the superintendents were already prominently identified with the local option party and had been assisting in organizing the campaign. How they could with honor and self-respect abandon the issue at that point was not clear to the officials. But the answer to the objections was clear and to the point. They were told to break any or all promises and to work for Penrose, because the United States Steel Corporation needed him in the Senate. It is probably unnecessary to add that Penrose carried Allegheny county.

Social Life

The question now rises,—and the answer must determine our judgment of the policies described,—what does it all mean to the men, and the families of men who work in the mills? What is the effect of it upon standards and ideals at the very heart of the community life? To know its effect you must see life in a steel worker's home. A week of heavy toil, during ten or eleven hours of daylight, six or seven days, and then an overturning of things and a week of night work, each shift thirteen or fourteen hours long, and the "mister" working while the children sleep, and sleeping while they play, —that is the regular round of events in the typical family while the weeks stretch to months and the months mount to years. "Home," said many a steel worker to me with grim bitterness, "is where I eat and sleep."

The library plays little part in the life of a twelve-hour workman, and the church, even with the men who do not work Sundays, and despite the efforts of the exceptional minister here and there, is losing its influence because of its failure to recognize and deal with social injustice in the community.

It necessarily follows that as books, lectures and concerts are shut off from the steel worker, so too are the better forms of social life. The younger men not infrequently take the time and trouble to dress for an evening of social enjoyment. There are few over thirty, however, who have not given up entirely social observances. But the natural desire for companionship cannot thus be stifled, and so the saloon comes forward as the social center. On Saturday evenings, especially after pay days, the saloons are crowded, and the workingmen find companionship and a chance to spend their money. It is a perfectly natural following of the line of least resistance that brings many of the men. They do not need to change their clothing and shave before being made welcome. They may come with the grime of the mill upon them and not feel out of place. In slack times when the mills are not running the saloon becomes a regular meeting place, and men go there primarily for companionship,—the drinking is secondary to that. Ordinarily you do not see much drunkenness. The men want to be fit for work the next day. But on holidays some go too far. The only men whom I found drunk in their own homes were furnacemen,—men who had been working for months without a holiday or a Sunday. They had had a brief holiday and they spent it in the only way they knew. The better class of steel workers who view their fellows with a sympathetic eye, explain holiday intoxication as a logical result of steady work and long days. After weeks and months of work, twelve hours a day, and no holidays, a man gets far behind in his accumulation of the pleasure that the world owes him. When a holiday comes it is all too short to collect the overdue bill,—and pleasure of a concentrated sort is sought to make up for lost time. Furthermore, the unskilled men are too unused to liberty to know how to use to advantage even a day.

The social spirit is not the only element in the popularity of the saloon. There are certain causes that make steel workers great users of alcoholic drinks. The heat of the mills, which permeates in greater or lesser degree every department, brings out the sweat and creates thirst. The men drink great quantities of water all through the day and they leave the mill at the end of a turn either nauseated from an excess of water or still thirsty. In either case they can find immediate relief in the saloon. The dust of the mills irritates the throat, and this sends many a man to his beer or whiskey. The great majority, however, are possessed of sincere belief that they must either drink or fail. A daily stimulant they consider essential to an endurance of the daily twelve-hour battle with heat and exhaustion. As a result, the saloons are taking more of the steel workers' money than any of the legitimate business establishments of the mill towns. I was told by a man who was in a position to know accurately the facts of the saloon business of McKeesport in 1906, that there were eighty saloons in this city of about 30,000 population. On the Thursdays preceding the semi-monthly pay days which fall on Fridays and Saturdays, the three leading saloon keepers of the city drew from their bank accounts from $1,200 to $1,500 each in dollar bills and small denominations, to be used as change. Other saloon keepers drew varying amounts and the total thus drawn each fortnight was over $60,000. On the Mondays after pay days the saloon keepers usually deposited double the amount drawn. These periodic leaps in deposits never failed to coincide with pay days, and the inevitable conclusion is that about $60,000 of steel workers' wages were regularly expended in the saloons within the two days.

If this seems overdrawn let me cite the case of George Holloway, who was blacklisted in 1901 after leading a strike in the Wood plant of the American Sheet and Tin Plate Company in McKeesport. With what was generally understood to be borrowed funds,—for Holloway was left almost penniless by the strike,—he started a saloon in McKeesport. I saw and talked with him in the fall of 1907, and he told me that in 1905, four years from the time of entering the business, he sold out. He had established a son in a saloon in the West and with the rest of his family he was living in McKeesport on the income of his investments, a retired capitalist. In the other mill towns there is every indication that the saloon business is as good as in McKeesport.

These are the things that go to make up life for the steel workers, a twelve-hour day for practically all, six, seven and even eight working days in a week, cultural opportunities denied, democratic aspirations choked, and a regime of coercion that holds sway even after the mill gate has been left behind, and the worker is on the street,—a citizen.

In view of all these things a look ahead is not only justified, but demanded. No thinking man believes that the labor problem can be settled by repressive measures. The employers themselves do not believe that this can be the end of it. During a long interview that I had with an official of one of the steel companies in Pittsburgh, in which I set forth the essential facts as presented in this article, he said to me: "The present situation can only be temporary. It would be too much to expect that the steel companies, when in complete control, would not go too far. It may be that they have already gone too far and it is certain that eventually the workmen will be driven to resist. They will revive their union; it is inevitable, and they will win back their old control. Then they will do just what they have always done before: become arrogant as they acquire more power and they will compel the manufacturers to fight them back to disorganization.

This is the movement in industry I think. There will always be a clash of interests,—there will always be industrial conflicts. But there will be a gain to society in each conflict. We won't go backward. Something will be gained every time and each new battle will be on a higher plane than the last." This is one employer's solution of the labor problem.

The Smoky City
by John T. Holdsworth

The smoke nuisance is here set down frankly and unreservedly as the greatest hindrance to Pittsburgh's economic progress. It is the one single problem imperatively demanding solution if the city is to take and maintain its proper rank in the industrial world. Long ago Pittsburgh assumed in pride the name "The Smoky City" which in an earlier economic era was an expression of its industrial activity and prosperity. In this day of civic enlightenment and business efficiency that name is at once the badge of public indifference and of industrial inefficiency. Thousands of people in this city, perhaps the majority, who have always lived amid the murk and the smoke which here is our common lot, believe that smoke and prosperity are synonymous. Some manufacturers still believe that they cannot suppress black smoke without increasing wages or fuel bills. "The more smoke the better times" is a saying that has become current in the community. In this belief the people have been indifferent or at least resigned to the soot and have stolidly borne the drains which it makes upon comfort, health and purse. It is certain, however, that if the people of Pittsburgh can have presented to them in a form which they can clearly understand a summary of the enormous toll annually exacted from them by the smoke nuisance, and every last cent of it absolutely unnecessary, then surely they will unite to banish it for all time.

Fundamentally the smoke nuisance is an economic problem. It increases the cost of living to every man, woman and child in this city. Smoke means waste, and waste of any kind means higher cost

Report of the Economic Survey of Pittsburgh (Pittsburgh, 1912), pp. 35–38.

of living. In the first place the smoke which now belches from a thousand chimney tops is the unmistakable evidence of enormous waste of the fuel possibilities of the coal being fed to the furnaces. Black smoke is simply unused carbon, wasted heat units; its emission creates additional waste. Leaving for a later discussion, the direct losses to the manufacturer due to imperfect combustion of coal, brief consideration may be given to the indirect losses to the citizen and taxpayer. . . .

In the annual report of the Pittsburgh Department of Public Health for 1910, the Chief Smoke Inspector says: "Demoralization and disease follow dirt, and there is nothing else known to man that can produce so much filth, dirt, demoralization and disease in a given time as the smoke from bituminous coal. The continual envelope of smoke in which the wives and children of our mill and factory employees are compelled to live not only dwarfs the children, but it destroys foliage and vegetation in all such districts by carrying tons upon tons of deadly gases through, and filtering them into, our atmosphere. This wholesale atmospheric vitiation should be stopped.******* The time has now arrived when a determined campaign must be inaugurated against the smoke produced by our metallurgical furnaces, many of which emit dense black smoke almost constantly. By pursuing the same vigorous and practical policy that has marked the progress of the City of Pittsburgh's successful campaign against the smoke from boiler stacks and chimneys, the 'furnace' smoke fallacy will soon be exploded."

It has been carefully estimated that the mills of Pittsburgh are responsible for from 50 to 60 per cent of the smoke, yet by some strange anomaly heating and puddling furnaces are exempted from the operation of the smoke ordinance. The present ordinance provides that "no steam boiler furnace or other furnace, *excepting in private residences, mill heating furnaces and puddling furnaces,* shall be constructed within the corporate limits of the City of Pittsburgh until the owner, agent or lessee shall first make written application at the office of the Chief Smoke Inspector for a certificate for that purpose, and shall furnish a written statement and drawings of the style and dimensions of such boiler or furnace, the height and size of stack or chimney, and the method or device for preventing the emission of dense black or dense gray smoke except for eight minutes in any one hour." The ordinance further provides that, with the exceptions noted above, all furnaces shall be so constructed or altered as to prevent smoke, and that no person shall be allowed the use of a furnace until it is constructed to meet this requirement.

Leaving aside the debatable question of its validity, this ordinance is defective in that it exempts the furnaces which are responsible for more than half the smoke nuisance. Some justification, perhaps, can be offered for the exemption of private residences, though it is probable that in order to make the ordinance proof against legal attack it must be drawn without any exemption. Furthermore, the smoke emitted from residence chimneys in this city, where natural gas is so largely used as a domestic fuel, is in a broad view of the question a negligible factor.

A much more important consideration than the mere administrative or punitive factors involved in this problem is that of efficiency and economy. It is passing strange that great corporations with millions of dollars invested, employing many highly paid managers and engineers, using up-to-date business methods, including cost accounting systems, employing, in some cases, efficiency engineers to bring about the most "scientific management," and ready to "scrap" any machine or appliance however expensive when something better can be secured to reduce the cost of manufacture—it is passing strange that these concerns go on year after year with little or no attempt to reduce the loss due to the smoke and gases which unburned now pollute the air. The only possible excuse for this indifference and waste, so entirely out of keeping with the general business methods employed, is the cheapness of fuel. With coal selling in the Pittsburgh District at prices ranging from $1.00 to $1.50 a ton, there does not appear to be much urgency for economizing on fuel. Cheap and good fuel in abundance is admittedly one of the chief advantages enjoyed by manufacturers in this District. But is there good reason in wasting a thing just because it is cheap? That was the practice in this region in the early days of natural gas and oil, and with what result? Like habits of prodigal wastefulness obtained in earlier days in the extractive industries such as farming, mining, timbering, and the whole country as a consequence is agitated over the question of conservation of natural resources. Yet in the manufacture of iron and steel and a score of other products, one of the most valuable of these resources, coal, is not only wasted but is permitted to become a menace to health and decent living, a tax upon every citizen, a scourge to vegetation, a defilement of buildings and merchandise, and a positive check upon civic and industrial progress,—all because it is cheap! Why should the energy of coal be allowed to run to waste any more than that of the laborer, of the machine, or of any other part of the productive process? Any one of these is evidence of inefficiency.

The objection that the economies to be effected by the smokeless combustion of cheap coal in the manufacture of iron and steel are so slight as not to warrant the expense of installing the proper devices, can be met with proof that large plants are now operating smokelessly in this state and elsewhere with considerable resulting economies in the coal supply. At Lebanon the American Steel & Manufacturing Company has adopted the plan of powdering the coal before supplying it to the furnaces with the result that its stacks are practically smokeless and the coal bills are considerably reduced. Some of the puddling and reheating furnaces at this plant have been using powdered coal as fuel for nine or ten years, and during the past three years the entire plant of 94 furnaces has been using powdered coal. The manager states that the change was made wholly for economic reasons. He further states that, as the men all work by the ton and can produce a greater output because they do not have to stop to clean the fire box every twelve hours, he could not, if he wished, return to the use of unpowdered coal as he would have a strike on hand at once. Other plants in the country, for example the Edison Manufacturing Company at Chicago, and the Phipps Power Station in this city, have demonstrated that coal, even though high in volatile matter, can be burned smokelessly and at a saving in expense. The plant that continues to smoke is not only guilty of gross disregard of the public health and comfort, but it stands charged with business inertia and inefficiency.

Housing Problems
by F. Elisabeth Crowell

To the average householder in any city the housing problem is largely a question of bricks and mortar or stone or wood plus a desirable location. In the rapid development of urban life, what were

"What Bad Housing Means to Pittsburgh," *Charities and the Commons,* 19 (March 7, 1908), pp. 1683–1697.

once considered luxuries grew to be regarded as modern conveniences and have now become necessities. These, of course, he must have. If he is a property owner, he grumbles about the taxes; if he leases his house from another, he grumbles about the rent, and here the story ends for him. He knows in a vague way that a tenth of the city's population, familiarly known as the "submerged," live under conditions and amid surroundings which are, to say the least, unpleasant, but beyond a comfortable feeling of gratitude that his lines have fallen in pleasant places, and a passing shade of careless pity for those other less fortunate ones, he gives no further thought to the subject. It has never occurred to him to consider the deeper issues underlying this matter of bad housing—considerations which have to do with the preservation of the public health, with the prevention of disease, and with the maintenance of certain recognized standards which make for the conservation of decency and morality among those who have been compelled by the pressure of economic forces to dwell in the adverse environment created by unsanitary, inadequate, or improper housing conditions.

Nature in forming the "Forks of the Ohio" designed a strategic point of unrivaled excellence, and our forebears of a century and a half ago were quick to recognize and utilize this point in their frontier warfare; but nature never intended these foot-hills of the Alleghenies, enclosed by these same "Forks," to be the site for a great city, with its teeming population. The physical conformation of the land covered by the city of Pittsburgh, with its succession of hills and dales, its limited area available for building sites, the obstacles to be overcome in the securing of adequate transportation facilities from one part of the city to another, all these considerations would seem to have militated seriously against the development of the frontier trading post into a modern city with its multitudinous activities. However, these disadvantages become of small moment when contrasted with the wealth of deposits hidden away in these same hills, which served as a magnet for the concentration of manufacture in this particular locality. The transportation facilities offered by the bordering rivers through their junction with the Ohio, was another important factor in determining the growth and importance of the settlement which had grown up near the fort.

To-day we have in Greater Pittsburgh, with its population of nearly 600,000, housing conditions which are inimical to public health and to private decency. It requires no skilled detective to ferret out these places, nor are they confined to the so-called "slums." They can be seen within five minutes' walk of the heart of the business district. They are duplicated in the Penn Avenue district, down in Soho, on the south side and on the north side. An equally bad condition obtains in the less thickly populated districts where houses have been built along abandoned water courses, known as "runs."

Inadequate, unsanitary toilet accommodations, insufficient water supply, cellar rooms unfit for human habitation, unsightly accumulations of rubbish, ashes and garbage in yards and cellars, dilapidated old shacks that look as if a puff of wind would demolish them:—such are the most glaring consequences resulting from the combination of private greed and public indifference. Add to this the frequent herding together of human beings like cattle in a pen, and one can form a fair picture of the conditions under which no small proportion of Pittsburgh's laboring population must make its homes and rear its families.

Within a few blocks of the court house, if a passerby would turn in casually at almost any alley, the chances are all in favor of his finding an old-fashioned privy vault. These vaults are an abomination at best, polluting the atmosphere and contributing a large quota to the mortality and morbidity statistics by serving as foci for the breeding of disease germs. All of them are foul, some of them indescribably so. It is undoubtedly true that the excessive typhoid rate in Pittsburgh has been considerably augmented by this widely accepted method of the disposal of sewage. The combination of an impure water supply with these primitive sanitary arrangements forms a vicious circle—the privy vaults serving to perpetuate conditions for which the water supply is primarily responsible. The new filtration plant will supposedly take care of the one source of infection. The Bureau of Health is laboring mightily to remedy the remaining evil, but it is sadly hampered by the limited capital at its disposal, as well as by a lack of proper support coming from public sentiment.

It has been estimated that 19,000 families in the old city alone are dependent upon privy vaults, a number of which are not even sewer connected. These vaults are not confined to any one section of Pittsburgh. Everywhere one goes they are to be found, tucked away obscurely in the corners of dark, noisome courts, flaunting themselves shamelessly at the edge of the street, clinging like limpets to the rocky sides of the hills, with never a concession to decency by having even a lattice surrounding them. The majority are easily accessible from the street, and when the doors are allowed to remain unlocked the condition of the compartments can better be imagined than described. The privy vault itself is flushed at irregular intervals, but there is always a residue of filth at the bottom. Frequently the surface waste water from the yard or court is supposed to drain into the privy well; the drain becomes obstructed at its junction with the vault and the waste water stands in greasy pools on the broken, uneven surface of the ground. I have seen vaults full to the brim and overflowing with the liquid filth; I have seen them draining down the side of a hill through an open wooden conduit in a neighbor's back yard, and emptying at the curb of a busy street in a thickly populated section of the city. Thence the sewage would find its way to the nearest street corner and at last into its proper receptacle—the public sewer. I have seen closet compartments built over long, wooden chutes which were supposed to empty into a running stream, which in its turn empties into the Ohio river. I use the word "supposed" advisedly. As a matter of fact the filth stood exposed on the ground at the edge of the "run," which would rise and wash it away when the river rose—an uncertain state of affairs both as to time and frequency of occurrence. This particular stream in question, Saw Mill Run, is now carrying off the sewage of about thirty-five thousand people. It drains that section of the city commonly known as Montooth, Beltzhoover, Mt. Washington, West Liberty and Elliott, and considerable territory not within the city limits. A local paper recently announced:

> Residents of the section drained by Saw Mill Run are beginning an agitation for the purpose of getting the city to build a sanitary sewer paralleling this stream.—The creek during most seasons of the year is shallow and the water polluted.

Another widespread evil, and one which probably bears most heavily upon the weary housewife whose work is never done, is the inadequate water supply. I am familiar with the oft-repeated statement that if these people lived in the country they would be obliged to carry water from the yard to the house; but conditions that may be tolerated on the farm or in a small village become intolerable when repeated in the congested quarters of an industrial city. Pittsburgh is a city of hills and mills and grime and smoke. It is difficult to keep clean under the most advantageous conditions. One would say that cleanliness was out of the question when water had to be carried not only from a hydrant in the court or yard, but up three or four flights of stairs as well, and carried not once but twice, for in these cases there is rarely any provision made for the disposal of waste water and this in turn must be carried downstairs and emptied into the yard drain. Is it any wonder that waste water is emptied from second story and third story windows and allowed to stand in the adjoining yard or court, whence it finds its way down through a narrow passageway between the houses and across the sidewalk into the street gutter? One ingenious second floor tenant hit upon the labor-saving device of installing a sink in the rear room of his apartment and running the waste pipe therefrom halfway across the first story extension; a wooden conduit served to continue the drain to the corner of the roof where connection was made with the rain leader, and so to the yard below.

Just opposite the Union Station there is a row of seven houses for which the sole water supply is one hydrant in the court; in the next court, another hydrant furnishes the water for the tenants of thirteen houses. These are not isolated examples. Similar instances might be cited in many portions of the city.

With regard to the inadequate water supply within the houses, this condition obtains principally in the old dwellings that have been converted into tenements, and to this class belong the great majority of Pittsburgh's tenements. The process of conversion usually means merely the crowding of three or more families into quarters originally intended for one or two families. It does not necessarily imply that any structural changes in the buildings have been made, or that the sanitary accommodations have been multiplied to meet the demands of the increased number of families. In such cases, one of the chief evils aside from the question of inconvenience, is the ruthless destruction of privacy that ensues. With no common hall, the usual means of access to the faucet is through the living room or rooms of another family. This is also true in some instances where sanitary closets have been installed within the house. When these sinks and closets are located in a common entry or passageway, a dirty, filthy condition of the fixture is to be expected. What is everybody's business is nobody's business. There is no placing the responsibility for the proper care of sink or toilet, and if out of repair they are allowed to continue in this condition for weeks and even months at a stretch.

The occupancy of cellar and basement rooms for living purposes is another growing evil resulting largely from the high rents and the lack of adequate housing accommodations to meet the need of a constantly increasing population. The excessive number of cellar and basement rooms in Pittsburgh is due partly to the hilly character of the land which renders the construction of a house on the edge of a declivity without one or more rooms of this type practically an impossibility. It is a question of how far rooms of this character strictly come under the definition of a cellar room as defined by law, but one fact is certain, however they may conform to the letter of the law, they are in direct contravention to the spirit thereof. Entirely below the ground level on one side, with adjoining rooms on another side, they may or may not have a window or door opening upon a narrow passageway, or a flight of stairs between this house and the next one. I have seen such rooms lighted by a small grating in the sidewalk (which practically meant no light at all), without ventilation, damp, utterly unfit for human habitation, serving as a bedroom for a whole family,—father, mother, and two or three children.

But the ordinary cellar or basement dwellings, as they are commonly known, exist in sufficient numbers to warrant more than a passing comment. They are an unmixed evil under any circumstances, whether occupied as kitchens or bedrooms, or both, as is frequently the case. During the past four weeks, with the co-operation of the Bureau of Health, 409 such rooms have been located in various sections of the city. Of this number 364 were cellar rooms as defined by law—that is, more than one-half the height of the room was below the ground level, and sixty-two of these rooms were occupied as sleeping rooms. Of the remaining fifty-five basement rooms, all were below the required height of rooms permitted to be occupied for living purposes (8 ½ feet) and nine of these were occupied as sleeping rooms.

As matters now stand, the Bureau of Health, lacking power to vacate with regard to unsanitary dwellings in general, is powerless to effect any remedy in the case of cellar rooms in one and two family houses. When rooms of this description are found to be occupied in tenement houses, by a worrying process of bringing suits under the tenement house law, the landlord can generally be forced to vacate such rooms. Inspection and reinspection is the only method of ensuring the observance of the law regarding the occupancy of these cellar rooms, the violation of which has become a fixed habit, a habit which adds no little to the revenue of the landlord or lessee, as the case may be.

For if the truth were known, the landlord in some cases is not immediately responsible for the renting of these cellar rooms as dwellings, although his remote responsibility is evident when one considers the exorbitant rents he demands, which make it imperative for the tenant to add to his income if any possible way presents itself. Having rented a five-room house, two stories and a cellar, the lessee proceeds to sub-let the two rooms on the second floor to one family, and the cellar to another. By charging the sub-tenants a little more than their *pro rata* share of the rent, he reduces his rent for the two remaining rooms considerably below what he would be compelled to pay for an apartment of two rooms that he might rent elsewhere. He has also done another thing; he has changed the character of the dwelling from a one-family dwelling to a tenement, and as a result we have the inadequate, unsanitary conditions previously noted. If the sub-tenants are further moved to increase their income by taking in lodgers or boarders, as is the usual custom among a large percentage of the foreign population, we have superimposed upon these various other evils a condition of overcrowding that serves to accentuate and intensify one hundredfold every bad condition of which specific mention has already been made. Foul closet compartments in the house or yard are made more foul; disorder and dirt become more and more the accepted order of things. Dark, unventilated rooms are made to do duty as sleeping rooms for six, eight, and ten, and even more lodgers; and when there is found sleeping in one room, which is the sole living room of the family, husband, wife, and children and two or more lodgers, one cannot but feel that the last word has been spoken, the last barrier of decency been thrown down. Where such conditions obtain as a result of the thrifty instinct of the tenant, it is bad enough in all conscience, but where the itching palm or the callous indifference of the landlord is part and parcel of a corporation whose wealth and power is one of the great world factors of to-day, even the most charitably inclined will be hard put to find any excuse.

Painters Row on the south side is a fair example of company owned houses where indifference is responsible for the long continuance of evil conditions. This property, owned by the United States Steel Corporation, consists of six rows of brick and frame houses; ninety-one families are living here. Twenty-two of these are without closet accommodations; and the water supply for the property is ridiculous in its inadequacy. A special investigation of this group of houses has been made and at the present time the company has promised to remedy the illegal conditions which have been found to exist in those buildings which come under the tenement house law.

With the private owner, the landlord, or "boss," the desire for the largest returns consistent with the smallest possible expenditure is the dominant motive in most cases.

There is a glaring example of this to be found in the old barracks on Basin alley, known as "Tammany Hall." Originally used as a planing mill, some nine years ago the owner determined to turn the building into a tenement. By an adroit manipulation of the proper authorities, permission to make the required changes was obtained, and to-day it presents one of the worst examples of bad housing to be found in any city in the country. A frame building of the flimsiest possible construction, with every available bit of space partitioned-off to make twenty-six rooms—a *cul-de-sac* here, a few steps there, narrow passageways leading off in every direction, with no fire escapes, with a minimum of light and air and a maximum of dirt and foul odors, it serves as "home" for twenty-five families. To see the place in all its hideousness it should be visited at night.

Accompanied by the chief of the Tenement House Bureau, I made a visit of inspection there at two o'clock on a Sunday morning. It was a cold, drizzly, desolate sort of a night without, but it was nothing compared with the desolation within. The air was heavy and malodorous. One passageway was lighted by an electric light in the outside alley; two others by smoking lanterns suspended by ropes from the ceiling. Two passageways were pitch dark. The occupants were sleeping heavily, in some instances the effect of too frequent imbibing a few hours previous, and in others the result of long, weary hours of toil. The fire danger seemed to overshadow every other evil, —a lamp carelessly overturned, a lighted match heedlessly thrown among some rubbish, and the old shell would burn like a tinder box. A few puffs of smoke would choke the narrow passageways, a single tongue of flame would destroy the ropes by which the lanterns were hanging and plunge the place into darkness. The confusion and the loss of human life that would ensue can easily be imagined.

I understand the owner has recently given out a contract for fire escapes in response to a severe prodding from the Tenement House Division, but this technical compliance with the fire escape laws means very little. In the first place the walls would seem too frail to allow of the secure fastening thereto of the fire escapes, and in the second place on account of the irregular construction it would seem an impossible problem to erect a sufficient number of fire escapes so that the seventy-two persons living there could be enabled to find their way to safety in case a fire should start.

The overcrowding was not so great as we expected to find. Indeed, it was to ascertain accurately the facts in this connection that our investigators timed their visit at the unearthly hour mentioned. The highest number found sleeping in a single room that night was five, but the number of occupants of a room is of course a variable quantity in places like this, and varies from week to week. A day inspection a few weeks before had elicited the following facts: Three rooms each were occupied by six persons; one room occupied by five persons, and two rooms each occupied by four. The rents are exorbitant, single rooms renting from four to seven dollars each per month. Several rooms are lighted by a sky-light only and are ventilated not at all—although the owner has complied with the letter of the law by cutting windows through into an adjoining passageway, which is dark and covered and renders the windows of no use whatever.

The sanitary accommodations are totally inadequate; eight flush closets in the yard, one hydrant in the yard and one in the rear entry to the second floor represent the sum total of what is offered to the tenants in this respect. There is also a hydrant in the kitchen of a restaurant on the first floor, but this is not accessible to any of the other tenants. As for the eight closets, they are shared with eighteen other families in adjoining houses, all on the same property and owned by the same landlord—forty-three families in all. In fact, "Tammany Hall" is usually meant to include these six houses as well as the old mill itself. Unsanitary conditions and overcrowding are quite as bad in these other houses as in "Tammany Hall" proper. One of the houses is a tenement housing twelve families in thirteen rooms. The water supply for these houses is obtained from one sink, on the second story porch, and the common hydrant in the yard. There is also a sink in one of the apartments, which, however, is not accessible to any of the other tenants.

A curious arrangement obtains here concerning the sub-letting of a number of the rooms, which is worthy of mention as a similar situation was found to exist in certain other tenements, especially where the Syrians and Arabians predominate. The store room on the first floor is rented by one man who conducts a general merchandise shop, and who also leases a number of rooms elsewhere in the building. These rooms he sub-lets to peddlers and their families either for a nominal sum of about fifty cents a month, or more often he charges no rent whatever, the understanding being that the peddlers buy all the supplies for their packs from the stock of wares in his store. The merchant's profits on his goods must be considerable when he can afford to house his patrons rent free in this manner.

"Tammany Hall" and the six adjoining houses bring in to their owner a monthly rental of about $430. His taxes amount to $442.71 *per annum,* leaving a net annual income of over $4,700., for precious little is spent upon repairs. In fact, no repairs could make "Tammany Hall" fit for human habitation.

It is possible to continue indefinitely the citation of such instances of overcrowding, with the resulting lack of proper sanitary accommodations. In one five-story brick tenement on Bedford avenue, containing 108 rooms, there are but twelve closets and four sinks in the entire building: six closets and a sink on the first floor, two closets and a sink on the second floor, the same on the third and fourth floors, and none on the fifth floor.

In another three-story brick tenement over on the south side, originally built for ten families and with a sufficient number of sinks and closets to meet the demands of that number, seven additional families have been crowded into the building by sub-letting eight rooms. These families have taken in boarders, and the condition of overcrowding resulting therefrom is as bad as can be found in the city. Of the eight rooms occupied by these families, each of seven contains a stove, table, chairs, and two or three beds, according to the number of boarders. The eighth room was extremely small and not used. In each of these seven rooms from five to eight persons cook, eat and sleep. A census of these rooms resulted in the following: One room occupied by a family of three and three boarders; one by a family of four and four boarders; one by a family of three and two boarders; one by a family of three and four boarders; one by a family of two and the wife's two sisters, and one by a family of two and the wife's sister and two boarders.

The closets in this tenement were in a very bad state of repair, with pipes leaking so that the wood floors of the compartments were soaked through and through. One closet had been out of repair for six months; two of the compartments were dark and four were unventilated. There was a sink on the first floor of each apartment but only four were trapped. Three room apartments rent for thirteen dollars a month and four room apartments for fifteen dollars.

One especially bad lot of tenements found in Soho consists of a row of five frame houses, two stories in front and five in the rear. The houses are in a dilapidated condition, the plumbing is defective, the outside stairs have broken treads, the porches are insufficiently braced, with sagging, broken flooring, and from one flight the hand rail is missing. There is a sink in each apartment, usually untrapped, and frequently both waste and water pipes leak badly. One unsewered vault represents the sole closet accommodations for the nineteen families living in this group of houses (including the boarders, a total of 151 persons). The vault is situated further down the hill and is reached by crossing a rickety platform so full of holes that its use is dangerous after nightfall. One especially large hole near the center of the platform was evidently used as a garbage dump, for directly below this particular hole there was an unsightly pile of garbage and refuse of every description.

The overcrowding in this house was another feature worthy of note. One room was occupied by ten boarders, two of whom were on a night shift and slept during the day, and there were two rooms each occupied by nine boarders, one room by eight, two by seven, three by six, two by five, one by four, one by three, and one star boarder had a room entirely to himself while the family of six slept in the kitchen. One of the rooms occupied by five boarders was a cellar room containing but one small window. Rents here are somewhat higher. Two room apartments bring from six to eight dollars and a half a month: three room apartments, from nine fifty to eleven dollars: the average rent a room being $3.35. The total yearly income from the property is about $1,800. The item of repairs is a negligible quantity here as in many other cases.

So far with reference to the disposal of sewage, special stress has been laid upon the archaic privy vaults with which the entire face of the city is pitted, but there is another state of affairs which obtains in many of the houses inspected which, if not quite as primitive is quite as intolerable when judged by the ordinary standards of sanitation. I refer to the so-called sanitary closets which have been installed in cellars, under sidewalks, and in small, unventilated, partitioned-off sections of living rooms. A combination of inferior workmanship and cheap material renders such closets little better than none at all. The water supply for flushing the bowls comes from an adjacent waste pipe, is totally inadequate, and during much of the time is conspicuous by its absence.

In a brick row of one family houses at Thirtieth and Spruce streets, owned by the Crucible Steel Company, there are nine such closets located under the sidewalk or court, and opening from the cellar kitchens. They are connected with the yard drain which is supposed to flush the bowls. Whenever the drain becomes obstructed the closets are without water, and according to the statement of one of the tenants this condition frequently endures for weeks at a time. About twice a year the company flushes the drain from a nearby hydrant. Provision for the lighting and ventilation of these closets is made by having an opening over the coal hole adjoining the closet compartment. Numerous cracks in the partitions between coal bins and closets allow a modicum of light and air to filter through. In winter the opening is securely covered in order to keep the cold out of the kitchen, so that practically the closets are dark, unventilated and unflushed during several months of the year.

In Negley Run the cellar closet appears to have a hold on the public fancy. Dark and difficult of access, such closets are hiding places for filth and rubbish and breeding places for disease. One such cellar that was inspected fairly beggars description. Before descending the cellar steps the stench warned one in advance of what might be expected. There were three closet compartments, one of which was unlocked and unspeakably filthy. The entire floor of the open space in the cellar, as well as of a partitioned-off portion, was literally covered with filth. In one corner a cluster of leaking water and waste pipes added their quota to the condition of affairs. Tenants of the apartment above stated that the pipes had been broken over a week. The extremely foul condition of the cellar was explained by the fact that the only entrance thereto was by steps leading down from the rear yard, and it would be most inconvenient to keep these heavy doors over the steps closed and locked. As a result, the cellar is a public privy for any chance passerby who wishes to make use of it. Evidently it is a convenient one.

In describing at such length these particular examples of bad housing conditions there has been no spirit of unfair discrimination and no intention of making a few "horrible examples" stand as a type of Pittsburgh's dwellings. These houses were chosen because they typify more completely all those features of the housing situation in Pittsburgh, which are found to exist in a greater or less degree all over the city, wherever bad housing conditions obtain. The specific conditions are no worse there than in many other houses except that these examples present the accumulation in one building of the whole variety of evils, phases of which are duplicated in hundreds, we may say thousands, of dwellings in Pittsburgh.

It has not been a pleasant tale in the telling and it makes anything but pleasant reading. The investigation of such conditions is repugnant and the description of them repulsive. The endurance of them is revolting. Under such conditions many a laboring man is forced to house his family and rear his children. Working years are reduced, efficiency impaired, because of these conditions which make so surely for disease and under-vitalization. The psychological effect of an overcrowded, unsanitary home upon the growing girl or boy cannot be estimated. The community at large suffers most of all; for not only disease but crime is bred in dark places.

These slum districts, excrescences on the city's fair surface, will increase and multiply unless there is a general awakening to a sense of civic responsibility in the matter of maintaining decent homes for decent people. I know the old discredited argument that many of these people have come from even worse conditions in their own land, and that they are willing to live thus. It is indeed because of such considerations that the grasping or callous landlord is encouraged to offer for rent old dwellings which make no pretense of complying with the requirements of either the tenement house law or the sanitary code. The real point is that the conditions described are not only unsanitary and indecent, they are illegal as well.

Children's Play
by Beulah Kennard

Play is a social inheritance. It represents social traditions as well as collective activity and has almost no existence away from group life. In primitive culture the child is given most of his education through forms of play. The essential facts concerning any stage of civilization may be learned from a study of its symbolic and imitative plays and games, and the quality of the common life may be learned from the richness of the material so obtained.

In this light even our American children of today are seen to be poorer in imagination, ideality, and invention than were their forefathers, for they have lost many of the old games without having gained new ones. But the children among the mills of Pittsburgh were usually of foreign parentage if not of foreign birth. The fact that this population was recruited yearly from the oppressed and impoverished peasants of southeastern Europe had much to do with the lack of play spirit here. These people seemingly are not rich in play traditions and customs, or they leave behind them those which they had at home. Under any circumstances, however, they must forget the ways of their old country and adopt the play traditions of the new one.

But what suggestion of play could parents or children find in a city of iron whose monster machinery rested neither day nor night? Their surroundings were ugly and forlorn. In many places green things could not grow because of the pall of smoke which swept heavily down, clouding the sunlight, and leaving a deposit of grime on everything, including the children. If the imagination is fed by sense impressions these children could have little idea of life other than that of mere existence for the sake of work. Wanting playground or play traditions, imagination or vitality, they literally did not know how to play.

Until the opening of the first playground by the Civic Club, in 1896, Pittsburgh, in her single-hearted devotion to business and her apparent indifference to any pleasure other than the satisfaction of success, had been a typical American industrial city. Her almost unlimited natural resources—her coal and iron and oil, which might

"The Playgrounds of Pittsburgh," *The Pittsburgh District: Civic Frontage* (New York: Survey Associates, Russell Sage Foundation, 1914), pp. 306–311.

have given the people a prosperous sense of leisure, her three noble rivers—had only served to make this "workshop of the world" a greater workshop, not to make it either beautiful or livable. From the hilltops one might see the outlines of the superb setting of this gate of the west, but at closer range the beauty was lost in narrow streets, incongruous, haphazard buildings, and smoke. Characteristically also, the city which had forgotten the meaning and the uses of leisure had forgotten the value of recreation. Perhaps the Scotch-Irish settlers of an earlier day, like our English cousins, "took their pleasures sadly," but it is surprising that the large numbers of play-loving Germans should have done so little to provide wholesome amusement for their families.

In 1896 Pittsburgh was in as great a need of play and of playgrounds as any city could well be. No town of its size in the country had so neglected to provide for public parks, of which there were then only two within the limits of the old city.

Of these, Highland Park was only a barren, almost treeless hill, crowned with a reservoir and encircled by a few carriage roads, and Schenley Park, which had been given to the city by Mrs. Schenley, the expatriated owner of large property holdings in the city, was a very uneven tract with valleys to be bridged and steep hillsides more ornamental than useful. A deep ravine separated this tract from the crowded section west of the park. It contained the city zoo and a fine conservatory, but was otherwise without any provision for recreation. Both parks were out of reach of the poor.

On the north side of the river the smaller city of Allegheny had planned better. Riverview Park was also on the edge of things, but through the heart of the city ran a long, narrow common which was accessible to the poorer sections. This common did not suggest or provide for play, but it was level, green, and shaded—a pleasant resting place for tired eyes. Mothers and nurses with very little children were often seen on its walks, and once a year the school children were entertained on the grass.

A City Without Play Space

Not in all the mill and tenement districts of Pittsburgh, not in the river wards, the Hill District, the South Side, in West End, or Hazelwood was there a foot of land for park or common with the exception of a little thirty-foot-wide strip of grass on Second Avenue near the court house, and upon this the adjoining property holders were looking with covetous eyes. Everywhere the bluffs rose at a very short distance from the rivers, crowding mills and mill workers into uncomfortably close quarters. How could we think of parks and playgrounds when all the land and even the river banks were needed for business?

Other writers in these volumes describe the physical and social make-up of Pittsburgh, but let us look at this city of crowded hillsides and teeming workers from the standpoint of childhood as these pioneers of play saw it before them in the nineties.

Many years before congestion began the small area of level ground downtown had been built over with old, one-family houses, and these were overflowing with a dense population for which there were neither enough rooms nor proper sanitary facilities. The tiny yards of these old houses were often filled with hovels or sheds used as dwellings, and those not built upon were filled with rubbish, even as they are today. The earlier residents of these neighborhoods had either moved away or been overwhelmed by successive waves of foreigners, an alien people with lower standards of living who had thronged through the city's gates and settled down in the most crowded districts. The situation was made much worse by the high rents which caused many families who occupied but two or three rooms to take as boarders the unmarried mill operatives, whose alternate night and day shifts compelled them to live near their work. Thousands of beds in these small and ill-ventilated quarters were thus occupied day and night, creating for the children of the family intolerable conditions. Play in a steaming kitchen or a home workshop is difficult, but play in the bedroom of sleeping boarders is impossible.[1] The only playground of these practically homeless children then was the street with its narrow sidewalks, and the space between the curbs, filled with a constantly increasing traffic.

Play space and acquaintanceship contended against the rivers and groups of rugged hills which segregated many sections with almost impassable boundaries, and these small populations were in turn often dominated by the masterful and prosaic mills. In the Penn Avenue district, for instance, was a dense tenement population of Italians, Poles, Irish, and Slavic people, with a growing colony of Greeks. The shops had strange names above their doors. The women wore kerchiefs on their heads and all the little girls seemed

1. See Byington, Margaret F.: Homestead: The Households of a Mill Town, pp. 135, 145. (The Pittsburgh Survey.)

to be carrying babies, while streets and alleys swarmed with children, children who would have been pretty had they not been so dirty.

At the West End were Welsh and Irish families who had lived among the mills for two generations. These showed greater signs of degeneracy than the more shifting Penn Avenue population. But what could be expected of people whose homes faced the open sides of a roaring steel mill and whose back windows were overshadowed by a railroad? They had not one green or beautiful spot for their eyes except the far-away tops of the hills above. Here the boys were nearly all sneak thieves and apparently had no sense of the right of property. They stole things of no value to them, and even stole from one another. A five-year-old girl in this neighborhood asked her teacher if she had ever ridden in the police wagon and was much surprised to learn that the teacher had not. She exclaimed proudly, "My pa has ridden in it four times and ma three, and when I'm big enough I'm going to ride in it, too."

Several of the mill districts were fallen from a better estate. A large section of the South Side and some of the wards in the city of Allegheny were settled many years ago by substantial German, Welsh, and Irish families, whose heads were mill operatives. Rents then were not so high, nor houses so poor, and these men could maintain comfortable homes and a fair standard of living, and give their children a good education. A radical change had taken place since the Slavs and Poles supplanted many of these older residents. Some of their homes have no floor except the ground, and no window glass.

Among the neighborhoods away from the shadow of the mill, the Hill District, with its Roumanians and Poles, its Italians, Syrians, and Armenians, and the large numbers of colored people crowded in between the conglomerate Jewish and Gentile peoples was full of local color and charm. The children of these people were found to be eager to learn how to become worthy citizens. There are, it is true, children in Pittsburgh for whom the word "America" has little meaning, who still feel the spell of the homeland. But these seem to be far outnumbered by the foster brothers of little Jacob Molinsky, who said, "My name is Polish, but I'm an American."

Loyal little souls! Their adopted country was treating them as the proverbial step-children are treated, and not as if they were her own.

Children of Work

So it was that in 1896, when the Civic Club, then recently formed and looking for work, saw the crowded streets and the yardless, forlorn homes of these children, it determined to take advantage of a law enacted the previous year and open the school yards as playgrounds. The first playground was started in a ward settled by middle class people. The club provided a few swings, toys, and sand, and by a fortunate "mistake" put two kindergartners in charge instead of one. In order to keep the teachers busy the visiting committee suggested that a little program be arranged dividing the time between stories, songs, directed games, and free play for the different groups of children. The playground in this district worked smoothly enough, though the teachers found that the children needed more assistance in their play than had been expected.

The committee then entered two mill neighborhoods and met the real difficulty. The members having never lived next to a mill and always having had yards and doorsteps of their own, could not understand that these children did not know how to play. The committee could not believe it. Some of them do not believe it now; they think that the children played while they were not looking. But the trained and experienced teachers soon discovered the spiritual starvation of their charges and set themselves immediately to do intensive work. The morning program began with a march around the yard led by a drummer boy in the full pride of his noise. Children came running from all directions. They sang and saluted the flag, and were then divided into groups for games and for free play in the sand piles and the swings. About the middle of the session, toys were put away and all the children were gathered into the kindergarten room where the teachers told stories, or taught kindergarten games and songs, accompanied by the piano. The trained teachers were usually assisted by volunteers from the committee who were not content to observe and criticize, but who spent many mornings guarding swings, taking care of babies in order to relieve the little sister-mothers, and telling stories, and who brought flowers each week for distribution. After the second year, the children's department of the Carnegie Library cooperated with the committee by sending trained storytellers to the playgrounds and by distributing books to the children.

Adult Play: Commercialized Vice
by James Forbes

Prostitution

A great money-making and money-spending community, Pittsburgh at the present stage of our social development inevitably became a center for commercialized prostitution. Its surplus of males is only less than that of a barracks town or mining camp. Managers and laborers are alike engaged in the harder physical processes of production. They are quartered as temporary sojourners where conventional restraints lose their accustomed force, and where vents for recreation such as more leisured communities provide are lacking. Link the promptings inherent in such a situation, on the one hand to the undisciplined spendings of sudden fortune makers, and on the other to the earnings of young salaried men and day laborers, both often insufficient for family life according to their standards, and you have a social order in which the mistress (or kept-woman) and the prostitute (or woman in whom many share) play their part despite the strict moral canons of an uncompromising church element in the community.

Not in Pittsburgh alone, but in all the nearby industrial towns of western Pennsylvania, Ohio, and West Virginia, there is an unnatural proportion of single men in mills and mines. Hundreds of footloose wage-earners from all parts of the industrial district look to the city when bent on having a "good time," making it, in the phrase of an old sporting man, "one big Saturday night town." Yet there can hardly be a sadder picture than the "parlor" in a disorderly house where sit the daughters of working people soliciting debauch at the hands of youths of their class. My belief is that labor unions are delinquent in not engaging aggressively in efforts to educate in their members a class consciousness without offense. A broader, a more inspiring propaganda, linked to that for higher wages, should be possible to such organizations as the United Mine Workers, the Amalgamated Association of Steel, Iron, and Tin Workers, and the various railroad brotherhoods. It is surely time for us to hear the last of "mill men's houses," "railroaders' houses," and so on, in Pittsburgh and elsewhere.

"The Reverse Side," *Wage-Earning Pittsburgh* (New York: Survey Associates, Russell Sage Foundation, 1911), pp. 348–350.

The situation which thus provokes illicit intercourse has been aggravated and exploited to the full by the business managers of vice. While prostitution has been covertly carried on in many parts of the city in flats or furnished rooms, there are two large districts which from time out of mind have been the markets for this traffic in women's bodies, by the women themselves and those who control them; and while the reform regime attempted to root out houses of prostitution from other parts of the city and to cut off the revenues of those which remained, the houses were officially tolerated within these areas.

How centrally situated is the chief of these districts may be appreciated from the fact that the Pittsburgh general post office has been in the heart of it. A step to the right or left from the southern half of Smithfield Street, the main business thoroughfare of the city, and one is surrounded by officially tolerated vice. Business buildings, fire company houses, hospitals, missions, railroad depots, the markets, the steamboat landings, and some of the hotels all rub shoulders with prostitution.

This is the section in and about lower Second Avenue in Pittsburgh proper. It lies in the territory between the heart of the business district and the Monongahela River, extending to Liberty Avenue at its lower end, and at its upper spreading through a nest of alleys lined with squalid dwellings which run up the Hill past Fifth to Wylie Avenue. Here the section flanks the tenement quarters where Jewish, Italian, and Negro households rear their children.

Prior to an expansion of the business section of the city and the establishment by the Wabash Railroad of a terminal midway to the Point, a large part of the entire area lying between lower Third Avenue and the Monongahela River was occupied by houses of ill-fame. Lower Second Avenue continued thereafter to be the main thoroughfare for these establishments, but commercial encroachment tended to spread them up both rivers along the line of Penn and Fifth avenues, and scatter them in certain sections of the East End. In the Second Avenue section alone there existed in the summer of 1907 over 200 brothels, a number considerably less than before the restrictive measures were enforced against them.[1]

The second vice district of long standing is situated across the

1. The once notorious "Yellow Row" stood idle and condemned at the time of the writer's visit, housing only an occasional squatter. This structure was torn down during Mayor Guthrie's administration.

river, adjacent to the workingmen's quarter in the former city of Allegheny. This district occupies a large area which may be said to be bounded by the railroad yards and the Allegheny River, and of which the principal thoroughfare is East Robinson Street.[2]

One beneficial result of the more rigid restriction of vice to these districts under the reform administration was the almost entire absence of "massage" or "manicure" parlors such as afford a cloak for prostitution in other large cities. At the more expensive restaurants, however, the kept-women of business men and politicians displayed themselves, expensively gowned, and they were often to be seen riding about in motor cars through the principal thoroughfares. At night, among the crowds at the downtown cafes and resorts were well dressed women who, in the residential sections where they lived, preserved more or less secrecy as to their mode of livelihood. Street walkers were very few, but there were indications that numbers of shop girls, office employes, and factory workers added to their incomes by occasional prostitution. All of these formed a fringe to the main body of the inmates of disorderly houses.

2. Closed in May, 1913, by the Morals Efficiency Commission.

PART TWO

Maturity & Obsolescence, 1914-1945

Introduction

The Pittsburgh Survey had emphasized the discrepancy between the industrial efficiency of the community and what Edward Devine called the "neglect of life, of health, of physical vigor" of the individual. The social institutions had to be modernized, raising them to the level of efficiency, planning, and imagination that characterized the industrial sector. But ironically, as the study included here by McLaughlin and Watkins suggests, the Pittsburgh economy had already peaked by the time of the Survey. It had reached a state of maturity by 1910, and the industrial sector would thereafter develop many of the rigidities attributed by the Survey investigators to the civic sector. Although the nineteenth century was a period of creative response to economic opportunities, the Pittsburgh economy would lag in the twentieth, unresponsive to changing technological and market circumstances.

During the growth period, extending from the 1870s through the first decade of the twentieth century, Pittsburgh manufacturers had exploited their competitive advantage in access to raw materials. The beehive ovens of the Connellsville coalfields in Fayette County produced the best metallurgical coke in the United States. At the time coke costs represented a crucial differential in pig iron (hence steel) costs. In time the Connellsville semi-monopoly in blast-fur-nace coke was undermined by the development of by-product coke ovens. Since these were more economical when situated near the furnaces rather than the mines, other deposits of coking coal be-came competitive. Access to new markets rather than one source of coking coal emerged as the major competitive advantage to the det-riment of the Pittsburgh region.

Meanwhile, in the decades before 1910, the Pittsburgh region had developed an economic mix that differentiated it from other metro-politan areas: an overspecialization in coal, iron, and steel produc-tion, heavy electrical machinery, and glass-clay-stone products, as well as a concentration of the labor force in the large plants neces-sary for those enterprises. Two other peculiarities evolved, associ-ated with this overspecialization and large-plant concentration. The coal industry resulted in the employment of a larger percentage of the labor force in the primary or extractive sector than other areas, and the region ranked low in tertiary employment (trade and ser-vices). Large-scale heavy industry did not provide the external econ-omies and inducements that gestated large numbers of small sup-pliers and businesses.

One thing that remained constant during the periods of growth and maturity was the determination of the steel industry to repress unionism. From the trauma of Homestead in 1892 through the great steel strike of 1919, the companies controlled their heterogeneous labor force through a combination of paternalism and power. The former was exemplified in the stock-sharing and other benefit pro-grams devised by the U.S. Steel Corporation after 1901 in an effort to secure the loyalty of the skilled worker. But, as the selections de-scribing the 1919 strike make clear, the ultimate deterrent was force. Given the political influence of the companies and employers in the mill towns of western Pennsylvania, the police power of the state was invariably mobilized in order to suppress strikes and dis-sent. The fundamental concept of unionism was rejected—that property rights, particularly in the corporate era, were not absolute, and that working conditions and wages were to be jointly deter-mined by capital and labor.

Previous selections by Byington and Roberts and two included here (Saposs's report on immigrant communities, and the Social Study of Pittsburgh) *illustrate another constant in the evolution of the Pittsburgh region: the persistence of ethnic identity, a phenomenon encouraged ecologically by the hilly terrain, which fragmented and isolated population groups. The significance of this phenomenon of ethnic cohesion and differentiation cannot be exaggerated. The ethnic group served the immigrant as a buffer against a strange, often hostile society. It provided a source of identity and belonging. Not least important, ethnicity was a significant dimension of the American tradition of voluntarism—the mobilization of resources and the creation of new institutions under voluntary auspices. Thus ethnic groups created an elaborate subculture, including churches, fraternal and mutual aid societies, newspapers, charitable and educational agencies, and many other organizations.*

Americans who complained of the unassimilation of the Slavic immigrant did not comprehend the functional significance of the ethnic subculture as a source of stability and social control. The Americanization process was necessarily a long-term, group phenomenon, and it was mediated by the ethnic subculture. Nowhere was it more important than in the coal and mill towns of western Pennsylvania, where the fraternal role of trade unions was limited, where a large population of unattached males existed, where the work regimen was severe. In a region whose environment and population mix was shaped by economic disciplines, the ethnic group became the leading source of communality.

The combination of a large working-class population and a socioeconomic elite that favored conformity to the economic verities, to salvation through work, was not a hospitable milieu for cultural innovation or vitality. To a much greater extent, the elites of cities like Boston and New York in the nineteenth century funneled wealth into the creation of cultural capital. With the exception of Andrew Carnegie, the Pittsburgh elite of the nineteenth century remained remarkably indifferent to cultural enterprise. The next selection, a devastating critique of Pittsburgh's social and cultural life in the 1930s was, despite journalistic simplification, essentially valid. Duffus stresses the suffocating impact of Scotch-Presbyterianism, and views Pittsburgh as the embodiment of a business culture, whose spokesmen gilded their materialism with a veneer of spirituality.

These views were substantiated by the Social Study of Pittsburgh, *directed by Philip Klein, a prominent New York social worker.*

This latter-day survey discerned two kinds of public opinion in Pittsburgh: dominant and minority. The former was created by the "economic hegemony of the industrial and financial corporations"; the conservative, if not fundamentalist, theology of the leading denominations; by the preeminence of employer compared to employee; by the "assumed superiority in endowment, culture, and moral qualities of the rich over the poor," and by the existence of a "tightly knit local social aristocracy" combining wealth, families, and prestige.

Dissent was not welcome in this self-contained empire. Indeed, the research project was designated a "social study" rather than a "survey" in deference to persisting resentment over the earlier investigation, which had "laid bare some of the social costs of the precipitous pursuit of power and wealth." The controlling conservatism expressed itself "in the sparse growth of militant organizations for social reform, in the meager representation of the community leaders in those in existence, and in the infertile nature of the soil for the dissemination of nonconformist ideas, for the growth of liberal groups, and for the defense of free speech, free assemblage, and academic freedom." Industrial strife, especially, promptly elicited an "outright denial of civil rights."

If the interwar years in Pittsburgh were bleak—culturally torpid and comparatively stagnant economically—they were equally unpromising in the area of environmental melioration. Little had been accomplished by way of smoke or flood control, the early-twentieth-century efforts to improve housing conditions through regulatory codes had minimal effect, and the city planning movement of the era had become more a matter of form than substance. Launched in a crusading spirit of regeneration, the city planning movement in Pittsburgh and elsewhere had aspired to supersede the entrepreneurial approach to city-building by a rationalistic determination of the "public interest." Before long, the City Planning Department was relegated to the backwater of municipal government. It lacked political authority and devoted its attention to the minutiae of zoning activities on the one hand, and the preparation of static, ineffectual master plans, on the other. As the article included here by Frederick Bigger indicates, it was not even the department but a private citizens' group that developed some approximation to a master plan in the 1920s. Elsewhere, Bigger had objected that public planning agencies were forced to "contrive results without having an adequate control over causes." The reality was that "mutual accom-

modation between the politician and the citizen with selfish interest limits the exercise of technical ability."

The most significant development in the quest for environmental melioration during the interwar years occurred under private rather than public auspices. This was the construction of Chatham Village, sponsored by the Buhl Foundation and described here in the article by Charles F. Lewis. Located in the Mount Washington section of the city, Chatham Village was conceived by the Buhl Foundation as a demonstration project. It hoped to prove that superior methods of residential subdivision and design were compatible with criteria of reasonable profit. Design innovations included the superblock unit of subdivision, differentiated street system, respect for topography and natural advantages of the site, and the grouping of open space ordinarily dissipated among roads, alleys or small lawns into large interior parks. The architects, Clarence Stein and Henry Wright, had already experimented with these principles at Sunnyside Gardens, Long Island, New York, and Radburn, New Jersey.

Although Chatham Village achieved an international renown, and became a mecca for architects and planners, it did not succeed in changing the character of ordinary commercial residential development in Pittsburgh. One problem was the large initial capital investment, another the self-imposed limitation of profits on the part of the Buhl Foundation, and a third the conservatism of the building industry, which favored stock plans and procedures already proven successful.

Government, during the interwar period, played a marginal role in the quest for environmental and social melioration. The reform movements of the early twentieth century had favored centralization of decision-making in civic affairs, the imposition of order and system as prevailed in the business sphere. This required an expansion of governmental authority, but the expanded role allocated to government was largely negative. The emphasis fell on regulatory functions. More positive, constructive initiative would occur under private or voluntary auspices. In other words, government would apply negative sanctions—zoning, smoke control, public health, housing codes—but would not actively intervene to build new houses or seriously compromise the decision-making initiative of corporate institutions. It was only the crisis situation confronted by the City of Pittsburgh at the end of World War II that precipitated a significant change in the role assigned to government.

The Economics of Maturity
by Glenn E. McLaughlin and Ralph J. Watkins

Within the nation are several older, more mature industrial areas. The experience of such an area may give some clues to the kinds of problems which arise in a mature economy: problems concerned with the creation of capital; with the outlet for savings; with the growing conservatism of investors; with the intensive use of capital and the mechanization of industry; with the application of capital to social needs; with the changing internal structure of the economy; and with the under-utilization of capital and labor. The Pittsburgh district is a mature industrial area whose growth trends began to taper off almost thirty years ago; and these problems there are acute ones. In the belief, therefore, that the Pittsburgh district offers an instructive case study of the problem of industrial growth in a mature economy, we shall turn our attention to a discussion of the clinical records of that regional economy.

Basic Nature of Pittsburgh Industries.
Pittsburgh is dominated by iron and steel, bituminous coal, electrical equipment, foundry and machine shop products (especially heavy machinery), and glass. These products, however, enter so widely into the making of consumer goods that changes in their output reflect general movements in industry. The major forms of industrial activity in the Pittsburgh district are all capital goods industries, but these industries have furnished the major basis for national industrial growth. The trends of Pittsburgh industry, therefore, are closely tied to the stage of development of industry in the country as a whole. Whenever the trends in manufacturing and construction in the country begin to flatten out, as in recent years, there is a sharp reduction in the new requirements for capital equipment and building materials. Thus, producers goods industries are peculiarly sensitive to broad industrial changes. Hence, Pittsburgh's industrial changes may in a measure indicate what may be anticipated in the national economy.

"The Problem of Industrial Growth in a Mature Economy," *American Economic Review,* 29 (March, 1939), Pt. 2, supplement, pp. 6–14. Reprinted by permission of the American Economic Association and the authors.

Comparison of Industrial Production Trends, Pittsburgh District and the United States.

The Pittsburgh industrial district had its rapid growth before 1909; until that time the annual rate of growth in industrial production in the district was greater than that in the United States. In the past thirty years, however, Pittsburgh has been in a comparatively mature stage of development and has been growing less rapidly than the country as a whole. Growth in industrial production in the district began to taper off noticeably after 1909, whereas national industrial production did not show definite signs of slowing down until after the World War. Industrially speaking, the Pittsburgh district reached maturity about two decades ahead of the country generally. Pittsburgh had its years of rapid industrial growth in the seventies, eighties, and nineties of the nineteenth century and in the first decade of the twentieth century, whereas national industrial growth has continued until recent years to feel the stimulation of rapid industrialization of the newer centers in the Midwest, in the South, in the Southwest, and on the Pacific Coast. Many of those centers will doubtless continue to grow rapidly, but areas of rapidly growing industrialization are becoming smaller as proportions of the total national economy. At the present time the composite industrial production trend line is advancing at about one-half per cent per year in the Pittsburgh district and at almost one and one-half per cent in the United States. The Pittsburgh district, because of the basic nature of its industries and because of its later stage of industrial development, may serve as a guide to later developments in the national economy.

Economic Development of the Pittsburgh District.

The first manufacturing industries in the Pittsburgh district were those supplying consumer goods for the local population and for settlers moving farther west. After a time this western community began to specialize more in the exploitation of local resources—in the making of iron, heavy machinery, glass, and pottery—and for the most part gave up supplying local consumers' needs for manufactured articles. Railroad operation reduced transportation costs and allowed the exchange of local specialties for eastern manufactures. Thus, during the latter half of the nineteenth century western Pennsylvania became firmly integrated into the national economy when

the district began to exploit its geographical position for the production of iron. The iron industry first became integrated in Pittsburgh,
where Connellsville coke was used with Lake Superior ore. Thus,
the main geographic advantages of the city in the iron industry consisted in its location near supplies of coal and near enough to Lake
Erie to obtain relatively low freight costs on necessary supplies of
ore.

During the 1870's industrial production in the Pittsburgh area
was growing at a rising rate. Both coal and steel were expanding
rapidly. Large amounts of capital were brought in from Philadelphia and New York, and the Pittsburgh district, which had
started to develop industrially much later than these seaboard regions, began to grow more rapidly. The maximum rate of increase
in population and in industrial population in the Pittsburgh area appears to have come during the 1880's. Population was increasing 4
per cent per year, largely owing to immigration. This influx was
brought about largely by the rapid expansion of the iron and steel
industry and the related increases in coal production. Great Bessemer converters and extensive crucible steel plants were constructed
during this and the preceding decades. The steel industry was growing at a fast pace, owing mainly to the substitution of steel for iron
in the making of railroad rails and structural forms. The Pittsburgh
area was clearly in the stage of rapid growth. During this decade the
annual growth of industrial production in the Pittsburgh district was
10 per cent, or double that in the United States. During the 1890's
the development of the open-hearth process greatly improved the
quality of steel and led to the acquisition of new markets and to the
further expansion of output. These gains, however, were not sufficient to maintain the rates of population and industrial growth, although the gains in each remained high. After 1900, expansion of
the local iron and steel industry began to slow up, and immigration
into the area was retarded. By 1910 the era of rapid population and
industrial growth was completed. In the decade ended in 1930 the
annual rate of population increase fell to 1.4 per cent, and the trend
in steel production became almost horizontal. Industrial production
continued to grow at about one-half per cent per year.

Present Growth Patterns of Major Industries.
Most of Pittsburgh's leading industries are comparatively old. The

steel industry there is characterized by a rate of growth not far from zero, and coal and coke production show declining trends. The district is so dominated by these and related industries that comparatively favorable rates of growth in glass, electrical equipment, and aluminum are of only minor assistance in raising the trend of total industrial output. Even if new industries appear, they will for a long time be dwarfed by the overwhelming importance of the older forms of economic activity. The absence of any new major activity in the twentieth century is worthy of note in connection with the marked retardation about 1909 in industrial growth and indirectly in population growth. Although none of the new important industries which have developed in the United States in the past forty years have taken root in Pittsburgh, many of them have been large consumers of coal, steel, heavy machinery, and glass, in part obtained from western Pennsylvania. Aluminum, electrical equipment, and glass are three industries which have apparently not yet reached maturity in the Pittsburgh district and which have continued to exercise a stimulating influence on manufacturing activity—even though overshadowed by coal and steel. Other forms of manufacturing which are growing rapidly are included mainly in the category of consumers' industries.

Structural Changes in the Pittsburgh District.
The major post-War changes affecting the industrial structure of the Pittsburgh district have been the decrease in coal production; the marked slowing down of expansion in manufacturing output; exceedingly rapid increases in service activities; the continued shift of manufacturing operations from the nucleus city to the smaller industrial cities in the periphery, especially along the Ohio, Monongahela, and Allegheny rivers; the increasing centralization of the district's service functions in Allegheny County, and mainly in Pittsburgh; and in many counties the decreasing relative importance of employment in mining and manufacturing and, within manufacturing industries, the decreasing relative importance of the iron and steel industry. Some of these diverse tendencies within the Pittsburgh district had their counterparts within the nation and thus reflected a general shift in the national economy under which fewer workers were required in coal mining and manufacturing and more in the manifold and growing trade and other service functions which

rising standards of living and increasing specialization demand. Other changes represent the rise of a metropolitan economy and the co-ordination of the various activities of the district on a regionalized basis. Thus, the increase in the number of persons engaged in service functions in Allegheny County reflects the growing extent to which the nucleus city and its environs take over trade and other service functions for a large metropolitan area and tributary economic region—functions concerned not merely with management control and financial direction but also with all the varied recreational, cultural, governmental, health, and social activities that go to make up the life of a region.

Effects of Slowing Down of Growth.

Retardation of industrial growth in the Pittsburgh district has been accompanied by large exports of capital to other parts of the country, for investment both in industries familiar to Pittsburghers and in newer forms of productive activity and by more intensive development and expansion of local industrial concerns. On the other hand, industrial maturity seems to have brought with it greater likelihood of under-utilization of labor and capital, greater susceptibility to wide cyclical swings in production and employment, and shortage of capital for social improvements.

Pittsburgh became an important investment center at about the time that it began to show signs of industrial maturity. Indeed, somewhat earlier there were evidences that capital and men were moving from Pittsburgh mainly to the West, South, and Southwest to establish newer concerns in the steel, coal, and petroleum industries. With the arrival of full maturity after the World War, Pittsburgh's need for "economic colonies" became acute, and large quantities of local savings—and War profits—were invested in other districts, primarily in steel and oil but also in sulphur, aluminum, glass, electrical equipment, food canning, public utilities, and a great variety of other forms of business. In part, outside investments have taken the form of branch plants of Pittsburgh-controlled concerns or of fellow subsidiaries where the Pittsburgh operating concern was controlled elsewhere. For example, large amounts of Pittsburgh profits must have gone into the development of the Gary steel district. More recently, the development of Pittsburgh as an important investment banking center, containing as it does one of the country's major underwriting groups for the sale of new securities, has facilitated the flow of Pittsburgh savings through investment channels to all parts of the country as well as abroad.

Industrial maturity and the absence of important new industries have meant that if Pittsburgh capital was to be invested locally it had to be used primarily in the further mechanization and rationalization of Pittsburgh's industries. This intensive investment is exemplified in the steel industry by the construction of continuous rolling mills, in the coal industry by mechanization of mining methods and transportation, and in the glass industry by the development of new manufacturing processes. Moreover, the turning back of capital into the same industry has required the careful study of investment opportunities and has led to the organization of large research laboratories in the district, particularly those in steel, coal, oil, glass, and aluminum. Some Pittsburgh capital no doubt is being used in the development of new local industries, but in such a mature area a large proportion of capital funds must be exported.

In the peak year of 1929 there was considerable under-utilization of capital and labor. In most of the months of that year from 5 to 10 per cent of the workers were entirely without jobs. Moreover, those who had jobs suffered appreciable loss of working time in that year, being idle in various months from 4 to 16 per cent of the time. For the normally gainfully employed population as a whole, total unemployment and underemployment of those with jobs have been estimated for 1929 as the equivalent of total unemployment of all workers, 14 per cent of the time. Average overcapacity of plant facilities during that year was probably of the same general order of magnitude or greater. From 1929 to 1932 the declines in employment and production were drastic. For example, man-hours in manufacturing industries fell 59 per cent from the 1929 average; and the volume of industrial production declined 62 per cent. Total unemployment at the low point (August, 1932), according to published estimates, amounted to almost 40 per cent of the normally gainfully employed population.

Although the evidence is not entirely convincing, the fifty-five-year record of industrial production in the Pittsburgh district seems to indicate that cyclical swings have become more severe and that under-utilization has tended to last longer as the economy has become more mature. This relationship is probably not a chance one, because a sharp upward trend in industrial production is exceedingly effective in wiping out the effects of past errors in judgment and in canceling the losses of depression. Thus a given depression is not so tragic in its consequences if growth is so rapid that the preceding peak is destined to be exceeded in level by the trough of the next depression. This relationship obtained in the Pittsburgh district during the seventies, eighties, and nineties and into the nineteen hundreds up to 1907. Thereafter, the story has been painfully different, so much so that the 1932 trough was lower than the trend value for 1901, and the low month of June, 1938, was only slightly above the 1901 average. Certainly, it can be said that the greater industrialization and urbanization that have come with increasing maturity have heightened the vulnerability of the district's population to cyclical swings. Moreover, the growing relative scale of monetary expenditures—another concomitant of maturity—has probably had the effect of increasing both intensity of cyclical fluctuations and vulnerability to depression.

Economic Outlook for the Pittsburgh District.
In summary, the economic outlook for the Pittsburgh district is that of a mature economy. No great change appears likely in the present annual increment of about 0.5 per cent per year in the trend of industrial production, and the rate of population growth in the 1920's of 1.4 per cent per year is almost certain to be lowered. The necessary acceleration of industrial growth adequate to support an annual increase in population in the Pittsburgh district of 1.4 per cent per year does not appear imminent. Unless the area witnesses another great expansion of service occupations, the basis for which is not in sight, continued migration to other districts appears probable.

Pittsburgh's industries are old and basic. They are dependent on such a great variety of consuming industries that only a general outburst of national productive activity is likely to lead to a material increase in their rates of growth. Moreover, since new industries of considerable size do not appear to be in prospect in the district in the immediate future, not more than a continuation of the slow-growth trends established during the past quarter of a century can be expected. Consequently, unless the rate of population growth drops or migration from the area continues, there is a strong probability of a slow decrease in per capita income.

In the Pittsburgh district, the demand for capital will probably be largely for the purpose of making replacements. Excess savings are likely in the main to be invested in other areas as in the past three decades. One of the major problems of industrial maturity is likely to be the shortage of capital for improving social conditions. Many social and governmental problems created during the boom stage of development have been left for solution in the stage of industrial maturity—when the cost can be least afforded. Moreover, the very effort to solve these problems is likely to aggravate their nature. When a region reaches industrial maturity, there is always the danger that industry may begin to move away from the area and from the problems which it has created, a movement that may likely be accelerated by efforts to solve those social problems created by prior growth. Further, those who have retained much of the profits of the period of rapid growth are likely to move along with their savings to other and greener pastures or at least to send their capital to more promising fields. Thus the social consciousness that develops with industrial maturity may develop too late for effective action. Its very development may, in fact, accelerate the processes of decay; and what was a mature area may become a depressed and stranded area. Some of these problems with respect to the improvement of living conditions and with respect to the solution of governmental problems threaten to become acute ones in the Pittsburgh district. Adequate housing and civic, recreational, and health facilities were not provided when the area was producing wealth rapidly. It may be impossible to provide these services at a time when most of the capital funds of the area are invested elsewhere. "It may be later than we think," but if it is too late—within the framework of an enterprise system—then from the people of that area we can, in our judgment, expect increasing pressures in the direction of public and joint private and public investment.

Conclusions.

Attention has been devoted in this paper to the Pittsburgh district as a case study in industrial maturity, in the conviction that Pittsburgh's experience with industrial maturity during the past three decades is instructive to the nation; that the sorts of social and economic problems encountered there are likely in some degree to be met with in the nation over the coming years. In order that we may bring into sharp relief what we consider the lessons of that experience, we shall now attempt to outline some of the problems of industrial maturity that we anticipate will require the attention of those in industry and government who must concern themselves with economic and social policy:

1. Slowing down of industrial trends means a diminished opportunity for investment and a discouragement to initiative.

2. Under these circumstances investors become increasingly cautious and conservative; investment is primarily for replacement and for the more intensive use of capital through mechanization and improvement of processes.

3. Both investors and enterprisers turn their attention to more promising fields elsewhere, thus seeking "economic colonies" for investment and development.

4. These tendencies further aggravate the problems of industrial growth since they tend to deprive the economy of both capital funds and aggressive enterprisers.

5. The slowing-down process of industrial maturity is likely to be especially devastating in its effects on real estate values, leading to stagnation or retrogression in these values and thereby cutting off the flow of investment into construction, with a consequent further depressing influence on industrial trends.

6. Industrial maturity is likely to bring with it more serious and more frequent periods of under-utilization of the factors of production.

7. Shortage of capital for social improvements develops just at the time when social consciousness emerges to demand such improvements. The political pressures supporting these demands are likely to lead to measures which further undermine that economy or weaken its position with respect to other economies which stand in a competitive relation to it, either as investment outlets or as market outlets.

In short, it is probably fair to say that an enterprise system functions best in an expanding economy; and that the appearance of industrial maturity raises profound questions concerning the ability of an enterprise system to produce a progressive evolution of the economy under conditions of maturity. We believe that it is essentially these questions which lie behind the transformation of economies throughout the world in recent years—transformations involving increasing public participation. The problem of the American economy is to adjust itself to these influences and at the same time to preserve the maximum benefits of an enterprise system. This problem is not a simple one; rather, it will require co-operation of a high order between industry and government—industrial statesmanship as well as political statesmanship.

The Steel Strike of 1919: Intimidation
by S. Adele Shaw

I arrived in Pittsburgh the evening of the third day of the steel strike. Through a gate to one side of me, as I stood in the Union Station, a line of foreigners perhaps twenty-five in number, Slavs and Poles, dressed in their dark "best" clothes, with mustaches brushed, their faces shining, passed to the New York emigrant train. Each man carried a large new leather suitcase, or occasionally the painted tin suitcase—a veritable trunk—appeared in the line. And there, not quite concealed by its wrapping, was the unmistakable portrait which one could picture in its setting over the mantel in the boarding-house just left. Men and baggage were leaving, as every night they leave from that station on that same train for New York and the "old country."

Scarcely had the gate closed on the emigrant workers when a guard threw open an entrance gate through which marched, erect and brisk, a squad of state constabulary—"Cossacks" they are called in the mill towns. Young men they were in perfect training—men with great projection of jaw developed, it almost seemed, to hold the black leather straps of their helmets firmly in place.

It was the following day that I came in closer contact with one of these troopers in Braddock, the town where the foundation of the Carnegie fortune was laid. I had been at labor headquarters and then, before calling on the town or mill officials, walked with the local head of the Committee for Organizing Iron and Steel Workers, down the street to see the mill with its protection of walls, guns and

"Closed Towns," *Survey,* 43 (November 8, 1919), pp. 58–61.

men. We neither stepped off the sidewalk of the main thoroughfare nor stopped as we looked at the mill on one side and the homes of workers on the other. We made no notes and spoke to no one we passed. Yet as we turned the corner, a trooper pushed the nose of his horse to my shoulder, dismounted and ordered us to stop. He searched the organizer and asked what he was doing in the town. The man presented his card.

"If I catch you loitering here one instant I'll arrest you." The jaw was unusually long.

"And *you, too,*" he snapped, turning to direct his attention to me.

"What are those pamphlets you are distributing?" He took the papers and book I carried.

"The Pittsburgh Sun and Chronicle Telegraph," I replied.

Corporal Smith took from me my book, my personal papers, a telegram of instructions from the editor of the SURVEY, the notes I had made on my visits to the towns, cards with addresses, etc. He returned my book and mounted his horse.

"When may I have my papers back?" I inquired.

"That's my business," retorted the corporal.

I.

Intimidation, not riot, is the word to describe the situation as I saw it the first week of the strike in the mill towns of western Pennsylvania. In addition to Braddock I visited Homestead, McKeesport and Duquesne in Allegheny County. Over each town hung an atmosphere heavy with suppression—a suppression personified on the surface by the troopers, but which dates back to '92, when the Carnegie Company under H. C. Frick broke the back of the union—a suppression engineered by the interlocking machinery of mill, town, county and state. It is this combination that the strikers are up against. It is the core of the present struggle. It explains more than anything else the demand of the workers to be heard—to be free men—free in their towns as well as in their work.

Backed by governor, sheriff and mayors, the iron will of the steel corporations has been clamped down upon the men at every turn in this, their first effort at self-assertion in from ten to thirty years. Two days before the strike was called, William S. Haddock, sheriff of Allegheny county, issued a proclamation prohibiting the gathering of three or more persons on highway or vacant property, and ordering the dispersing of persons "unlawfully, riotously and tumultuously" assembled together. This proclamation under the sheriff's own interpretation prohibited all outdoor meetings, the making of remarks derogatory to public officials and the expression of "radical" sentiments. The interpretation of the words "derogatory" and "radical" he left with town officials or his local representative.

Despite this order, strikers have attempted to hold outdoor meetings, basing their action on their constitutional right to freedom of speech. Early in the first week a thousand of them crossed the city line from McKeesport into Glassport borough at three in the afternoon. Glassport authorities did not protest, but seven of the state police and county deputies appeared, dispersed the men, and arrested the leaders on charge of riot. The toll was four injured. Since that time the sheriff has prohibited the holding of any meetings in Glassport, indoors or out. Asked why he had taken such action when the Glassport authorities had not objected to the meetings, he said that since the mayor of McKeesport had prohibited meetings it "would not be fair to him if the sheriff did not prohibit them in the adjoining borough."

In North Clairton, just beyond, strikers were holding a meeting the Sunday before the strike in a field where local authorities had, previous to the sheriff's proclamation, given the men permission to meet. The meeting was proceeding peaceably when suddenly seven or eight troopers broke it up and took five men under arrest. Thirty-six more of the men were arrested a day or two following the meeting. The majority were held for "inciting to riot." Bail was placed at from $1,000 to $2,500 and pending the hearings ten days later, the men had to put up a total bail of over $43,000.

In Braddock, both outdoor and indoor meetings had been held previous to the sheriff's proclamation. At the first attempt, during the summer, the organizers had been arrested to be sure. But at their hearing Squire Holzman said he "refused to do the dirty work of the burgess." The men were released. During the strike, indoor meetings continued. So Braddock afforded me not only fresh impressions of a steel town in the midst of the strike but also of the sort of strikers' meetings prohibited in other boroughs which did not share in even Braddock's restricted measure of industrial liberty.

Braddock lies on the right bank of the Monongahela just below McKeesport and across the river from Homestead. It is the typical steel-mill town, with the works on the level by the river, the foreign districts close about, the railroad and steel car lines running through the business sections, dividing the industrial district from the residences of Americans and officials on the hillside. There are the Edgar Thomson Steel Works, the original plant of the Carnegie Steel Company, where Carnegie and Schwab got their start; the Carrie furnaces of the same company which makes metal for the Homestead works; the American Steel and Wire Company, a subsidiary of the corporation, and the McClintic-Marshall Construction Company, called by labor organizers "the greatest labor-hating concern in America."

"No trouble here at all" was the invariable answer from town and mill officials when asked how things were going. A cold dead calm had descended upon the town. The stacks of the mills seemed scarcely breathing. The air was cleared of dust and soot and the blue sky shone above. Along the main street a steady stream of foreigners passed—not loitering nor in groups—but walking seemingly in full enjoyment of their right to be dressed up and look at the shops or partake of the town's amusements, yet on the alert. To many of them it was a new experience. They had christened the first day of the strike "Labor's Day."

Yet police and plainclothesmen were everywhere in evidence and an occasional trooper passed on his horse. Nearer the Edgar Thomson works the state police, who earlier in the day patrol the foreign districts, were guarding the men who came out. I saw but a handful—perhaps twelve—young men and Negroes, with their dinner buckets, their faces smirched with soot. At the entrance to the works the mill police stood on watch on the porch of the guard house, guns at their feet. Deputies and plainclothesmen stood by. Troopers patrolled up and down before the high concrete wall with its iron gates—a wall which gives the mill the appearance of a medieval town. Behind the wall the mill officials and the majority of the workers—many of them Negroes—worked, slept and ate. Where the railroad tracks enter the mill, two small wooden guard houses had been erected. The front walls were of wood below and corrugated iron above. Between the two materials there was an open space perhaps two feet wide, through which the deputies could be seen. In these shacks on either side of the tracks the strikers believed machine guns were set for action. Below the tracks, the street opposite the mill and those leading out from it were lined with workingmen's houses. Children played on the filthy bricks and in the dirt by the curb.

In the evening I went to a meeting of strikers. All was quiet as I made my way toward the river. Down a poorly lighted street, so dark I could scarcely see the curb, I found the men standing, filling the vacant lot before the door of the hall which was packed, and on the sidewalks and street, but not blocking either. There was neither noise nor excitement. "Mother Jones goin' to speak." "Come on, lady." And the men held up their arms to open a passage for me. The hall was jammed. Sweat stood on every forehead.

The first speaker was J. G. Brown of the Pittsburgh strike committee. I had heard him the summer before in the mill towns telling the men what the eight-hour day would mean for them and their families, urging them to take out their papers and become citizens, and never failing to impress upon them the necessity of obeying the laws of the town, state and the country. Then came the deep clear voice of a woman, filling every corner of the hall. I stood on tiptoe and saw the grey hair of Mother Jones, the woman agitator of the mining districts of Colorado and West Virginia, who with the rough speech and ready invective of the old-time labor spellbinder, has exerted a powerful influence over the striking steel workers. At her first words there was complete silence. Though practically all were foreigners, not a man in the hall appeared to miss a word. "We're going to have a hell of a fight here, boys," she said and went on:

> We are to find out whether Pennsylvania belongs to Gary or to Uncle Sam. If it belongs to Gary we are going to take it away from him. We can scare and starve and lick the whole gang when we get ready. . . . The eyes of the world are on us today. They want to see if America can make the fight. . . . Our boys went over there. You were told to clean up the Kaiser. Well, you did it. And now we're going to clean up the damned Kaisers at home. . . . They sit up and smoke seventy-five cent cigars and have a lackey bring them champagne. They have stomachs two miles long and two miles wide and we fill them. . . . Remember when all was dark in Europe and Columbus said, "I see a new land," they laughed. But the Queen of Spain sold her jewels and Columbus went to it. . . . He died in poverty, but he gave us this nation and you and I aren't going to let Gary take it from us. . . . If he wants fourteen hours he can go in and work it himself. . . . We don't want guns. We want to destroy guns. We want honest men to keep the peace. We want music and playgrounds and the things to make life worth while. . . . Now, you fellows go on out. I want to talk to the other boys.

Pittsburgh Newspapers and
the Steel Strike of 1919

Four hundred issues of the seven daily English-language newspapers in Pittsburgh were examined as they appeared during the first two months of the steel strike (September 22 to late November, 1919).

The seven papers have circulations running from 60,000 to over 100,000 each, and together constitute the dominant press influence for a large area around Pittsburgh, extending north to Erie, Pa., west to Youngstown, O., south to Wheeling, W. Va., and each toward the center of Pennsylvania, where the circulation of Philadelphia papers is more important. . . .

Undiscriminating readers must have gained the impression that the men on strike in the steel industry were disloyal and un-American by virtue of entertaining some revolutionary economic theory. Had readers sought to find out what this theory was they would have had little trouble in finding in the newspaper columns extracts from Foster's "red book." Had they sought from the newspapers information of the actual demands of the strikers, they would have found from September 22 to the end of December scarcely a reference beyond statements to the effect that the demands amounted, according to Mr. Gary and other Steel Corporation officials, to "the closed shop." They would have learned nothing of the resentment which stirred a good many citizens of Pittsburgh against the suppression of free speech and other constitutional guarantees. Incidentally readers would have gained the impression that the clergymen of the district were opposed to the strike because almost all comment from clergymen quoted by the newspapers had this aspect.

Undiscriminating readers must have come to the conclusion that the district was being saved from a revolution by the efforts of the local authorities and the State Constabulary.

The investigator came into contact with a number of discriminating Pittsburgh readers, however, who had reached the conclusion that they could not learn from their papers the true facts regarding the strike and must rely on newspapers and magazines published elsewhere than in Pittsburgh.

"The Pittsburgh Newspapers and the Steel Strike," *Supplementary Reports of the Investigators to the Commission of Inquiry, The Interchurch World Movement* (New York: Harcourt, Brace and Company, 1921), pp. 90, 95.

The Immigrant Community
and the Steel Strike of 1919
by David J. Saposs

European Background of Strikers

The bulk of the strikers are of the "new immigration" and chiefly
Slavs. The principal Jugo-Slav workers are Serbs and Croatians.
Slovaks, from what is now the Czechoslovakian Republic, make up
a large percentage in many mills. Russian and Austrian Poles, as
they called themselves when they emigrated, form the largest single
racial blocks in other mills. Hungarians, Roumanians, Italians,
Greeks and Lithuanians comprise smaller or larger percentages in
certain mills, one race tending to crowd others out and to monopo-
lize a plant or at least a department. A dozen other nationalities of
the "new immigration" are represented, from Ukrainians (Little
Russians) to Horvaths (Jugo-Slavs), from Great Russians to Turks,
from Finns and Jews to Syrians and Armenians. The "new immigration" of course is predominantly Balkan or Southeastern
European.

Very few of these immigrant workers in the steel mills are from
industrial communities. Outside of Hungary and Italy, the regions
from which the steel workers come are almost wholly agricultural.
This horde of immigrants reached America entirely unacquainted
with modern industry and practically ignorant of the existence of labor organizations. Whatever schooling they have is of a primary
and rudimentary nature, acquired chiefly as a part of religious training. Their only previous experience as workers was as agriculturists
and most of their life in the old country was spent in small farming
villages.

The Hungarians are the principal exception, in that a good portion of them come from industrial centers and mining communities.
These naturally have a working acquaintance, at least, with labor
organizations and labor conceptions. Most of them are socialists,
since Hungarian labor organizations are politically socialist by tradition. The few Finns in the industry are strongly socialist and very
clannish. Italians who come from North Italian industrial centers

"The Mind of Immigrant Communities in the Pittsburgh District," *Supplementary
Reports of the Investigators to the Commission of Inquiry, The Interchurch World
Movement* (New York: Harcourt, Brace and Company, 1921, pp. 226–242.

also are acquainted with labor organization ideas and often with socialist principles. Most of the Italian steel workers, however, come from Sicily or from other backward communities.

For the most part the steel workers were previously wholly unacquainted with modern industry and labor organizations.

Sources of Immigrant Information and Leadership

Transplanted into a highly developed and complex industrial country, totally different from their former home, they seek guidance and leadership principally for the purpose of adapting themselves to their new surroundings. Their immediate sources of information and guidance are the local club or individual relatives or other fellow countrymen. It is the immigrant of a few years' experience here who guides them to jobs, familiarizes them with routine and procedure in the plant, enables them to find homes and to furnish them if they have families. At the club, they meet fellow countrymen who gladly give them their conception of America. If they can read, they also find here newspapers in their own language which keep them informed of developments at home as well as of news in this country. In church they are enabled to maintain the habits and traditions of their old country. Quite generally, their priest also is a counselor and a guide.

But these local sources of information naturally look for guidance to higher and better informed channels, since they themselves are practically isolated or too steadily at their work to seek this information independently. Even the priest must have a higher and an outside source for his knowledge of developments in America. Quite often he too has been transplanted from an agricultural to an industrial country.

In the final analysis, the immigrant workers look for guidance and for interpretation of America to leaders of their own nationality, who are generally associated with a benefit society or are editors of a newspaper. Almost every benefit society has a weekly paper of its own, and there are some independent papers with influence among the immigrant workers.

The national leaders themselves are not workingmen, and, with a few minor exceptions, were not workingmen in the old country. They come from middle-class families and are imbued with middle-class notions. In this country, while their entire constituency and following are made up of workingmen, the leaders live among and associate with middle-class people and read the usual papers in English.

In their desire to be of service to their fellow countrymen, or to develop a clientele off whom to make a living, the leaders naturally try to devise societies or other agencies to serve their countrymen. In doing this they overlook the principal problem confronting the immigrant as a worker. For a professional man ordinarily does not need the kind of organization to protect his economic interests which a workingman needs. He is fairly conversant with the business or the profession that he is in; he has a certain amount of initiative and bargaining ability so that he can protect himself as an individual. What he needs is protection against exigencies beyond his control such as sickness insurance, death losses, etc. He also wants a club for social intercourse.

All immigrant leaders from their own experience also realize the difficulties of adaptation for those who are unacquainted with the language. They remember how they were imposed upon and how perhaps they were persecuted by the police or other civil authorities. Hence, guiding themselves by their own experience and not seriously studying the conditions and the needs of the immigrant workers, these leaders provide protection for their fellow countrymen as if they were business or professional men, not immigrants and workers. So it happens that these immigrant nationalities have highly developed benefit societies and social clubs in every community, but almost no organizations to protect their economic interests as workers.

The only exceptions of importance are the Hungarians. Since a large number of these workers come from industrial and mining centers, acquainted with protective economic organization, their leaders are of a different type. Many of them were workingmen or otherwise connected with the labor movement in Hungary and know what workingmen need. Consequently, while they realize that their fellow countrymen (as strangers in a new country) need benefit societies and protection against persecution and imposition, they also seek economic protective organizations as wage workers. Hence, we have in this country the Hungarian workmen's benefit societies based upon a philosophy and preaching ideals entirely different from the societies of the other immigrant workers. This is also true to some extent among the Italians. But while both Italians and Hungarians educate their fellows as workers, they rarely develop labor organizations of their own.

Among the other nationalities a few leaders have recently organized radical and socialist papers and societies. They are a very small percentage and so far have not succeeded in counteracting the influence of the middle-class immigrant leaders, who got in on the ground floor.

It is interesting to contrast the run of immigrants in the steel mills with such nationalities as the Finns and the Jews, both of whom have but few representatives in the steel industry. The immigrants from these two races are largely from Russian industrial and commercial centers. Owing to the persecution of the Czar, they developed a definite working-class philosophy. Hence, while their leaders also come from the middle class, they have a distinct knowledge of and adherence to workingmen's notions. They educate their fellow countrymen in working-class concepts, founding organizations based fundamentally on working-class needs. They have benefit societies, they have clubs, but the underlying doctrines of these are working class rather than middle class. Naturally, the newspapers which they publish reflect working-class philosophy. The chief Jewish working-class paper has a circulation of 300,000. They have numerous magazines and extensive workingmen's educational societies. This is true of the Finns likewise, although they are very few in number. They have four workingmen's daily papers, one monthly magazine and one quarterly, edited as working-class periodicals. Naturally, these races have also developed independent labor unions and labor leaders, although they generally work in harmony with the "American" labor movement.

The difference between the leaders of the vast majority of workers in the steel industry and the leaders of the Jewish and Finnish workers can be stated as follows: *The leaders of the immigrant workers in the steel industry might be termed clansmen.* A clansman in this sense would be a person accustomed to profit from the helplessness of his fellow countrymen. He generally has qualities of leadership, is somewhat better educated than his fellows, has a little more initiative and is more adaptable to a new environment. He comes from a family which even in the old country has been accustomed to profit by the helplessness of fellow countrymen.

He is seldom one of the working masses in upbringing or in intellectual outlook. He generally has a highly developed business instinct. With business motives, he assumes leadership because it is financially profitable. Whether honest or dishonest, he is bound to lead them in accordance with his business ideals and his conception of a business society.

The leaders of Jewish and Finnish workers, on the other hand, might be termed intellectuals. They are generally students and idealists, men who not only sympathize with the political oppression of their fellow countrymen, as do the leaders of the immigrant workers in the steel mills, but who also have studied the economic life of their fellow immigrants and have a thorough knowledge of their economic problems. They have developed primarily into crusaders and evangelists who see more clearly the economic condition under which their people labor. They undertake leadership from idealistic motives rather than for business ends.

Church and Pastors

The priest and preacher of the immigrant workers in steel communities as a rule gets his philosophy from the nationalistic leaders and foreign language press of the business stamp. His industrial conceptions are those of the secular leaders. He is often unacquainted with the labor movement, except as he has indirectly heard or read about it. He is generally on good terms with the management of the plants where his parishioners work. The management usually makes an effort to cultivate the friendship of the priest and contributes to his church. He, therefore, would be inclined to act as an interpreter of America and its industrial problems from the viewpoint of the employer.

Amalgamation, Industrial and Economic

By organizing their fellow countrymen into benefit societies and clubs on nationalistic lines, the leaders naturally emphasize segregation. It is charged that this explains why employers have fostered these societies and cultivated the friendship of the priest and financed his church. There are, however, deeper forces working underground which are breaking up these nationalistic segregations and which develop a spirit of fellow-feeling and solidarity among the immigrant workers in the iron and steel industry. Forces leading to economic and industrial amalgamation, although often poorly guided, are overcoming the stimulated forces that make for nationalism and segregation.

In the mill, immigrant workers of various nationalities work side by side. They learn to know each other, they learn to work in harmony with each other, but, above all, because of the discrimination against all of them as "hunkies" and foreigners, they develop a feeling of fellowship which cuts across racial and nationalistic animosities. This is an inevitable, natural and unforced development based on common experience and common grievances. At the same time it intensifies rather than overcomes the cleavage with the English-speaking worker.

Labor organizations, out of self-protection, undertake to develop conscious industrial and economic amalgamation by organizing all the workers on an equality. Among the Jews and the Finns, where their own national leaders are cognizant of this need, the old American trade unions do not need to develop foreign language organizers. All that is necessary is to cooperate with the labor leaders of those nationalities.

Among the great majority of immigrant workers in the steel industry, just as in the coal and metalliferous mines, and later in the packing industry where their nationalistic leaders had neglected the economic interests of their fellow countrymen, the American trade unions began to develop a new type of leader who could organize the immigrant workers. This marks the advent, then, of what is known as the foreign language organizer in A. F. of L. unions. These are young fellows with initiative and more than the usual amount of intelligence, who possibly have some knowledge of trade unions in Europe, but who learned their unionism chiefly in this country through the guidance and tutoring of native-born trade unionists. These become the economic leaders of their fellow countrymen. They are mainly responsible for organization among immigrant workers in this country.

The I.W.W. has followed a similar policy, generally more aggressively than the A. F. of L., and almost always more democratically, which explains some of its successes in initiating organization among immigrant workers.

The first A. F. of L. union to try this policy with great success was the United Mine Workers (coal). The old Western Federation of Miners (metalliferous mines), now known as the Mine, Mill and

Smelter Workers, also uses the method with great effect. Mr. Fitzpatrick and Mr. Foster followed this policy in the packing industry and applied it in the iron and steel industry.

With a little information on trade unionism and on their immediate needs as wage earners, the immigrant workers in organized industries begin to assert themselves, and, while not challenging their old leaders, proceed to impress their own point of view upon their benefit societies and newspapers.

Since these benefit societies are democratically controlled, they often amend their constitutions by committing the societies to trade unionism, urging the members to join unions, and providing for the expulsion of members who break strikes.

From their newspapers, they begin to demand labor news and discussions of industrial problems. They force the discussion of specific strikes through communications to the newspapers. Thus the workers in unorganized industries first learn of trade unions and of what their members claim for unions.

(It is interesting to note that not only have the nationalistic leaders or clansmen been ignorant of the desires of their fellow countrymen, but that organizations like the Inter-Racial Council make the same error. Editors of foreign language papers in Pittsburgh refused to subscribe to the Inter-Racial Council's advertising and news because they said that their readers were not interested in the news matter which the council supplied. They want news on industry and labor, not on political happenings in Washington, which seem to them remote.)

Those of the workers who cannot read, hear labor problems discussed at their clubs. In the course of their migrations, workers from unionized industries bring news of the doings of the union and its results. Other workers read newspapers aloud, giving the news of conditions in other places and in other industries. If the information which comes to their attention stands out in contrast to conditions in unorganized territories where the management is arbitrary and working conditions and wages not as favorable, they note it. The workers of the various nationalities, although living apart, worshiping at separate churches, and attending separate clubs, readily begin to feel common interests based on common grievances.

Thus conditions ripen for labor organization. Workers begin to look for the union to come to organize them. This explains why in many towns little exhortation was necessary in organizing the iron and steel workers. In dozens of towns single mass meetings resulted immediately in thousands of applications for union membership. The Fitzpatrick-Foster committee had very loose and unsystematic methods, but the immigrant workers joined readily and placed large confidence in this mushroom organization; many who were not members responded to its strike call.

Alignment of Forces in Steel Strike

Within the effective strike areas, immigrants walked out practically as units. Those who remained at work were of two classes. First there were those who expected to return to the old country in the following spring or summer. Contrary to the impression conveyed by the American press, the immigrants who worked during the strike were the ones least interested in the welfare of this country; *those who struck were the ones who have their homes and families here and who intend to remain and make this their permanent home.*

A second element among immigrants who did not strike was from races with few representatives in this country or with so few workers in the iron and steel industry that it was either financially or otherwise impossible to secure organizers who spoke their language. Such nationalities have very few papers in their own language and no previous knowledge of trade unionism.

When the dominant institutions of the community, controlled by native-born Americans, opposed the strike and raised the race issue through ministers, newspapers, civil authorities, etc., the immigrant strikers were not entirely surprised. It was the customary practice in steel towns and they were used to it, except that the "alien" cry was more violent during the strike.

In general, the immigrant strikers' own priests and clansmen leaders, as well as their newspapers, did not support the strike. This also did not surprise the strikers. Guided by commercial philosophy, surrounded by Americans whose respect they value highly, it is natural that the clan leaders quailed before epithets and charges of "bolshevism." The friendship of many of these leaders was cultivated by the large steel corporations; they were placed under obligations to the corporations or overwhelmed by unexpected friendliness. One Pittsburgh leader said that he and his colleagues were greatly embarrassed by the steel strike, since the Steel Corporation had contributed a "large" sum of money, the exact amount of which he refused to divulge, to the Red Cross of his nationality. He considered the strike of his fellow countrymen as "base ingratitude." In another case, strikers charged that the editor of a foreign language paper was bought by the steel interests. He ran nine articles in his weekly against the strike; he told an investigator that he had them translated into English at the rate of fifteen dollars per article, but he was not in a position to supply the copy as he had turned it over to a certain person. When asked for the name of the person so that the translated copy might be inspected, he said that the person had sent it to "someone in New York." When told that the investigator intended going to New York and would like to ask permission to see these articles, the editor refused to give the name of the person in New York.

For the most part these leaders seemed honest in their opposition to the strike. There were two reasons for this: The national leaders are frequently more interested in the future of their newly emancipated European fatherlands than in this country. Some of the leaders interviewed told the investigator that they considered it inadvisable for their compatriots to embark upon a long strike and spend all their savings when they should be making preparations to return to their own country next spring or summer. By spending their savings, they would be penniless and would either remain here or visit the old country as poor people. They felt that their fellow countrymen should bear the bad conditions for one winter longer and save up money to take back to the old country. They explained that the immigrants who worked during the strike had definitely decided to return to the old country.

The other outstanding reason is probably as "un-American" and is to some extent copied from the English-speaking public and press. The latter constantly pointed out to the American workmen that this was a strike of foreigners and incidentally asserted that these foreigners or aliens were essentially Bolshevists and enemies of law and order. The immigrant leaders opposed the strike by arguing that American labor unions never cared for the immigrant, that they were using the immigrant as a cat's-paw to strike to improve conditions "for the American workers who did not even go on strike." The editor-leaders in the same pronouncements pointed out that the chief labor leaders were Americans and declared that Americans called out the immigrant workers and double-crossed them by letting the Americans stay at work.

Another argument which the editor-leaders used effectively was that the A. F. of L. "had always been against immigrant workers"; also that this was not the first strike which Americans had called and then remained at work. Thus, just as the English press and public were raising anti-foreign prejudice, so the immigrant press and leaders tried to raise anti-American prejudice.

Solidarity of Rank and File

Notwithstanding that the immigrant leaders and their newspapers almost wholly opposed the steel strike, few dared make the opposition very open and blunt. In private the editors explained that the workers were leaning to unionism in general and they did not dare oppose the strike too openly for that reason. One editor explained that a competitor of his in Chicago had openly opposed the strike and had lost almost all his subscribers and was on the verge of bankruptcy. He said that he was more "foxy" and instead of openly opposing the strike he published nothing in favor of it; in fact, he refrained from discussing it entirely and indirectly "warned his fellow countrymen to be law-abiding," not to listen to "agitators," and above all things not to be "ungrateful to this country which had done so much in emancipating their fatherlands." He said he followed the policy of the English papers by intimating that instead of a strike against the Steel Corporation it was a revolution against the government.

Of the nine foreign-language papers whose editors were visited in Pittsburgh, only two were openly for the strike, one a Hungarian weekly with only 2,000 circulation, the editor really making most of his income from job printing, and the other a Russo-Carpathian paper with a circulation of 4,500, which favored the strike because its immediate rival openly opposed it. Another paper supplied fair information on the strike. The editor is a conscientious and scholarly man who, despite his business and professional associations, seems to be more in touch with his fellow countrymen. Two papers openly opposed the strike, one a weekly of 6,000 circulation, which printed the nine articles against the strike already referred to. The other paper is published in Homestead and has a large circulation. The remaining four papers did not come out openly against the strike, although their editors were distinctly opposed to it. These editors said that the societies of which the papers are the official organs are composed almost wholly of workers in the iron and steel and mining industries and that they did not dare openly to oppose labor organizations or strike.

The determination of the immigrant workers, with their firm conviction that they had grievances, was curiously attested by their attitude to their old-time leaders. In instances where newspapers opposed the strike, the workers repudiated them and registered vigorous protests. For almost the first time the immigrant workers dared to defy the dominant elements, their old leaders and newspapers, and followed the National Committee for Organizing the Iron and Steel Industry. Apparently this was because only the latter recognized their grievances. Immigrants who differed in language and had their traditional nationalistic animosities accentuated during the war, cast away their race prejudices and struck together. This was further evidence that the strike was a strike of rank and file where leadership was secondary.

Immigrant Rebellion

The determination of the immigrant worker to assert himself, in spite of all the opposition of dominant opinion in his own community, was the chief reason why the foreign and the English press, and especially the "American" elements of society, considered the strike as having deeper motives than mere demands of ordinary trade unionism. Not only the mill managers, but all the governing classes in steel towns were accustomed to seeing the immigrant docile and submissive; to them any strike was indeed a revolution. Formerly the immigrant obeyed orders without questioning. He did the unpleasant work, the heavy and exhausting work, and never asked the reason why.

He had submitted for years to militaristic mill discipline. In the community he had acted in the same way. He had lived his life away from the others, at first purposely keeping out of their way. Then as he became "Americanized," he began in recent years to assert himself as a member of the community. As one "American" minister explained it, "The foreigner wants too much; he owns the largest churches in the community, is buying up the property, and is now even running his own candidates for political office."

While it was natural that the immigrant should arrive at this state of mind in the course of adapting himself to his new surroundings and gradually becoming acclimated—that is Americanized—this assertive state of mind seems recently to have concentrated on economic problems and conditions. At his clubs and by fellow countrymen who had worked elsewhere, he was being told that better conditions existed in unionized industries, particularly that there was no twelve-hour day where there were unions. Also he began to believe that these betterments could be acquired through united action under the leadership of labor organizations.

Most important, the immigrant in the steel mills had tasted better conditions during the war. He had had an opportunity to earn more by working on the better paying jobs, for the first time he had been treated considerately by the foreman, etc. In the community, he had also been looked upon differently, that is, either as an "American" or as a worthy ally. At "home," his fellow countrymen were becoming free citizens in nations rid of autocrats.

The immigrant worker took these new developments seriously and was very much disillusioned after the signing of the armistice when the employers and the dominant elements in the community took the attitude that, now the war was over, it was time to return to all the old conditions. The immigrant was again a "hunkie." This was the last straw. Thereafter he waited for anybody to lead him into the promised land.

Thus the strike was also an outburst of the inhibited instincts for self-expression. If the immigrant worker had not tasted the satisfactions of recognized self-expression during the war, it would have required a more intensive and systematic campaign to organize him. It might also have been very difficult to get him to strike in the face of approaching winter. It was because the immigrant's deepest emotions and instincts were stirred that this huge and unprecedented strike was possible. The immigrant wanted not only better wages and shorter hours. He resented being treated as a chattel or a "hunkie." He was no longer content with being ridiculed and scorned and considered only good enough for the dirty work. He had caught the rivalry of the steel industry—that if any one is worth anything he is promoted from one job to another with the prospect of ultimately being a roller. This incentive had before the war existed only for the "American": it was felt that the "hunkie" needed no incentive. Therefore, steel officials as well as the highly skilled American workers and others in the community were frightened when the immigrant worker asserted himself as if he were on an equal footing with them.

Disillusionment

Many of the strikers said that if the strike was lost they would never return to the mill. Even those who had been born in this country but were sons of immigrant workers on strike said they would return to their fathers' countries, which were become independent and free nations, rather than remain in the mills under old conditions. Most of the immigrant leaders interviewed held the opinion that if the strike was lost the immigrants in great numbers would return to the old country. In previous years, when there was not this alternative, immigrant workers who were defeated in strikes in other industries would sullenly return to work. In such cases their efficiency was impaired and they were fertile ground for I.W.W. and other revolutionary seed. A cause of I.W.W.-ism is despondency; hence, the strength of I.W.W. belief in sabotage. A self-respecting workman, strong enough to meet any opponent on an equal footing, hardly ever resorts to underhand ways. He will when he thinks he has been downed unfairly. Thus sabotage commonly follows lost strikes among "American" workmen as well as among "foreigners." As a result, the whole moral fiber of the worker is affected. He loses faith in the worthwhileness of work, he loses faith in orderly methods of changing the conditions of work.

The Ethnic Community
by Philip Klein

Nationality Communities

Wherever a considerable aggregation of families having the same nationality background succeeds in establishing their homes, there a "nationality community" has sprung up. Italian, Greek, Polish, whatever the group may be, if it has any social vitality and economic

A Social Study of Pittsburgh: Community Problems and Social Services of Allegheny County (New York: Columbia University Press, 1938), pp. 248–264. Reprinted by permission of the publisher and the author.

security, its life finds expression in a series of enterprises, individual and corporate, which serve its particular needs—churches, parochial schools, lodges, newspapers, stores—conducted in the language and according to the traditional demands of each group. By means of innumerable interrelations between its members and functionaries such a community develops a coherent and characterful life of its own.

It is a mistake to imagine that foreign-born communities are simply replicas of life in the country of origin or that the traits that appear in the members of such communities are explicable simply as the immigrants' "cultural background." The social process is much more complex. Some clues to this background can be gained by considering the general characteristics of peasant communities of Eastern Europe as they were in the nineteenth century. Thus they were known to, and are remembered by, large numbers of America's foreign-born population. Before the advent of the automobile, which is still used only on a small scale in Eastern Europe as compared to American rural areas, many peasant communities had little contact with the rest of the world. Life moved slowly from generation to generation. Innumerable villages retained traits which characterized them in the Middle Ages. Customs and obligations long established as helpful in the hard struggle for a livelihood or as contributing to the meager pleasures of peasant life through the centuries acquired all the significance of eternal verities. Against these focal values new ideas had relatively little weight.

In a peasant community most of the families are likely to be related by blood or by marriage. The position and satisfaction of each member depends on the strength and property of his family group, on the number of fields or cattle the family own, on the dowry it can provide its daughters, and on the inheritance to which the sons look forward. Each member almost from infancy contributes his labor to the family's good, and only the outcast has no claim to share whatever security the group can provide. Innumerable records of peasant emigration illustrate the fact that in the communities where emigration becomes a tradition the departure of the individual is less often an assertion of an individualistic will than a part of a family plan through which to solve its problem of poverty—to pay off a mortgage, to buy additional land, or to provide for a younger son. In other words, life is corporate, and the corporation is the family. At the head of each family is the father, a sovereign both in rights and in responsibilities.

However, the emigrant, from the moment his departure is decided on, is imperceptibly modified by the individualistic experience he is undergoing. His traditional outlook on life is subject to disorganization. Moreover, everything he experiences in America has a more casual, more complex, and at the same time more self-centered quality. His success depends on his own prowess. His companions are intent on personal pleasure and adornment. The fact that his family have owned acres for many generations contributes nothing toward his prestige. He is no longer surrounded by the only people to whom from the cradle he has felt allegiance, that is, to his kin and village. The wonder is that the claim of distant relatives in so many instances survives long years of separation, even when illiteracy had reduced the exchange of letters to meager communications dictated to a third person.

The average immigrant colony goes through several phases of development. The early years of a colony composed of unskilled laborers is apt to show many characteristics which may also be found in a frontier American town. Saloon, dance hall, boarding home, are the conveniences which spring up in the casual life of any early settlement.

The flotsam and jetsam of immigrant life gradually develop coherence and institutional life becomes possible. In some nationalities, perhaps most strongly among Italians, there is a tendency for immigrants from the same village or district in the home country to cluster in the same American neighborhood. Under unfavorable conditions this cohesiveness may outlast the period in which it is essential to the immigrant's economic and emotional security. It may become an atrophied social process, isolating a minority group from relationship to the larger society in which it lives. The normal trend in Allegheny County has been marked by a gradual geographical dispersion from the first settlements in the hollow or on the river front to various better residential districts. With this geographic dispersion normally goes a branching out of interest and enterprise which, unless it is blocked, tends gradually to relate the erstwhile immigrant to many aspects of American life, although he may long retain his affiliation in his own nationality community.

The nationality communities in and around Pittsburgh are well known. There is considerable variation in the type of institution which may become of central importance in each immigrant community. Among Czechs, for instance, the Sokol (Gymnastic Society) is of central importance; among Italians it is difficult to develop any organization because of the supreme importance of family ties and village ties. Among immigrants who have enjoyed educational advantages and have lived in urban districts the institutional patterns which evolve are apt to be complex, representing a variety of specialized cultural interests, such as literary and dramatic societies, political organizations, and so forth.

Among nationality groups in whose tradition the Church has played an important role, the Church is likely to be transplanted with great strength and to afford a channel of cultural continuity which makes for stability of character during the difficult years before cultural adjustment to American life can take place. Among the Greeks, the Poles, the Russians, and to a large extent among the Slovaks, the Church becomes a center of community life, an expression of deep-rooted cultural form, as well as of religious practices. It is likely to draw to itself functions which in the country of origin belonged to the political community. Support of the Church is imposed on all members as a tax, which may be quite heavy. Within the parish societies the activities may vary greatly in value, but at best they conserve habits of cooperation and mutual responsibility, and they may be important in offering opportunity for recreation and the preservation of beautiful and cultural traditions. Many of the Catholic churches maintain parochial schools. In others a weekly language school is provided to instruct the children in the mother tongue of their parents, thus contributing to the safeguarding of family solidarity.

The mother in one Italian family was urged by a social worker to move to a better neighborhood. It was pointed out that she could attend the American Catholic Church there. She protested that she much preferred putting up with her present less desirable neighborhood because the church was served by an Italian priest. She explained: "I want my own religion for the children."

In any immigrant group the daily hazards of life very soon prompt some sort of organization for mutual aid. A few pennies are saved by each individual from weekly earnings and are turned over to a saloon keeper or a boarding home keeper to be kept in a pool available in case of sickness or accident. This was the typical beginning of the lodge. Many nationalities, especially Slavs, Hungarians, and Germans, are apt to build a "hall" as the center of their social activities. These halls are found in every community in Allegheny County where nationality groups live in sufficient numbers to be able to finance the enterprise. As community centers of foreign nationality life, these nationality halls are of great importance. They may be owned by a large number of individual shareholders, or a group of lodges may hold the shares. Occasionally a hall is erected by a few individuals as a business enterprise, profit on which is made by letting out the hall to local lodges or any other organizations. Individuals may hire the assembly room for weddings or other festivities. In addition to the secular halls there are others connected with parish churches.

In Tarentum, for example, there are approximately 3,000 Slovak families. The Lipa Hall there was built in 1918. It is supported by a number of Slovak societies including the Sokol, the National Slovak Society, and the First Catholic Union. Each one holds a share worth $35. In addition there are about 560 "members" who pay 25 cents each month to help support the house. The membership has been growing recently. Twenty-five percent of the Slovak children in the community are said to belong. There are two gymnastic classes for children under sixteen years which meet twice each week.

In a number of the communities in the Allegheny Valley the nationality halls have mural decorations which are painted by the same artist. One which represents the dual orientation of the members' interests is worthy of note. On both sides of the stage are portraits—on the right, President Roosevelt; on the left, President Masaryk of Czechoslovakia. On the side walls are scenes from the homeland: on one side, a towering feudal castle, a peasant boy and girl on a village street, and a legendary meeting of a knight and the virgin. On the other side, a river scene with a "No hunting, no fishing" sign suggests that the locale is American. In other halls there were photographs and calendars having pictures of various American presidents. Washington, Lincoln, and Roosevelt seem to have been the favorite choices.

The typical nationality hall is a rectangular building of two or more floors. On the ground floor is a large room with a bar, pool table, and tables and chairs. There are several additional rooms, usually including a kitchen and small business offices, on the ground floor. On the second floor is usually a large assembly room, with gymnasium equipment and a stage.[1]

The nationality hall is usually in charge of a resident steward and his wife. The steward is elected from the regular membership and receives either a salary or a commission on drinks. The use of nationality halls varies greatly. In some lodges quite elaborate operettas and plays are performed several times during the winter. Recently there has been a revival in the popularity of musical programs, which have thus far been sponsored primarily by some of the nationality churches and performed in church halls. The beautiful choir trained by Father Staroski of the Greek Catholic Church, on the South Side of Pittsburgh, is an example. Father Popovitch's choir at St. Savia, in McKeesport, is also notable. This movement is now spreading from the churches to some of the lay groups, who perhaps recognize the appreciation to be won from the American people by this contribution to community culture.

In some instances the halls also provided reading matter for their members. It was usual to find the daily papers, both in English and in the mother tongue of the group. In one nationality hall is a small library from which the members may borrow books to be kept by them for several weeks; in another, plans are now under way to raise money for a new book collection. The interest of this group tends toward study of economic problems and radical political theories. One member pointed out that their hall was the center for any enterprise the group wished to consider. Here money had been raised to send to the homeland during the World War. Here also Liberty Bond campaigns were inaugurated. In Tarentum an attempt was made to measure the importance of the two nationality halls as recreational resources. We were told that whereas ten of the Slovak boys used the local Y.M.C.A., 268 members belonging to the national Sokol met in the Lipa Hall, while 400 were members of the Junior Lodge, and 183, of the Senior Lodge, which meet in the parish hall. In Tarentum 25 percent of the Slovaks are said to belong to the national hall. A larger percentage probably are members of the Catholic lodges.

It is difficult for Americans, particularly for the older generation, to appreciate the social importance of these "national halls." In a

1. Nationality halls were visited during the study in McKeesport, Tarentum, Coverdale, Springdale, and East Deer Township.

setting belonging to the group, where the members feel free from the inhibiting presence of superior-feeling and authoritative Americans, the genuine interests and enterprise of nationality groups have free play. In a number of places the importance of both lodges and national halls seems indeed to be diminishing, but in many they are still the center of plans for mutual aid.

The secretary of a small lodge in East Deer Township explained that in case a lodge member was injured, it would be the duty of the secretary to see that he was taken to the hospital. If he were killed, the lodge must do more than pay his insurance benefits. The members would meet and talk over a plan to help his widow and children.

Drinking is not disapproved by the community, and the men frequently stop at the hall for a drink after work in the mine is over for the day; on holidays they drink heavily, and, as is traditional in the homeland, no one is too much shocked at the man who gets drunk. It was said that the women drink very moderately, as they believe in this way they are more able to restrain their husbands. In the national hall at Tarentum the steward explained that children under sixteen are never permitted in the pool room and bar. They enter by a separate entrance and go upstairs to the large gymnasium where gymnastic drills are held twice each week.

Since the depression, lodge activities have been failing for lack of funds. One informant mentioned that members lacked money for carfare as well as for decent clothes in which to attend social functions. "Somehow we don't feel like celebrations since things had gotten so bad," one woman said. Two club leaders spoke of the great difficulty of getting leaders for the Sokol, as it requires intensive work. Several Sokol lodges are adopting the English language for their instruction in order to hold the younger members. It is generally recognized that the young people tend to drift away, and there is a marked effort to develop new programs to attract them. This is partly a question of sheer business. The lodges cannot remain solvent if their membership becomes predominantly a group of aged and infirm. Yet this is a real possibility which confronts them.

Mixed Immigrant Communities

Not every settlement of the foreign-born is large enough to produce a well-knit community life. Where the employment policies of American industry in the county have resulted in attracting a mixture of many nationalities, each one too small to develop its own cultural institutions, the result would seem to be a culturally incoherent aggregation of "foreigners," which even more than the urban immigrant colony is slow to overcome the prejudices of older American residents of the countryside.

The observer, alert to problems of the immigrant, is immediately struck by the cultural impoverishment and social disorganization of such a community.[2] The usual hedonistic diversions are certainly present: the movie, the bowling alley, the saloon, and the dance hall. But, whereas in the well-developed nationality community the encroachment of these commercial enterprises is likely to be tempered by traditional activities of more cultural significance, such as those offered by gymnastic societies, singing, dramatic clubs, or literary clubs, in the mixed immigrant community these are either entirely absent or they are conducted intermittently and on a peculiarly meager level. In its early history, this type of community tends to be disunited, broken into component cultural fractions. After a time—if one may judge by what has happened in the communities studied—cultural prejudices recede, alliances are made, and joint activities become possible; but lacking conservative cultural roots, the interests of the population are shallow except where economic grievances constitute a real and deep-seated common experience.

It is to these small and resourceless settlements, which have come into being in all parts of the country in response to the needs of industry, that the Protestant mission tends to come. Unhappily, however devoted their efforts to care for the needs of the population, the ultimate effect in spiritual life is likely to be still further demoralization. This is because religion, at least in its forms of expression and its definition of belief, springs also out of the depths of a people's culture and is inextricably interwoven with it. Sudden transitions can hardly be made without threat to the depths and richness of religious life. Some individuals seem capable of finding the universal meanings which make it possible to pass from one form of religious experience to another without loss of inspiration or spiritual integrity. But for the average person, and above all for the peasant who does not live according to abstract concepts, form and essence are one.

2. Almost any of the mining towns offer examples of this type. Coverdale and Russelton may well be studied as mixed immigrant communities.

Reaction like that of the Italian woman who prefers a long trip once or twice a year to a distant Italian Catholic parish to the regular ministration of a local Irish Catholic church, because as she puts it: "I like my Italian religion," is found frequently among just those whose personalities are nourished by strongly rooted loyalties. If such strong preferences are felt within the broad framework of the Catholic Church, it is even more true when the transition is from Catholic to Protestant worship. A Slovak miner's wife said: "I'd rather send my children to my own church even if we have to pay there and at the Mission they give you all sorts of presents." Yet, without doubt, the missions have a certain popularity, not wholly explained by their offering of a combination of religious and material advantages. It may be partly because of the warmth and friendliness of many of the workers, as well as because they often provide the only organized social services available in the settlement.

New Americans in McKeesport

In order to obtain some idea of the situation of new Americans when considered in their relationships within one local community an attempt was made during this inquiry to construct an integrated, if brief, picture of the organized life of new Americans in one of the industrial communities of Allegheny County.

The city of McKeesport was selected because of the number of nationalities there, their size and their stability.[3] The 1930 census shows that the immigrants and their children are outstripping the native-born residents of McKeesport in number in almost the exact ratio observed for the county as a whole. Of the total population of 54,632, the foreign-born and those of native birth and of foreign or mixed parentage numbered 32,154, or 58 percent of the total population.[4] If one classifies together the foreign stock from Great Britain, Ireland, Germany, Sweden, and other northwestern countries of Europe, they constitute approximately 38 percent of the foreign stock.[5] These nationalities are often referred to as "the old immigra-

3. Twenty-six individuals were interviewed. The majority of interviews lasted from one to two hours and several persons were seen more than once. A variety of reports available through the courtesy of the International Institute and of several nationality organizations were examined.

4. Fifteenth Census of the United States, 1930, *Population,* Vol. III, Pt. 2, Table 15, p. 688.

5. *Ibid.,* Tables 18 and 19, pp. 702 and 706.

tion," because people from these countries came to the United States in large groups and had well established communities here before the mass emigration from southeastern European countries commenced in the eighties. It will be noted that the largest single group of the foreign-born according to country of birth, as recorded in the 1930 census, is that of Czechoslovakian nativity, who, together with their children, number 6,505. The second largest group recorded belongs to the "old immigration," 3,633 Germans. The Polish stock, 3,586, come next. Then there is a drop of 2,387 Italians, 2,219 Hungarians, and 2,161 Jugoslavs.[6]

These census figures are, of course, only roughly indicative. The census enumerators cannot go beyond the information given by foreign-born residents, and many immigrants are exceedingly hazy in their knowledge of European geography. Census enumeration, morever follows the political boundaries created at the close of the World War. Thus, for example, Czechoslovakian origin may represent culturally diverse Slovaks, Hungarians, and Czechs. In McKeesport the Czechoslovak group consists almost exclusively of Slovaks.

The coming of the "newer immigrants" to McKeesport was an event in the history of local industry and illustrates the general pattern of immigrant accretion referred to earlier. The National Tube Company was established in 1872, and the population therafter grew rapidly.[7] In each stage of the growth of the immigrant settlements the needs of the industries have been the potent drawing force.[8] These same industries are still the chief employers of foreign labor. A former employee of the company tells how at one time the National Tube Company brought in carloads of Mexicans, who were first housed in company barracks. After several years the demand for this labor failed, and they were left to find their way back to Mexico or to other employment as best they might. A few Mexican families living in wretched quarters in the first ward are the his-

6. *Ibid.*

7. As one landmark of the newer immigration, one may take Rev. Daroczy's report that the first Hungarian (or Magyar) family settled in McKeesport in 1881 (newspaper article by the Rev. Daroczy on "Magyar Culture in McKeesport," in the *Daily News,* March 5, 1935).

8. An unpublished survey of McKeesport made in 1930–31 gives as the principal employers: the National Tube Company, 7,200 employees; the National Sheet & Tin Plate Company, 1,800 employees; the Firth Sterling Steel Company, 550 employees; and the Fort Pitt Casting Company, 300 employees.

torical survival of this industrial chapter.

While, of course, the bulk of new Americans belong to the laboring mass, there are also an increasing number of successful enterprises in the business world conducted by new Americans. The Italians have been most active in undertaking independent enterprises, but there are scattered instances of business enterprise on the part of other nationalities. There are two hotels in McKeesport, and the smaller one of the two is owned and operated by a Slovak. The four moving picture theaters are owned by Austrian Jews. There is a large printing establishment operated by the United Societies of Greek Catholic Religion. A large bakery is operated by a Hungarian. A real estate and insurance business, by a Slovak. The local agent for the Frigidaire is a Jugoslav.

These illustrations perhaps suggest the trend toward economic success among many members of nationality groups. Inevitably there has come with it a growing interest in civic affairs, which is expressing itself in political organization. For instance, each of the Slavic groups in McKeesport has a political club. These have been united in the past two years in the "Slavic Political Federation," which also has a woman's branch. There is as yet, we were told, no clear-cut trend of political thought in this group or any definite conviction concerning the Republican and Democratic parties. In the last election, however, they were overwhelmingly Democratic.

The tendency is for politicians to respect requests coming from any organized body of voters. It is said that the individual foreign-born person has little chance to overcome the discrimination against him unless he can bring the influence of such an organized group into play. Thus, for instance, during the days of prohibition a Hungarian applying for a position on the police force was told that he would have to be recommended by a certain Hungarian Club known to have bootlegging interests, since the administration could not appoint a man against the wishes of this organization which controlled many votes.[9] Incidentally, this situation would seem to provide a new and vital reason for the survival of the nationality organization.

A student of the local situation reports:[10]

> To the uneducated European peasant who has been accustomed to the autocratic control of the village by the local official corresponding to the mayor of an American city, the city official is omnipotent. It is almost impossible to con-

9. Reported in an unpublished survey of McKeesport.
10. *Ibid.*

vince the average foreigner that the mayor, the ward politician or the local representative in either the State or Federal legislature cannot set aside laws to grant a favor to anyone loyal to the party. The extent to which this faith in the politician enters into community life in McKeesport is almost unbelievable. The politicians frequently seem to be favored by Providence, for in numerous cases, where in the natural course of events, the desired end would be gained with no intervention, and could not possibly be hastened, some local politicians have written a letter just in time to get all the credit for the success which was inevitable. Aldermen[11] make a practice of filling out petitions for the entry of relatives of naturalized citizens and sending them to the local representatives in Congress instead of to the State Department. The voter then gets the impression that he is indebted to the Congressman and to the party for the admission of his relative, who would have been admitted if the man himself had sent the petition to the State Department instead of paying a fee to the alderman for unnecessary red tape. The alderman and notary public make a living from the foreigner in McKeesport. High fees are often demanded, and many services, such as filling out applications for citizenship papers, which could be done by any private citizen or social agency, are regularly performed by these petty officials for a fee, because the foreigner thinks he must go to an official for such services or they would not be legal. Many domestic and neighborhood difficulties are taken to aldermen who require high fees and accomplish little in many cases.

Almost every nationality group has many organizations which furnish potential support for politicians. At special affairs held by these organizations public officials are usually the most honored guests and speakers. Especially is this true just before election, when political candidates spend Sunday afternoon making the rounds of these meetings. To the simple-minded foreigner, with a peasant background, it is a great honor to have the mayor or other officials attend their affairs, and one visit of an hour or two nets the party several hundred votes, with a few drinks on the side. . . .

The successful politician in McKeesport must be affable enough to win the loyalty of the foreign element, diplomatic enough to respect the interests of powerful industries without drawing forth open criticisms, and tactful enough to keep his eyes closed to the activities of local bootleggers and gamblers. It is not surprising that civic improvements are slow in coming, for many of the most needed improvements, such as better city planning, conflict with the interests of the industries to whom the official feels he owes more than to the voter.[12]

With regard to McKeesport one may ask how far older American groups who control the cultural and civic institutions invite participation by the "new Americans." One may hear much talk in McKeesport about the failure of the "foreigners" to become Americanized. Yet when one examines the membership lists of American enterprises, one rarely discovers a name suggesting that the

11. Local magistrates.
12. Interview with a social worker in McKeesport.

McKeesport inhabitants of southeastern European stock have a chance to see more of America than school, mill, shops, and movies! For instance, the Kiwanis, the Lions, the Optimists, are said not to have extended their membership to citizens of foreign stock. There are one or two successful Slavic and Italian businessmen among the Rotarians. According to a social worker formerly in McKeesport, a number of men of various nationalities are members of the American Legion, but these same men do not belong to the fraternal orders or other groups predominantly American. Among women's groups, there is the same distinction.[13] The College Club, for instance, has only on rare occasions admitted a college graduate whose family belongs to one of the "nationality" groups. The Women's Club is said to have a closed membership limited to fifty; the Junior Auxiliary is of similar type. The Mothers' Club has made no effort to include mothers from "nationality" groups. Even the Catholic Church organizations, such as the Catholic Daughters of America and the St. Vincent de Paul Society, have few members with foreign background. The Chamber of Commerce is indeed a point of contact, and it was noticeable with what pride some of the businessmen among new Americans mentioned the doings at the Chamber of Commerce luncheons and spoke of their success in raising money in their own nationality groups for some of the civic enterprises sponsored by the Chamber, such as funds for the Boy Scouts, the Hospital, and the Helping Hand. There is a psychological clue here which should be noted. There seemed to be little interest among the nationality leaders in supporting social services rendered by Americans for "the foreign people." This may well be because an appeal based on the fact that the unfortunate are their own people identifies them still further with a status of inferiority and lack of adjustment to American life which they desire at all costs to escape. There was pride, however, in having been asked and having contributed to a variety of causes sponsored by the Chamber of Commerce in behalf of the whole community, especially when there was recognition of the contribution as coming from a particular group.

It was mentioned several times that the school board in McKeesport did not discriminate against girls of foreign parentage

13. At the time this study was made, there was no parent-teachers' association in the schools—an organization which might have served to bring new Americans into helpful contact with community situations.

in the appointment of teachers. This was a happy contrast to the evidence on this point obtained in some of the other towns of the county. It is reported that the Public Library has a few Croatian books and a collection of two hundred books in the Hungarian language selection by the scholarly Hungarian pastor, whose congregation helped raise the money for the purchase of these books. The books are well selected and are in frequent use. Most of them represent the best type of fiction, both modern and of an earlier period.[14]

In social work the only participation of nationality leaders on a constructive democratic basis was found to be in the International Institute and on the Recreation Committee of the Community Council. Four of the nineteen members of the latter were of foreign background. There was little opportunity to find out how active the new American members of the Recreation Committee have been or whether their interest has been aroused and held.

Although there are many reasons why immigrants of each nationality build up their own institutions, their exclusion from American organizations and from close contact with the American world of ideas probably contributes more than anything else to the longevity of the nationality communities.

As an example of a nationality community in McKeesport, the community of the Slovaks will be briefly described. In any immigrant community there are likely to be factions of which a wise community organizer will have to be aware. Some of the divisions reflect the European inheritance. There are, for instance, the Slovaks who tend to favor the Hungarians, whereas others favor the Czechoslovak government. Some Carpatho-Russians are fervent Russophiles, while others are Czechoslovak in their loyalties, although in Europe they are all today politically under Czechoslovakia. The di-

14. In this connection it may be mentioned that in the New York Public Library there are collections of books of particular interest to the different language groups. In 1898 the trustees of the Webster Free Library, now a branch of the New York Public Library, appropriated $30 for the purchase of Bohemian books. The project of developing the library as a center of Czechoslovak art, music, drama, and literature has slowly grown. The entire Czechoslovak book collection now numbers 10,000 volumes. Efforts have been made to draw the interest of foreign-born groups in a great variety of ways. One plan which proved very successful in one branch was to give a puppet show to which the Porto Rican school children and their parents were invited. It was given in the language of the parents invited. The show was followed by a visit around the library and an explanation of its purpose. There resulted a marked increase in the willingness of parents to let their children go to the library.

visions may also be defined in religious terms; Roman Catholic, Protestant, Greek Catholic, and freethinkers have various alliances and hostilities. As soon attempt to organize a Southern community in the United States without reference to Negro-white cleavage as to proceed in a nationality community without being aware of traditional conflicts.

In the Slovak group, as in many other groups, the Church is the vital center of social life, the strongest element of continuity transplanted from the past. The multiple activities affiliated with the Church fulfill many needs. As one example one may take the largest Slovak parish, which is the Roman Catholic "Holy Trinity." Organized in 1893, it now has eight hundred families. The priest, an American, relates that in the seminary he and several others were ordered to study the Slovak language with a view to being put in charge of a Slovak parish. When he first came to McKeesport, he says, "there was a riot." The people wanted a Slovak priest. However, he stayed on and has built up a strong organization. He seems to be greatly respected, and "performs the services quite correctly!" He preaches in Slovak (even though it is imperfect Slovak). Holy Trinity parish has, like all Catholic churches, a number of clubs for all ages and both sexes—"Ladies' Rosary," "Young Ladies' Sodality," "Young Men's Lyceum," and the "Holy Name Society" for men. The St. Vincent de Paul Society has ten members who are very active in parish visiting. The society has given $400 to $500 in relief each year. These church societies provide a social outlet for the members, usually are a source of support for the Church, and offer some opportunity for moral and religious influence.

The parochial school has 434 pupils. Five local lodges of the Slovak Catholic Union are organized under the sponsorship of this church, meet at the parochial school hall, and have a membership of several hundred each. Church lodges are similar to the nonsectarian type, collecting dues on life insurance policies issued by the National Union. The local lodge carries a sick-benefit fund. In addition the members of the lodge meet for a variety of social entertainments. The distinctive feature of the church lodge is that it is under the guidance of the spiritual advisor, the priest, and much of its activity is devoted to raising funds for various church purposes.

Another large Slovak parish is that of the Czechoslovak National Church of St. Peter and St. Paul, organized in 1925 with a membership of five hundred. An important denomination in McKeesport

which includes many Slovaks, as well as Carpatho-Russians, is
Greek Catholic rite, represented by the congregation of St. Nicholas, organized in 1901. This church represents a compromise between the Eastern orthodox ritual and recognition of the supremacy
of the Roman Catholic pope. Until recently the clergy have been allowed to continue their ancient custom of marriage. Recently the
order of the bishop, at papal behest, abolishing this right has been
threatening a split in the Church. There is also an interesting question of language. Since the ninth century the Church has used the
old Slavonic language. Today when this language is increasingly remote from the vernacular spoken by the laity, it has been proposed
by some of the younger members to substitute English. The Catholic Church urges the adoption of Latin. These details illustrate the
elaborate and deeply historical cultural issues, often rather remote
from actualities of life in America, which still occupy the interests of
these congregations. Belonging to St. Nicholas Church are a mixture of Russians (Carpatho-Russians), Hungarians, Slovaks and
some Croatians, totaling about 1,500 members. The church owns
several pieces of property, including a parish house where the usual
church societies meet. The language school for children, customary
among practically all immigrant groups, gives instruction in old
Slavonic which is useful for participation in the church service, but
does not serve the usual purpose of foreign-language schools of
strengthening the family by teaching the children the language of
their parents. In the Church of St. Nicholas the course in the eccle-
siastical language lasts six years; lessons are given every Saturday
and daily for nine weeks during summer vacation! Under the spiritual direction of the priest there are several lodges affiliated with the
United Societies of Greek Catholic Religion, a national fraternal
organization. It has been said that the church societies lack vitality,
are meager in program and narrow in outlook. It was not possible to
investigate this aspect. Monthly dues of one dollar paid to the
church are obligatory for every family; otherwise Easter confession
and communion may be withheld, and this action carries the dire
threat of eternal punishment.

The local priest is interested in the social problems of his parishioners. He feels that the young people representing the grand-
children of those who immigrated are a fine group and are increasingly interested in the Church. The young people in the choir give

several dramatic performances during the winter and have numerous "sociables." His ideas on the role of social agencies are suggestive and may be significant. For example, he does not think the Church should distribute relief. This should be done by social agencies. He is glad to have the social agencies consult him, as they frequently do, with regard to the need of a particular family; but, he observes, social agencies need the advice of people who understand the lives of the immigrants. Three women in his parish are receiving Mothers' Assistance. He is now trying to get old-age pensions for two members. In spite of this interest and of his efforts on behalf of his parishioners it is evident that Father "X" knows very little about the way American social agencies operate.

The fraternal benefit society, "United Societies of Greek Catholic Religion," has headquarters in McKeesport, which results in a center of activity and interest for the local Greek Catholics. There are fourteen local lodges, totaling about eight hundred senior and one thousand junior members in McKeesport. The headquarters publishes a weekly newspaper, *Enlightenment.*

The Slovak National Hall in McKeesport is a large three-story brick building, located on White Street, that is, in a poor neighborhood. It has the usual equipment of assembly room with stage, gymnasium, bar, pool room, and small offices. It is owned by private stockholders who rent out the rooms for profit to any organization. The Sokols hire it for gymnastic drills at a low rental.

Reference has been made to the Federation of Slavic Political Clubs. This movement started about two years ago in an attempt to get all the Slavic groups in McKeesport united—the Poles, the Slovaks, and the various Jugo-Slav groups. Obviously there is potential economic, as well as political, strength in such a union; but it is too early to predict its significance. At present the group is active just before elections. In McKeesport the organization hopes ultimately to succeed in electing Slavic people to office, but at present they back the ticket put into the field by one of the other parties if the group is favorably disposed to its promoters. It is associated with a national movement of this same type.

The Sokol movement is the typical expression of Czechoslovak cultural life. Sokol means eagle, the bird of strength and courage. Sokols were organized in Europe to foster, through gymnastic training, moral discipline, and comradely loyalty, the union of the Czech people at a time when, under the domination of Austria, the privileges of political organizations were denied them. Sokols became the symbol of devotion to the cause of Czechoslovak nationality. As the Falcons were organized among the Poles at the time of foreign domination, possibly both movements were originally inspired by the German "Turnverein" which came into being early in the nineteenth century, during the period when the younger generation of Germans felt the spirit of revolt against the domination of Napoleon. In America these organizations have lost much of their nationalistic vitality but they have survived largely because of their athletic interests. Membership in Sokol depends on a standard of conduct approved by the group and doubtless is a regulating influence. Recently insurance features have been added, and the new projects of Sokol leaders include proposals for summer camps, for dramatics, and for musical programs. The local Sokol lodges in McKeesport seem feeble. It is said that there is a diminishing interest in the traditional gymnastic drills and that there are many factional disputes. The depression also has contributed to the falling off of paid memberships.

The Jugoslavs are few in number, and their organizations are split by bitter political disputes which reflect the divisions now keeping these groups apart in Europe. Of the three Jugoslav groups—Serbians, Croatians, and Slovenians—the first two are found in McKeesport. Serbian life centers around the Serbian Orthodox Church of St. Sava. There are 120 families from McKeesport in the parish and 90 families from Duquesne.

There are five Hungarian church congregations in McKeesport—the Roman Catholic, the Magyar Reformed Church, the Hungarian Greek Catholic, the Baptist, and the Free Magyar Reformed Church. Inevitably there is a hard struggle for existence in each one. The Hungarian Hall is on Market Street and in general pattern is similar to the hall of the Slovaks. Americans have expressed the opinion that this hall is a demoralizing influence because of the drinking and card playing that goes on, but inquiry from thoughtful and intelligent persons of the groups themselves gives a different impression.

Some additional foreign-nationality clubs found in the new McKeesport directory are: the American-Russian Self-Culture Club; the American Serbian Club; the Hungarian Social Circle; the

Italian Social Union; and the German Turn- and Gesangverein. This list is by no means exhaustive.

Enough has been said perhaps in these brief notes on some of the nationality communities in McKeesport to suggest that in trying to understand the community life of the foreign cultural groups in a local community reference must be made both to the social and institutional life developed here and to the cultural loyalties which have their roots in the countries of their origin.

Country-wide Nationality Fraternal Societies

The local community of each nationality group tends to link itself with communities of like nationality in other localities. This complicated "interlinkage" comes about not only through the intermarriage of individual families, not only through the constant interchange of information regarding employment opportunities, business developments, and professional services but also by means of common enterprises which become incorporated in large national or supernational federations. Thus, local fraternal lodges are united in various "unions," "alliances," or "societies," and these federations in turn stimulate the creation of new local lodges. Through annual conventions the developments of policy and program are coordinated.

Through the agency of permanent national headquarters the national organizations either directly administer or contribute to the support of a large variety of institutions and services which serve the purposes of the group. A function common to all these national societies is the issuance of insurance policies to their members and the publication of a newspaper or periodical. In addition there are undertakings expressive of the interests of each group. Some maintain educational institutions or scholarships, summer camps or gymnastic organizations. Some are linked to religious denominations and some are nonsectarian.

Thus, these fraternal societies tend to become extensive enterprises of mixed social, business, and political character. The relationship between members is one of "brotherhood," so that a member need never feel bereft of human relationship wherever he can find other members of his fraternal order. For the immigrant this fact has been an immeasurable support. Among the older generation the fraternal orders with their subsidiary lodges still tend to be

the center of social life. As was pointed out with reference to the local lodges, the allegiance of the younger generation hangs in the balance. All the societies, conscious of the danger of disintegration as
the older generation dies off, are making a bid for the support of
youth. This leads to many interesting modifications in program and
procedure.

Is Pittsburgh Civilized?
by R. L. Duffus

I

The city of Pittsburgh is a lurid example of that supreme paradox of
the modern age—that our civilization rests upon coal and iron and
that in almost every spot where coal and iron are brought together
civilization is blighted and begrimed. So it has been in that region
which used to be called Merrie England. So it is in Western Pennsylvania. The blight is not Pittsburgh's alone. Pittsburgh is only a
larger Braddock, Homestead, or McKeesport. From whatever direction one approaches the once lovely conjunction of the Allegheny
and the Monongahela the devastation of progress is apparent. Quiet
valleys have been inundated with slag, defaced with refuse, marred
by hideous buildings. Streams have been polluted with sewage and
the waste from the mills. Life for the majority of the population has
been rendered unspeakably pinched and dingy. Too obviously the
people have served the machines, not the machines the people.

   This is what might be called the technological blight of heavy industry. It might be mitigated. Perhaps it cannot be wholly avoided.
But Pittsburgh has suffered under another blight—that of almost
absolute power without a corresponding sense of responsibility. I do
not propose to peer into the city's political cesspools. That has been
done already more than once by courageous individuals who have
descended into depths blacker and inhabited by stranger forms of
life than any that William Beebe has been able to penetrate in his re-

"Is Pittsburgh Civilized?" *Harper's Monthly Magazine,* 161 (October, 1930), pp.
537–545. Copyright 1930 by Harper's Magazine. Reprinted from the October,
1930 issue by special permission.

cent deep-sea explorations off Nonsuch Island. I will confine myself to saying that if the crime and corruption of Pittsburgh were not so well organized the city would probably rank ahead of Chicago in popular disrepute as the Bad Boy of American cities. The reasons for this state of affairs are fairly obvious. The murders which have given Chicago its bad name are the results of a struggle for power, which in turn is due to the failure of any one faction to secure and hold a firm grip on the community. In Pittsburgh the underlings can and often do murder one another. But gangster methods are for the small fry. They cannot upset the system because the stability of the system is guaranteed by the rigid control of the city's economic and political life by a small group of respectable persons at the top.

I do not for a moment believe that these persons deliberately will the rottenness at the bottom or are even aware of much of it. They are nevertheless the final arbiters in any situation in which they care to interfere. The supreme crime in Pittsburgh is not murder or robbery or pilfering from the public treasury or violation of the Eighteenth Amendment or even Sabbath-breaking—it is a willful defiance of the little group of Scotch-Presbyterians who regard themselves as having been elected by Providence to be the city's masters, and who are, in fact, its masters. If any large American city is so narrowly, so religiously, I might even say so conscientiously dominated by so small a group I have yet to hear of it. And this statement brings me to the point of view from which I wish to examine Pittsburgh. Here is a city in which the theory of *laissez faire* has been allowed to work itself out almost without let or hindrance. It has been built on gigantic material production with as much profit-taking as the traffic would bear. It ought to be an individualist's Utopia. What kind of Utopia is it, judged by the higher standards of civilization?

I might try to find an answer to this question by an analysis of wages, housing conditions, and standards of living. That these are not up to the ideal level anyone may satisfy himself by the simple process of strolling about the industrial portions of the city and observing for himself how the great masses of the people live. If he is still curious he may re-read the old *Pittsburgh Survey* and the records of sociological inquiries which have been made since that historic document appeared. The Pittsburgh worker too often lives amid ugliness and dirt, in congested quarters, next door to vice and crime. He lacks anything like adequate facilities for recreation. It is a common saying that the old Presbyterian iron-masters believed that when a workingman was not at home or in the mills he ought to be in church. Though the Citizens' Committee on City Plan, with one of the Mellons on its board of directors and the tactful and tireless Frederick Bigger as its technical expert, has succeeded, among other achievements, in getting a number of new playgrounds, there is not much evidence that the old point of view has altered. Labor, as industrial Pittsburgh still sees it, is just another raw material, to be bought as cheaply as possible. The city's masters are often compared with the feudal overlords of medieval Europe. But with one or two exceptions they have never displayed the slightest trace of that sense of responsibility which was the essence of feudalism. If the market wage was not a living wage so much the worse for those who were forced to accept it.

But economic reforms are, after all, only a means to an end. The end is the "good life." The "good life" implies an all-round development of human nature, so that an individual will be not merely a workingman, a businessman, or a church member but a practitioner in several fields of the fine art of living. Culture of this sort has been the fine flower of many wealthy societies in the past. It has been the only valuable residue of such societies. What evidence is there that the wealth of Pittsburgh is producing or can produce this flower? What have the rulers of the city done with the civilizing power that is so abundantly theirs? Have they civilized their city? Have they civilized themselves? It is impossible to give an encouraging answer. Pittsburgh has the wealth to buy a high degree of civilization. It remains, on the whole, barbaric. To illustrate what I mean I should like to call attention to certain aspects of this glorified and incongruously pious mining camp, this churchly city where clergymen are silent in the presence of political and commercial corruption but call down damnation on the heads of those who dare to hold symphony concerts on Sunday.

II

The forces which make the pattern of life in Pittsburgh are economic and religious. That is to say, they are Scotch-Irish and Presbyterian. It is probably a fact that no breed of men, not even the New Englanders, have been as successful as the Scotch-Irish in combining dividends in this world with a sense of security in the next. The Scotch-Irish, including the notable Mellon family, had the first pickings of the enormous wealth in and around Pittsburgh. They made a thorough job of it, not only without a sense of sin but with a sincere conviction that they were thereby serving the God of their fathers. They went to church regularly, ruled their families with rods of iron, and counted their pennies. To this day church membership is essential to participation in the higher social life of Pittsburgh. "What you want to do to promote yourself in Pittsburgh," said an old timer to an ambitious new arrival, "is to buy yourself a hundred-thousand-dollar house and join the proper church." This remark is guaranteed to be authentic. The situation could not have been summed up more neatly.

Because the leading families are Presbyterian, the church would seem to be the "proper" one. But there are qualifications to this rule. Anyone wishing to do so and willing to submit to its rule of life may, of course, come into the Presbyterian fold. Admission to the inner circle is another thing. An obscure newcomer might as well aspire to be one of the original twelve disciples. It is wiser, as a rule, for the newly arrived family of some means to hitch up with the Episcopalians, who stand high socially in Pittsburgh as they do in other cities—including, perhaps, the celestial city. To do so shows a commendable degree of modesty, since the new arrival thus refrains from claiming too close a fellowship with the established Presbyterian aristocracy. It is especially wise if he is a salaried employee of some hard-bitten Presbyterian, even though his salary may sometimes be large enough to give him the spending power of a millionaire. Above all, no one who aspires to reach the supreme social heights should be a Catholic or a Jew. Nor will any Catholic or Jew, as a rule, rise high in the employ of a Presbyterian manufacturer or banker.

Newly fledged as the Pittsburgh aristocracy is—or perhaps because it is newly fledged—it has a narrowness and arrogance which rather startle visitors from more democratic communities. These traits do not show themselves in swagger or ostentation. Pittsburgh women of the highest rank may sometimes be seen doing their own marketing, or going from shop to shop comparing prices. I was told of one dear old lady who went on putting up her own preserves with her own hands long after her husband had become a multimillionaire. Andrew W. Mellon himself, whose very presence creates a holy of holies, is one of the gentlest, shyest and most mild-spoken of men. In former years. Mr. Mellon used to be a regular attendant at meetings of the Board of Trustees of the Carnegie Institute, of which he and his brother, R. B. Mellon, are members. Usually he said nothing. One day he mildly proposed that a painting by a certain Pittsburgh artist be acquired for the museum. A temperamental fellow trustee, with a lack of reverence almost unique in Pittsburgh, lit into the suggestion. He said the Pittsburgher couldn't paint—expressing a rather common belief among the elite that no Pittsburgher can paint. Mr. Mellon blushed. "My cousin," he said mildly, "knows something about these things and he says he's a very good artist." Then he subsided and spoke no more.

Mr. Mellon, to be sure, does not have to be assertive. His wealth and power speak for him. Some of the lesser aristocrats, whose pinfeathers are still damp, have to go to more trouble. There is a story of a certain business man who called at the office of a local steel company with an order for three-quarters of a million dollars' worth of material. Half an hour later he was back with a second order for the same amount. He explained that he had intended to place this order with another company. He had gone to the company's headquarters and was about to step into the empty elevator when the attendant motioned him back. Another man stepped in, the door was closed and the elevator shot up. "Why did you do that?" he asked the starter. The man looked at him incredulously. "Don't you know," he demanded, "that you can't ride up in the same elevator with C. G. Brown?" The eminent Mr. Brown's dignity was thus preserved, though at the cost of a little business which would otherwise have gone to the company of which he was president.

A certain highly paid executive was ingenuous enough to move out to Sewickley Heights, most exclusive of suburbs, and build himself a hundred-and-fifty-thousand-dollar house next door to his employer's splendid mansion. To his astonishment and dismay the employer's wife snubbed the executive's wife, and at the end of a year the rash intruder took his family and his goods and migrated to Cleveland. The explanation was simple. A hired man is a hired man, no matter how large his salary. Owners and hired men cannot mingle on equal terms, nor can their families. Wise hired men, not yet sanctified by great possessions, join a certain country club where they meet others of their kind. Then they bide their time in patience.

Ultimately, if the Presbyterian God who directs affairs in Pittsburgh sees fit to smile on them, they may be admitted to the sacred Rolling Rock club, whose membership list is hand-picked by the Mellons.

But it may be set down as an axiom that the solid basis of Pittsburgh society is money and that no achievement and no personal charm not abundantly gilded can effect an entrance. An actor, artist or author of recognized standing in his field will be received in Pittsburgh if he happens to have social connections there. Otherwise he will not. I asked a lady who knew about such things if this barrier were not sometimes spontaneously overcome by visiting celebrities. But she remained firm. "There never would arise in Pittsburgh," she assured me, "a spontaneous invitation." So that was that. The inevitable result is that society in Pittsburgh is dull. It lacks the performing bears and trained seals from the stage, concert hall, studio, or writer's den who are to be found in similar circles in more sophisticated cities. The intellectual and artistic society of Pittsburgh is not "high" society. It forms a group of its own, and its church affiliations, if any, are likely to be Unitarian. Scores of men and women who would be welcomed wherever a respect for scholarly or aesthetic achievements counted for something remain obscure in Pittsburgh. Artists and scholars at the Carnegie Institute or the University of Pittsburgh, scientists at work in the great Westinghouse laboratories changing the face of human life—such persons are ranked in Pittsburgh above the clerks and mechanics but infinitely below any solemn ass with the soul of an ant who may have inherited a few million dollars from a Presbyterian ancestor. This tendency exists in any society based, as American society mainly is, on wealth. But I doubt that it is as strong in any notable American city as it is in Pittsburgh.

In characterizing Pittsburgh society as dull I did not mean to imply that it is dull for those who are a part of it. It is probably dull only for those whose intellectual interests are keen and whose sympathies are broad. It has plenty of amusements and of course plenty of money to spend on them. There are at least five hunt clubs, or country clubs of which riding to hounds is a feature, in the neighborhood of Pittsburgh. It is a little difficult to think of the descendants of the straitlaced Presbyterian stock putting on red coats and galloping over the countryside after an elusive fox, but the thing does happen. I suspect, too, that forbidden beverages occasionally trickle down thirsty throats after a hard morning's ride, a round of golf or an evening of dancing. But there is no historic antipathy between hard-shell religion and hard liquor. Mr. Andrew Mellon's grandfather had a distillery on the ancestral farm and the Mellons themselves, as is well known, have owned distillery stock in more recent years. One must make allowances, too, for the difference between the older and the younger sets. But comparatively speaking and as a group Pittsburgh society is probably pretty well disciplined. Such of its entertaining as is not done in the country clubs takes place in the spacious homes, most of them in the suburbs of Pittsburgh. Pittsburgh has only two large hotels, neither one much frequented by the exclusives, and there is no decent nightclub life.

It would be rash to give Pittsburgh's Four Hundred a certificate of purity on such negative evidence as this. But the indications are that when prominent Pittsburghers wish to indulge in what are known in the cinema world as orgies they come to New York to do it. They have their foibles, like the rest of mankind, but they do not flaunt them. I doubt that as a class they have the generosity and enthusiasm necessary for splendid sinning. When the choice must be made they are hypocritical, not brazen. In public places, at least, the code of proper behavior is enforced with relentless severity. Not so very long ago a man of some wealth and other social pretensions came to Pittsburgh to associate himself with one of the local enterprises. His wife remained behind while he was looking about for a suitable residence. In a hotel lobby one morning he met a woman who happened to be a friend of the family and unthinkingly asked her to lunch. Next day an associate took him aside. "I've been told," said the associate, "that you were seen lunching with a lady at the William Penn." "Well, what of it?" demanded the newcomer. "My wife knows her. She's a neighbor of ours back home." The Pittsburgher solemnly shook his head. "It may be all right where you came from," he said, "but you mustn't do that sort of thing here."

The system is inevitably selective. Lively and unconventional persons find it unendurable and make their escape. The stodgy remain. The literary and artistic annals of Pittsburgh are rich with the names of gifted individuals who could not stand the atmosphere of their home town and who got away as soon as they could. Mary

Cassatt, the painter, was an early and notable example, and of a more recent generation are William Singer, whose landscapes have won favor, Frank Vittor the sculptor, Gertrude Stein, Robinson Jeffers, and Gilbert Seldes. Some of these were from the upper crust of Pittsburgh life and some were not. None of them could find a career in Pittsburgh, even if they could have endured the Pittsburgh folk ways. One young woman, the daughter of an eminent family, shook the dust of her native hills from her shoes and fled to New York. She took with her a small but intelligent dog named Jock. Sometimes, for the edification of her irreverent New York friends, she would say to the dog, "I'm going back to Pittsburgh, Jock." Upon which Jock, sensible animal that he was, would lie down and die.

III

In setting forth these dismal facts I am not, of course, unaware of certain inspiring exceptions. Andrew Carnegie did not originally intend to establish either a Museum of Art or a College of Fine Arts. He was, in a way, bullied into doing both. But he did recognize, more splendidly than any Pittsburgher before or since, the moral obligation of great wealth. He could not make Pittsburgh creative but he did establish a center where the friends of the arts could rally. The Mellons, on at least one recent occasion, have financed the International Exhibition at the Carnegie Institute, and they have given handsomely to the University of Pittsburgh. The late Henry Clay Frick was a philanthropist as well as a collector of note. There are a number of respectable private collections of objects of art in and around Pittsburgh, and doubtless some of them will go to the Art Department of the Institute when the owners move on to the Presbyterian section of the future life.

Several years ago the Rev. Charles F. Potter made what was described as a cultural survey of a number of American cities, with special attention to their reading habits. He put Pittsburgh at the bottom, Columbus, Ohio, second, and Cleveland—which was the unkindest cut of all from the patriotic Pittsburgher's point of view —at the top. The Rev. Mr. Potter's results were looked at askance in some quarters as not being founded on a sufficient number of graphs, charts, tables, case histories, and other such sociological impedimenta. They expressed, however, an emotional attitude which every student of Pittsburgh culture will understand. I am happy to say that I cannot be quite as severe as the Rev. Mr. Potter. Pittsburgh did, indeed, earn a place in the list of the country's ten worst book towns which the *Publishers' Weekly* compiled last winter. On the other hand, it does possess some lively book stores and an active Booksellers' Association. One store has attracted as many as 30,000 patrons to its book counters in five days by its "book fair." Brentano's recently established a branch store in the city, which I assume was done after some canvassing of the commercial possibilities of the neighborhood. But I am inclined to believe that the undoubted resourcefulness and perspicacity of the Pittsburgh booksellers is akin to the same qualities in those who hunt for water in the desert. The book retailer has to be good or his children will go hungry.

The public library system, thanks to Mr. Carnegie's generosity and to the efforts of some tireless librarians, is also good. Its book circulation per capita is higher than that of New York City or St. Louis, though it is only three-fifths or so of the exceptionally extensive per capita circulation of the Cleveland Library. But the man in the street, with comparatively little money and no social position to speak of, can always be made to do quite a lot of reading if he is intelligently approached. In Pittsburgh he has comparatively few recreations of any other sort. But for those who can afford to hunt foxes or whack golf balls about, reading seems to be a last resort. Music is not quite in the same predicament, perhaps because it has a slightly greater social significance. Yet when the city's music lovers proposed to have symphony concerts on Sunday they met with stubborn opposition from the Presbyterian die-hards, fortified by Pennsylvania's antique blue laws. The concerts were held, but permission to sell tickets at the door was refused. The logic behind the opposition was simple and old-fashioned. People ought not to be entertained on Sunday. They ought to think about their souls. They ought to be bored. They ought to go to church and bolster up the self-esteem of the preachers. Of course the well-to-do could frequent their country clubs. In fact, being God's delegates on earth, they could do about as they liked. It was the middle and lower classes who had to be protected against having fun. Even the Carnegie Library had to put up a stiff fight before it succeeded in giving out books on the Sabbath day. But I do not wish to blame religion entirely for Pittsburgh's philistinism. A prominent element in the city has long held that culture or anything else which does not produce dividends is superfluous. "That man," one illustrious Pittsburgher is quoted as saying, "possesses more useless information than anyone I ever met." The attitude is said to be thoroughly typical.

It is not, of course, universal. The city has its saving remnant, to whose public-spiritedness one may well take off his hat. Two wealthy Pittsburgh women recently gave libraries to two nearby factory towns. One of them, having seen and admired a certain Pompeiian red in her travels abroad, took special pains to work that red into her library and make a truly beautiful building. Some of the solidest citizens have given valuable time to the still embryonic city plan. Men like Arthur E. Braun, treasurer of the plan committee, would be an asset to any city. Yet when all the reasonable additions and subtractions are made, the culture and the public-spiritedness of the ruling class in Pittsburgh are in the red. That class has taken with an exacting hand all that the city and the region had to give. As a class its gifts in return have been mean and niggardly. It has been deficient in sympathy and in imagination and that deficiency reveals itself in the unnecessary grime and sordidness of a once beautiful city.

Must we then despair of anything good coming out of Pittsburgh? I do not think the case is quite as bad as that. It is a governing group that has failed, not a whole city. The Presbyterian bloc are not Pittsburgh, nor will they always have the power and dominion that they now possess. New figures are coming up. Edgar Kaufmann, son of a Jewish peddler, has just completed what is perhaps the most beautiful department store in the United States, if not in the world. When he wanted murals symbolizing the life and aspirations of the city he called in Boardman Robinson to do them and Robinson did do them with distinguished success. This is perhaps a little nearer to creative art than the importation of almost any number of Flemish paintings. Father Coakley has set a new standard for all denominations by his Church of the Sacred Heart. Frank Nicola long ago projected the beautiful Schenley Farms development, near the park given to the city by Mrs. Mary E. Schenley some forty years ago. Pittsburgh's newest bridges have received awards for their aesthetic merits. Two boulevards going up the hill from the heart of the city afford picturesque views of the valleys of the Monongahela and the Allegheny, though truth compels me to add that I have painfully tramped the entire length of both thoroughfares but have yet to see a single motorist slowing down for a single second to contemplate the scenery.

The International Exhibition is, of course, only incidentally a Pittsburgh affair. Some Pittsburgh artists believe, whether correctly or not I cannot say, that in the American section of the Exhibition the dice are heavily loaded against local talent. In the last few years some two hundred paintings have been sold during these annual shows—not all of them, of course, to Pittsburghers. The attendance, over a six-weeks period, rose from 53,990 ten years ago to 132,544 last winter. This total obviously includes a considerable number of the common people of Pittsburgh—Poles, Russians, Slavs, Lithuanians, and Czechs, in clean shirts and Sunday clothes but with the grime of the mill under their finger nails. Children of these immigrant races come to Carnegie Tech to study the fine arts, though if they show ability and are gifted with horse sense they generally go somewhere else to practice them. At least they go somewhere else to get a reputation. If they then come home with a New York or Parisian O.K., Pittsburgh is willing to look at their stuff.

If Pittsburgh's industries were not so heavy there might be a larger market for domestic talent. There is a small market now. Not long ago the Westinghouse Company purloined an instructor from the Carnegie College of Fine Arts with the intention of making its household electrical products more aesthetic. The same company sent thirty of its engineers to the art classes so that they might be at least casually reminded that there was something besides stresses, strains, and formulas in the world. Pittsburgh has a stained glass industry of which some of its citizens are rightly proud. But on the whole the things that are made in and around the city do not lend themselves to artistic treatment. Pig iron is pig iron, a rail is a rail, and a steel girder is a steel girder. The thing to do is to make them strong and durable. The making is a heroic process, even now when you may walk through a steel mill in full swing and see only a handful of men pulling levers. But the making of steel and the bossing of men who make steel seems to impart a metallic quality to human nature. An outsider who said that the process was brutalizing might be merely turning a phrase. But that word was deliberately applied by a man with whom I talked and who has known Pittsburgh, high and low, for some thirty years. If Pittsburgh could diversify, as

Cleveland has done, there might be a liberation of the human spirit. But the owners of Pittsburgh are doing well as things are. Why should they liberate the human spirit? They will encourage industrial research to produce more cheaply and even more safely. There are a dozen important research laboratories in the Pittsburgh region. One of these, the Mellon Institute of Industrial Research, is responsible in large part for the elimination of four-fifths of the smoke that regularly inundated the city prior to 1914. But the smoke that blinds men to beauty—that is another matter.

IV

The inhabitants of Pittsburgh may well object to having their own town singled out for criticism in this egregious manner. It will be a most encouraging symptom if they do. To some degree their resentment will be justified. The barbarism of their city has both general and specific causes. Its general cause is the machine age itself and the excessive individualism which characterizes that age. Pittsburgh, like much of the rest of America, is suffering from the delusion that the means are more important than the end—that what men do with the various commodities mentioned in the Census of Manufactures is more important than what they do with their own lives. Neither New York, nor Chicago, nor Cleveland, nor any other American city can plead not guilty to that indictment. But in the cities mentioned the ruling classes—for I think that even in this great democracy we may speak quite frankly of ruling classes—have progressed beyond the mere accumulation of money and power and the disposal thereof for their own pleasure. To put the same thing in another way, they have arrived in some conspicuous and influential instances at a broader conception of what the pleasures of a civilized life are. I am speaking, of course, in comparative terms. I would not class even Cleveland, which actually takes pains to acquire works of art of the "Cleveland School" for its Museum, with Paris or Vienna. It is just that Cleveland and one or two other American communities have advanced somewhat beyond the troglodytic stage. Pittsburgh, because of its unfortunate combination of cultural narrowness and refractory materials, has lingered far behind.

It is a pity, too. I never visit Pittsburgh without a sense of a splendid vision waiting to be realized. The wooded hills, the rivers well worthy of the noble names they bear, the play of light on mist and smoke, the sturdiness of the people one sees on the streets, the sense of power behind the grimness—these are raw materials hardly yet exploited yet capable of producing infinite riches. But the Anglo-Saxons who have done so well with coal and iron have left these other mines unworked. And for that reason I believe that the scepter will in time pass from them and that a truly civilized Pittsburgh will be built by the races they thought only good enough for the sweat and dirt of the mills. It is a bitter saying among the Pittsburgh minority that what the city needs is a few first-class funerals. I am not savage enough to subscribe to that formula. But Pittsburgh does need one large and comprehensive funeral—it needs to bury John Calvin so deep that he will never get up again.

Planning in Pittsburgh
by Frederick Bigger

If the city of Pittsburgh and adjacent territory were to be viewed from above, when the late afternoon sun brings into high relief the slopes of the ridges and the multitude of serrated hills, there would come instantly to mind a picture of the human brain with all its convolutions bared to view. There would appear, however, one marked difference, in that the landscape is distinctly divided into three major parts. Two large rivers, the Allegheny and the Monongahela, wind through the hills, gradually converging to form the Ohio River at the so-called "Point District," where lies the downtown business district, a small approximately level area of less than two hundred acres.

These rivers lie each in a valley, often rather narrow, sharply defined by high and steep hills. In many cases the hills rise so close to the water's edge as to leave but a narrow shelf, wide enough only for a highway or a railroad, or perhaps both. Here and there a minor valley, more or less ample, breaks through the barrier of hills to bring its tributary creek to the river.

Sporadically, through the river valley are towns and villages occupying low land, or the easier slopes where the hills recede farther

"The Anatomy of Pittsburgh—And Its Challenge to the Planner," *American Architect and Architecture,* 151 (December, 1937), pp. 52–54.

from the river, the latter sweeping in a great arc around the town. The highways and railroads following the river, bordered by industrial plants or straggling houses, appear as tenuous connections between the thriving towns. In fact, an aerial observer would not see below him one single compact city, nor would he discover any indication of that topographically meaningless boundary line within which lies the political unit of the City of Pittsburgh with its irregular area of about fifty-five square miles.

Some of the hills are covered with streets and buildings; others stand steep, barren, and unbuildable. Great hillsides and bluffs overlook thriving communities, and form barriers compelling circuitous travel and long detours in passing from one part of the city to another. The hills throughout the district, varying as much as 500 feet in elevation, afford striking views.

From this general description it will be readily believed that in Pittsburgh are many more or less isolated settlements and communities, difficult or indirect of access. It is said that quite a number of these districts are never visited by residents of other parts of the city, and close observation leads one to accept the statement as true.

The difficulties and cost of imposing modern urban conditions upon this western Pennsylvania topography emphasize the compelling forces that have driven human beings to build a city here. Not only does one marvel at the temerity of men before such an undertaking, but even more is one astonished that these physical difficulties failed, during so many generations, to impress the leaders of the community with the supernecessity for broad-visioned and coordinated planning.

The seven hundred thousand people within the city are the nucleus of a metropolitan district, comprising seventy-five to eighty separate political units and a population exceeding a million and a quarter persons, most of whom live within sixty-six square miles lying in or adjacent to the major river valleys. In contrast to this, Allegheny County contains 725 square miles. Regardless of the County boundary, a circle of thirty-mile radius with Pittsburgh as the center would include something like 150 separately incorporated communities.

As an industrial center the census records of recent decades continuously have shown less than forty per cent of the population to be native white persons of native parentage. The remainder is in large blocs of native-white-of-foreign-parentage, foreign born, and negro. The foreign born, of many nationalities, have displayed the usual tendency to live in groups according to nationality. This tendency, combined with classifications of an economic character, which heretofore have seemed inevitable, often is intensified further by the physical segregation induced by the rough topography. When there is superimposed upon all this a political system and custom making it possible for the inferior politician to play off one district against another, the combined difficulties create of themselves an insistent demand for simplification and coordination.

What about planning? In the year 1764 the first plan of streets and building lots was laid out, covering the small area bounded by Market, Ferry and Water Streets and Second Avenue (now called Boulevard of the Allies). Twenty years later, in 1784, a plan was laid out for the whole of what we now know as the downtown business district, or "Golden Triangle." From that time on, piece by piece, the land was cut up into building lots, and the streets were gradually extended. It was a piecemeal process, with too much of accident and chance and with no general comprehensive planning or control of the expanding community. This continued for 126 years, until 1910, when the City Planning Commission was created and assigned the task of examining the things that had been done; of appraising the need for correction of early mistakes; of studying the possibilities of creating a more orderly arrangement of streets and open spaces; of attacking the problem of how best to make a city suitable to modern conditions and ways of living. Then for a period of about seven years, 1910 to 1918, the Commission tried to adjust itself to its huge task, and a beginning was made. During the past nineteen years there has been slow but substantial progress—much more than the average citizen realizes. No small part of the accomplishment in planning is due to the privately financed Citizens Committee on City Plan which was organized in 1918. Its six comprehensive city plan reports are almost completely valid yet, and official plans since made are largely based upon them. That citizen group, which was incorporated in 1920 under a title, Municipal Planning Association, was largely quiescent between 1933 and 1937, but is now revived and active.

In Pittsburgh, architectural planning and design have been subjected to the same kinds of handicap of financial and legal procedure that have operated in all American cities. During the depression much discussion has been given to these matters. They have received some consideration by architects, who themselves can do little to cope with the special forces that dominate planning and design. Whether a building of architectural excellence shall remain in existence or be swept away in rapid speculative evolution of business or residential localities will always be a significant matter with respect to architecture and city building.

If we admit that urban zoning laws have been only a first *and not too successful step in protecting neighborhoods* and in stabilizing different sections of the community, we must also admit that few buildings seem to need to be more than good enough in quality of design and material to live through a financial period of uncertain duration. With real home ownership extremely limited in proportion to the entire population, and with buildings of all kinds treated as exchangeable commodities in a speculative or investment market, it is small wonder that urban land uses are continually changing and that the objective of architectural excellence should be either entirely neglected or very limited in its acceptance.

So long as the designer is expected to produce first a building to earn for its owner more money, rather than to satisfy, in an adequate and beautiful way, a human need or a social purpose, just so long will architectural excellence have limited and short-lived expression. This assertion might be amplified extensively.

We need not assume that only particular housing projects are subject to the uncertainties of unstable and uncontrolled city growth. Certainly, all residential development, most business district development (including practically all of the same neighborhood business developments), and at least some of the industrial areas, are subject to the same uncertainty. Maladjustments are encouraged by reason of lack of control; and it is clear that the community must learn how to devise and apply reasonable regulations which will encourage more harmonious development and greater stability of neighborhoods and of property values.

Mr. Frederic A. Delano, Chairman of the National Resources Committee, said: "When you consider that most of the altruistic housing projects are based on amortization in thirty to sixty years, it seems ridiculous to talk about them if there is not some definite plan of stabilization. . . . So, I appeal to you . . . that you give close attention to stabilization of value."

The foregoing remarks were prompted by a discussion in which one of the speakers looked askance upon housing which is or becomes a multitude of separate ownerships, and housing which is on a purely speculative basis, because of the lack of stability inherent in developments of this sort. Individual owners are reluctant to act collectively for their own protection, and singly they are unable to cope with the disintegrating forces that surround them. Speculative building projects are based on the intention to get the most out of the community with the least possible contribution by the speculator. If the planner of the community is to deal with the relationships of dwellings to other buildings, to streets, and to open spaces, then he must look with favor upon long-term-investment housing on a large scale, upon co-partnership housing, and upon limited-dividend-and-rental housing, all of which require certain stability and continuity of existence within the urban pattern.

By way of illustration, it is worth mentioning that the City Planning Commission from time to time opposes the changing of zone classification which would allow large multi-family buildings (apartments) to replace an outmoded mansion or a group of old and small houses. In many such cases no community need whatever for the proposed apartment can be cited, but only the desire of the property owner to market his property at a higher value. Frequently, within a very short distance of the site in question there exist large areas of property zoned to permit apartments but not built up with such buildings. To grant the request would handicap this latter property. It would give the successful applicant a monopoly within a locality where his neighbors would have their properties damaged in character and value because of the introduction of the unharmonious new structure; and meantime they could not hope to get an income from apartments similar to his because of lack of demand. What, then, is the alternative? Obviously, it is to devise means of stabilizing neighborhoods, either by real estate deed restrictions or more permanent zoning, and to adjust the property valuations if necessary, so that the smaller dwellings may continue to exist, or be increased in number, without changing the essential character and the value of the neighborhood.

Beyond these maladjustments which we have been discussing, there are other factors which influence the scope and permanence of architectural planning and design. Bad city planning, layout of streets and building blocks which are not only bad in themselves but also badly adjusted to uneven topography, inappropriateness of land subdivision which has been based on sales and quick profit rather than on harmonious and consistent community planning—these factors are very significant.

In Pittsburgh, for example, with rough and difficult topography, we could have a more efficient street system if there were larger blocks and perhaps but half as many streets. This would afford opportunities for designing an entire block of buildings as an entity, with more adequately disposed open spaces, more charm, more stability for long-term investments or for owner-occupied dwellings. An excellent example of this is Chatham Village, a well designed entity of many moderate-rent dwellings held under one ownership. Here, the site planner and the architect worked hand in hand to design the remodeling of the ground, the location of streets, the grouping of buildings of different sizes, in harmonious relationship to the streets and to the open spaces surrounding the buildings. This is the kind of development which could not have been expected under the traditional policy of "every lot owner for himself." Chatham Village is a long-term investment, the value of which over a long period is assured by the fact that it has been designed in this manner, and that it is largely self-contained.

What could have been achieved if the development of Pittsburgh's topography for urban uses had been properly planned in the beginning? If that had been done, we should have been able to reduce the total cost of streets, while allowing the thoroughfares individually to be more spacious and in many instances of easier gradients. We could have reduced the cost of underground utility systems, i.e., the initial cost as well as the cost of maintenance and operation. We could have allowed the originally beautiful hillsides and ravines to remain intact as parks, or be developed as the large estates of well-to-do owners, that is, owners who could afford to pay the greater cost of building residences on difficult hillside sites. Concurrently, we should have avoided that kind of land subdivision which has produced many small and steep lots on hillsides and ravines, speculatively created and sold to poorer people who are less able to build on these more difficult sites. We should have had fewer abandoned or low-grade lot developments for the city to take over and hold, doubtful of what is best to do with them.

The physical problems themselves are enormously difficult in Pittsburgh. Here, as elsewhere, and regardless of their difficulty, the physical problems go hand in hand with the economic and social forces with which the planner must try to cope.

No one will deny that there remain a few places in the City of Pittsburgh not spoiled, a few places where buildings of architectural merit are properly placed and still in no immediate danger of deterioration because of the breakdown of the neighborhood. However, it is small wonder that this city should be called by some a city of lost architectural opportunities. If one is not reconciled to the past mutilations, how much less can one become reconciled to the continuation of these mutilations. If they are to be stopped, we must revise some of our procedures in city development, and exercise controls that will allow architectural planning and design to accomplish all that it is capable of accomplishing, both for the social good of the community and for its beauty.

PART THREE

Renaissance

Introduction

World War II catapulted Pittsburgh out of the Depression, but there was little cause for optimism. Business leaders recognized that critical choices had to be made. In simplest terms, the choice was between abandonment and wholesale reconstruction. Air pollution produced darkness at high noon, the road system was obsolete, the housing stock was old and substandard, the economic structure was better suited to the nineteenth century. Many corporations were contemplating removal of their headquarters to other cities.

A Fortune Magazine *article of 1947 vividly portrays the postwar executive elite which was instrumental in salvaging the city. It revolved, in turn, around Richard King Mellon, whose decision to remain and rebuild was the single most critical factor. A second key figure was Mayor David Lawrence, whose career is described in the selection by Frank Hawkins. The collaboration of Mellon and Lawrence provided a bipartisan political basis for the reconstruction effort.*

The Pittsburgh Renaissance represented an object lesson in elite-initiated environmental and economic change, the catalytic role of a small, but cohesive, influential and determined element of the social structure. Through Lawrence and his control of the Democratic party machinery, it was able to broaden its base of support. Institutionally, the Renaissance was based upon the promotional efforts of the Allegheny Conference on Community Development, founded by Mellon in 1943. It worked closely with the Pennsylvania Economy League, Western Division (founded in 1935), and the Pittsburgh Regional Planning Association (founded in 1938). Also significant in the Renaissance effort were offshoots of the Allegheny Conference such as the Regional Industrial Development Corporation (1955) and ACTION-Housing (1957). This constellation of organizations, revolving around the Allegheny Conference, represented a forceful combination of power, research, and technical proficiency.

In the final analysis, the Renaissance was dependent upon the ability of the corporate leadership to utilize the resources and power of all levels of government. Economic modernization, the reconstruction of the central business district, in particular, could not occur in the absence of smoke control, flood control, or the improvement of local transportation facilities. Related to the extraordinary success of the Renaissance in nurturing a corporate-governmental symbiosis was the extensive use of the public authority expedient. The list included the Urban Redevelopment Authority, Parking Authority, Public Auditorium Authority, Allegheny County Sanitary Authority, and Tunnel Authority.

The concrete achievements of the Renaissance in the first decade are described in the article by Park Martin, then executive director of the Allegheny Conference. The widespread consensus of the first decade, however, diminished in the 1960s in the face of criticism that many social problems were neglected. The major initiative of the Renaissance in dealing with the social dimensions of renewal had been the organization of ACTION-Housing in 1957. The Pennsylvania Economy League had, in fact, directly linked the future of the renewal program with the need for construction of moderate cost housing to accommodate displaced families. Under the leadership of Bernard Loshbough, ACTION-Housing developed an ambitious, innovative program, including the sponsorship of new and rehabilitated housing, community organization, and research. A series of ACTION-Housing reports is included here, illustrating the nature of the experiments in new and rehabilitated housing.

ACTION-Housing published an urban renewal impact study in the 1960s, which documented the magnitude of the housing problem in the city and county. Almost half the housing units, 238,000, were built before 1920, and more than 90,000 dated from before 1900. New construction added housing at the rate of about 5,000 units a year, one percent of inventory. Some 22.3 percent of all county housing units were deficient in one or more respects, but 81 percent of the deficient units were in Pittsburgh and other older settlement areas. The report demonstrated the degree to which the housing problem was racially differentiated. The black population of Pittsburgh had increased from 12 percent in 1950 to 16 percent in 1960. The 134,000 blacks of Allegheny County were concentrated in three areas of the city: East Liberty, Lower North Side, and Hill District. It was found that some 56 percent of black-occupied housing in the county was deficient, compared to 20 percent for the white population; and the black population was concentrated in those areas most affected by urban redevelopment plans, thus suffering the main burden of disruption and relocation.

In Pittsburgh and other cities, postwar urban renewal was characterized by large-scale clearance, emphasis upon the central business district, and indifference to the impact of renewal upon family and neighborhood life. The community organization efforts of AC-TION-Housing represented an early and ambitious effort to supplement the physical side of renewal with concern over social aspects. It devised a strategy which it called neighborhood urban extension. This represented, to some extent, a departure from the norm of elite initiative.

As originally conceived, the objective of urban extension was perhaps too exalted and ambitious: to "transform declining residential areas of cities into modern, attractive, well-ordered neighborhoods that possess a genuine sense of community, and to achieve this change largely through the efforts of neighborhood people themselves, utilizing the vast resources of the city." Following a three-year pilot project in Homewood-Brushton, ACTION-Housing launched a five-year extension program in three neighborhoods. The neighborhoods were selected in collaboration with the City Planning Department, the Mayor's Office, and the Urban Redevelopment Authority.

The work in Homewood-Brushton continued. This neighborhood had undergone a drastic transformation in population during the 1950s: from 77 percent white in 1950 to 34 percent in 1960. It con-

tained a large number of welfare families, delinquency and crime rates were high. The second neighborhood, Hazelwood, was still relatively stable but threatened. Situated along the Monongahela River, two miles southeast of the downtown area, it encompassed most of the city's fifteenth ward. Composed of lower-middle-income families, its environment was dominated by a Jones and Laughlin plant. The white population had dropped from 18,000 in 1950 to 14,000 in 1960, while the black population increased from 2,000 to more than 2,500. Only 10 percent of high school graduates entered college, compared to 30 percent for the City of Pittsburgh. Urban extension planners emphasized the need for conservation type renewal in Hazelwood, and attention to such potential social problems as adolescent racial tensions and juvenile delinquency. Perry Hilltop, the third extension neighborhood, was located on the upper North Side. It was almost entirely residential and white. Problems included incipient blight, racial tensions related to the construction of Northview Heights, a public housing project, and the inconvenience of old, small commercial facilities.

Neighborhood urban extension served a number of useful purposes. It led to many small, but concrete improvements in physical facilities and social conditions. It involved neighborhood residents to a greater degree than previously. And it suggested a supplementary concept of urban renewal: more diffuse, neighborhood-centered, and attuned to social problems.

ACTION-Housing's urban extension program had modified the predominantly central business district emphasis of the Renaissance, but the civil disorders of 1968 dramatized the fact that the black community had not viewed postwar renewal as a source of melioration. The black population, it was claimed, had been "excluded from the Pittsburgh consensus. Its demands have not been heard, its needs have not been met."[1] More broadly, critics of the Renaissance viewed the problems of the black community in the broader context of neighborhood powerlessness, and advocated the delegation of effective decision-making authority to "neighborhood people."

Although components of the Anti-Poverty crusade of the 1960s, such as Community Action and Model Cities, contributed to a greater emphasis upon neighborhood needs and materially benefited

1. *Pittsburgh Point,* June 13, 1968, p. 4.

*the black population, discontent increased within the white ethnic
population. This was partly a result of the heightened minority
group consciousness generated by the civil rights movement, partly
a result of the belief that federal anti-poverty programs ignored the
poor white population. Indeed, ethnic affiliation had always been
central to an understanding of Pittsburgh's social system, and was
reflected in political voting patterns. Although the ferment of the
1960s and early 1970s did not, in fact, result in a significant restruc-
turing of power, it did shatter the façade of consensus achieved in
the early Renaissance, and directed greater attention to neighborhood-centered needs of the black and ethnic populations.*

A New Civic Elite

Night travelers to Pittsburgh late last year had the unnerving experience of coming into a city illuminated largely by candles. And the
farther they went into the dimmed-out city, the deeper grew the
sense of having strayed into some darker century or into that ice age
projected by the gloomier prophets of industrial paralysis. Pittsburgh was in the grip of a twenty-seven-day power strike, the first
major strike against a public power utility in the history of the country. It was also in the grip of a transportation tie-up, pulled tight by
picket lines after the head of the independent power workers' union,
a mild-looking young man named George Mueller, was jailed on an
injunction and contempt-of-court proceedings. At the same time a
fifty-three-day hotel workers' strike was in progress, and visitors
found themselves shunted into strange hotels in outlying towns,
commuting miles each day into the beleaguered city.

No streetcars and few buses were running. A picket-line tie-up of
coal trucks knocked out the central steam plant heating most of the
big downtown buildings, and department stores, restaurants, and
other businesses closed down for lack of light and heat. Office workers hitchhiked in and out of town as best they could, climbed long
flights of dark stairs to work, huddled in coats and sweaters in

"Pittsburgh's New Powers," *Fortune,* 35 (February, 1947), pp. 69–74, 76–77, 182,
184, 186. Reprinted from the February, 1947 issue of Fortune Magazine by special
permission; © 1947 Time Inc.

stone-cold offices. Elevator service was strictly rationed. Morning and night, traffic jammed up for miles on the boulevards, bridges, and tunnels converging on the triangle of narrow downtown streets. At dusk the city sank into grim shadow. Finally, as the strike lengthened, huge steam boilers were rushed in from the oil fields, black and rusty, and set up naked in the streets to heat the skyscrapers. Mobile power generators were rolled up beside the big stores to supply light for reopening trade. In the racket and glare of these monsters Pittsburgh appeared more than ever a city under siege. By the time the strike ended in arbitration, even conservative Pittsburghers were ready to admit that it had been badly and stubbornly handled on both sides. For twenty-seven days Pittsburgh had felt, for lack of a common meeting ground, the terrible power of industrial discontent to cripple even the heaviest and proudest concentration of U.S. industrialism.

Pittsburgh Is Worried

The power strike was not Pittsburgh's first but second, and the longest breakdown of its kind within the year—a year that included a twenty-six-day steel strike, a 114-day electrical workers' strike, two coal strikes totaling sixty-three days, and an assortment of some eighty other labor disturbances that all together left Pittsburgh with scarcely a strikeless day on its calendar. Other cities and industrial areas may show the same pattern for strike-ridden 1946, but with nothing like the basic force and continuity of Pittsburgh. There is something elemental and portentous in this area. Pittsburgh today is not only the capital of big industry but the capital of big labor, the birthplace, headquarters, and testing ground of the mightiest C.I.O. union. Pittsburgh in its postwar tensions, changes, contrasts, shifts of power, and plans for the future may well epitomize the problems of an advanced industrial society and its chances for survival.

Pittsburgh is situated, as the geography books say, at the confluence of the Allegheny and Monongahela rivers, in an industrial area of some two million souls, built upon mighty underpinnings of coal, steel, and glass. In the roaring decades following the Civil War, when Pittsburgh was supplying the iron and steel for building the North and opening the West, the growth of this area was one of the raw wonders of the nineteenth-century world. Great mills proliferated up and down the narrow riverbanks, the building city staggered helter-skelter up precipitous hills and valleys, and some of the

greatest of U.S. fortunes were laid. By 1900 more wealth had probably been beaten and torn from the 750 square miles of Allegheny
County, whose capital is Pittsburgh, than from any like plot on
earth. The cast-iron Gothic character of that era, Scotch-Irish Presbyterian in its origins, is still heavy upon the whole region, its architecture, its attitudes, and its outlook.

The first shiver in Pittsburgh's iron self-confidence came in the
chill thirties, when the great freeze hit its heavy industries harder
than any other. For the first time Pittsburgh turned its attention in-
ward and began to talk of "maturity," of having reached its peak, of
preparing for decline. War swept these introspections aside. With its
mills flaming and thundering night and day, Pittsburgh surpassed
even the tonnage peaks of its heyday—in four years of war rolling
out $19 billion in war production, about 70 million ingot tons of
steel, to reassert its title as the steel capital of the world. But in the
first full year of peace the old doubts began to return, though backlogs of civilian orders stood mountain-high, and earnings—despite
all the dislocations of strikes, shortages, and slowdowns—seemed
likely to top any prewar year. For one thing, the war had brought no
new industries, only an expansion of the existing heavy plant that
for years had swung Pittsburgh up and down with every gyration of
the business cycle. For another, as 1946 ran out, the huge backlogs
were suspected of having false bottoms.

Looking at itself after its Herculean war labors, Pittsburgh saw
itself older, grimier, more unlovely than ever. The war years had put
another thick, black coat of tarnish on the Golden Triangle, had
added another stratum to the giant, barren slag heaps in its front
yard. Out through the mill towns—Homestead, McKees Rocks,
Aliquippa, Monessen, Ambridge, to give old griefs a habitation and
a name—straggled the untidy heritage of nineteenth-century plan-
lessness, a vast slum, a hurt to the eyes. Back on Pittsburgh's door-
step and more aggravated than ever was a housing problem that is
among the worst in the country, a shortage of twenty years' standing, with over 40 per cent of the area's dwelling units unfit or inadequate for habitation, less than 40 per cent of them tenant-owned,
and some 25 per cent crowded at the one-person-per-room level established as a standard minimum for health. Pittsburgh also has a
smoke problem, a river-pollution problem, a flood problem, an ur-
ban-blight problem, a traffic problem—all the accumulating ills of
aging urban areas everywhere, but with a special, harsh, industrial

edge in Pittsburgh's rugged topography. In the hard light and let-down of victory, Pittsburgh suddenly found itself tired of its dirt, chaos, and congestion.

This is a great change for Pittsburgh. And, indeed, Pittsburgh is changed from the days when it shrugged off such problems. In 1943, even before the war ended, a citizens' committee, heavy with the biggest financial and industrial names in Pittsburgh, sat down to consider long-range plans for cleaning and rebuilding the city—and the first stages of its program are already moving into action. For the first time the industrial elite has moved in to initiate and push a broad-scale civic-improvement program. Pittsburgh is worried. It is worried about the shift of steel to the West and the decentralizing pattern of postwar industry. It is worried about the dwindling mar-kets in bituminous. It is worried about its continued imbalance of heavy industry and its failure to attract more diversified, lighter in-dustry to the area. It is haunted still by the memory of the late great depression, the idle men in the streets, the streets greasy with river damp. The balance sheets look good now, and, if all goes reasonably well, it can look forward to three or four years of boom production filling the world's banked-up needs for peacetime durable goods. This may be Pittsburgh's last chance, it thinks, to reverse the course of urban decay and industrial decline—and, considering the chafing unrest of urban industrial populations everywhere, it may be none too soon.

Pittsburgh Is Changing

The blunt fact about Pittsburgh's changing scene is that a new gen-eration is in power. It is a change more complete than has yet been realized. It begins in the Mellon empire, extends through Big Steel, and runs through the other power groupings that make up the com-plex hierarchy of Pittsburgh. The war brought it of age. Except for one or two isolated, elderly figures, the old generation is no more. Out in Pittsburgh's once fashionable East End the great, gray, chill mansions of the late Richard Beatty Mellon and Andrew William Mellon, the fabulous brothers who built a small bank into an indus-trial empire, have long been vacated—R. B.'s having been razed and its surrounding acres turned into a public park. Most of the other stiff, baronial mansions of that era along Pittsburgh's upper Fifth Avenue have gone the same route to save taxes or to settle estates. The new generation prefers to live up the smart country lanes of Fox

Chapel, on the rolling, close-clipped acres around Sewickley, or in the fox-hunting country around Ligonier. It is a freer, though only slightly less aloof, generation than that of its icy elders.

When Andrew Mellon died in 1937, the succession to the throne fell to Richard Beatty's only son, Richard King, then thirty-eight. Andy's only son, Paul, a slim, scholarly young man, more interested in literature than balance sheets, had made it plain upon his graduation from Yale in 1929 that he wanted no part of banking and finance. Young Dick was an entirely different type, fond of horses, big-game hunting, and accounting. Groomed in the family's intricate finances by his father, and proving an apt pupil, Dick held sixteen directorships in as many corporations by the time his father died in 1933. One of his earliest positions was treasurer and Director of the Ligonier Valley Railroad, an obscure Mellon bauble that old Judge Thomas Mellon had once turned over to R. B. and Thomas to cut their teeth on. By the time Richard King Mellon became titular head of the empire in 1937, he had slipped into some twenty directorships that stake out the Mellon interests in some of the greatest U.S. corporations.

It was no sinecure. A cardinal principle in the Mellon code had been to keep a close eye and grip upon those enterprises in which Mellon money held a dominant stock interest. It was this, as much as a strong family attachment to Pittsburgh, which located the now $650-million Gulf Oil Corp. and $80-million Koppers Co., Inc., in the Golden Triangle along with the other Mellon-controlled colossi, when both companies might more easily have been set up elsewhere. The elder Mellons believed in putting all their eggs in the Pittsburgh basket, and watching the basket. With the passing of the patriarchs, however, there was a strong and natural tendency among the corporations to assert more and more autonomy. Most were in the hands of seasoned, Mellon-picked management—men like Colonel J. Frank Drake of Gulf and Arthur Vining Davis of Aluminum Co. of America—and the ascension of a young, untried captain to the bridge invited a test of power, or at least a period of watchful waiting. This test had just begun to work itself out when war intervened and Colonel Richard King Mellon went off to Harrisburg to head Pennsylvania's Selective Service.

Mr. Mellon Goes to Work

Almost as soon as Dick Mellon doffed his uniform in May, 1945, things began to happen. The first of the major Mellon actions last spring was to create a new organization called T. Mellon & Sons—a title that is a sentimental throwback to the original banking house on Smithfield Street where Judge Thomas Mellon and his elder sons, James and Thomas, opened for business in 1870. The new enterprise with the old name was a puzzle to Pittsburgh. It was not a new banking house, nor a holding company to contain the vast Mellon interests, nor a charitable institution for the final disposal of the Mellon fortune. T. Mellon & Sons is a nonprofit organization without assets or much visible machinery—an organization of a kind found only in England to serve old industrial families. It was set up with the purpose of consolidating the younger Mellon interests in Pittsburgh, and studying technical, social, and economic affairs—potentials of new investments—for the advisement of the family. Asked to elucidate further, Dick Mellon said: "We are going to work again."

T. Mellon & Sons, in structure, is a directory of the present Mellon family. Surrounding Dick Mellon in the presidency is a tight little inner circle of four Vice Presidents who have come to be his closest lieutenants and advisers: Alan M. Scaife, scion of an old Pittsburgh steel family, who married Dick's sister, Sarah; Adolph W. Schmidt, smart corporate brain, who married a Mellon relative; George W. Wyckoff, another Pittsburgh steel heir, a friend and classmate of Paul Mellon; and Arthur B. Van Buskirk, who carries the Mellon ball in the new civic projects. On the Board of Governors of the new company, along with these officers and other Mellonmen, is Paul Mellon, who has a big estate in Virginia, and has recently shown the continuing trend of his interests by putting up $4,500,000 to endow a new liberal-arts college near Pittsfield, Massachusetts, along the seminar lines of St. John's College at Annapolis. Also associated in the new organization are Sarah Mellon Scaife and Ailsa Mellon Bruce, Andrew's only daughter, who lives in New York. Meetings of T. Mellon & Sons are designed to get the family around a table to talk over and integrate high policy. Each member, however, retains his or her own holdings and may act independently. "A very simple arrangement that works," is the way the Mellons describe it, "a kind of family sewing circle."

Some powerful sewing was soon going forward. One of the first results of the family council was the surprising merger last September of Mellon National Bank, keystone of the banking empire, with Union Trust Co. of Pittsburgh, integrator of the Mellon corporate holdings, into the Mellon National Bank & Trust Co., with total resources of over $1 billion. In the chairmanship of this financial centerpiece sits Dick Mellon, with Frank R. Denton, who was snapped up by the Mellons as a smart, young bank examiner in 1929, as Vice Chairman and chief administrative officer. Then in double-quick order came the merger of Mellon Securities Corp. into the First Boston Corp. to separate the Mellon name from security distribution and form the country's largest investment-banking house, with combined assets of $338 million. Associated with these sweeping changes were the previous merger of Mellon Indemnity Corp., and the earlier joining of Mellon-controlled Pittsburgh Coal with the once Rockefeller-controlled Consolidation Coal to form $105-million Pittsburgh Consolidation Coal Co., by far the biggest commercial coal operation in the world.

The significance of this gigantic tightening and coordination of the Mellon empire is that it is the announced prelude to expansion, a new foray of Mellon money into new investments. In the 1880's a modest investment in a struggling little company attempting to manufacture aluminum led to Alcoa. During World War I a $300,000 stake in by-product coke-oven patents grew into Koppers Co. In the technological ferment following this war there are even wider opportunities, and the Mellon third generation means to realize them. The real effect of T. Mellon & Sons is to consolidate the new generation in control, confirm the developing leadership of Richard King Mellon, and ensure the continued survival and enlargement of the empire.

The third generation, with a strong assist from war, has so far made a good job of surviving. Taking 1939 as a base year, the tally sheet for the main Mellon-dominated enterprises in 1945, the year the war ended, looked like this: Gulf Oil's assets up 25 per cent to $653 million, net earnings up 195 per cent to $45 million; Alcoa's assets up 66 per cent to $417 million, net earnings down 46 per cent (on war-contract cancellations) to $20 million; Koppers' assets down 38 per cent to $81 million, net earnings up 65 per cent to $3 million. Pittsburgh Consolidation Coal, merged late in 1945, showed combined net earnings of $5 million against 1939 deficits for the two companies totaling nearly $2 million.

Altogether, and including the banking enterprises, the total assets of the inner Mellon citadel now stand at an all-time high of nearly $3 billion. This, of course, does not represent the total net worth of the Mellon family. Nor does it include the Mellon holdings in First Boston Corp., heavy holdings in many industrial, transportation, and utility companies, blocks of Pittsburgh real estate, and other odds and ends. Surviving the depression, the New Deal, and war, in a milieu increasingly hostile to such giant accumulations, the Mellon empire remains as one of the largest working fortunes in the Western world.

The major fact about T. Mellon & Sons, significant to Pittsburgh and the nation alike, is that the new generation is not only bent upon an aggressive capitalistic offensive to establish new industries, but is committed to bending a large part of its energies to civic rebuilding on a new scale. Since 1900, Pittsburgh has had no less than six master plans drawn up for a broad-scale rehabilitation of the city, but nothing ever came of them. Nothing moves in Pittsburgh without the Mellons, and the elder Mellons never moved in that direction. Their philanthropies took as ruggedly individualistic a form as their enterprises. Significant of the changed times is the fact that Dick Mellon now sits as president of the Pittsburgh Regional Planning Association, a post in which it would be difficult to imagine his forebears. The new movement under way to rebuild Pittsburgh embraces a much wider circle than the Mellons, but few Pittsburghers underestimate their power in it. It is an experiment in survival worth watching.

The New Generation Spreads Out
The rise of a new generation in management, and a new attitude in local responsibility, is a postwar-Pittsburgh phenomenon. Its quickening effect is beginning to appear in many quarters. Down the street from the ponderous Greek portico of Mellon National is the heavy baroque façade of Peoples First National, on the corner of Fifth and Wood, the nearest rival to the Mellons in the banking field. It has a young new President and a newly streamlined organization. Peoples First National is the product of another merger last summer, between Peoples-Pittsburgh Trust Co. and majority-owned First National, to eliminate competition and simplify operations in a single institution with total resources of $375 million. Into

its presidency moved smart, forty-one-year-old Robert C. Downie, fresh from a bang-up job as Army chief of the Pittsburgh Ordnance District.

Peoples First National does not compare in scale or structure with the Mellon group. No single family or group of stockholders controls it, and it has no line of controlling interest in a galaxy of huge industrial corporations such as characterizes the Mellon setup. It once tried to create such an empire. For years an intensely bitter struggle went on with the Mellon group as John Hartwell Hillman Jr. and associates, controlling figures in the bank, attempted to create around the old Peoples-Pittsburgh Trust a family empire to rival the Mellons'. Hillman is still the largest single stockholder, but his interest now amounts to only 4 per cent, and the Hillmans are no longer in active direction or control. Grouped around the present Peoples First National, but in nothing more than a banking relationship, are: $450-million Westinghouse Electric Corp., whose home plant sprawls for miles up East Pittsburgh's Turtle Creek Valley; $22-million United Engineering & Foundry Co., leading maker of heavy steel-mill machinery and equipment; $46-million Blaw-Knox Co., specialty steel fabricator; $22-million Rockwell Manufacturing Co., maker of meters, valves, machine tools; and other lesser industrial satellites. Most of these also do business with the Mellons.

This does not unduly excite President Downie, who believes that the intense rivalries and individualism of the past generation are out of date and nonproductive. His bank will compete hard for business, but otherwise remain on the best possible terms with the Mellons or any other competitors. Downie has had a swift rise since he came out of the University of Pittsburgh law school in 1932 to become counsel for Dravo Corp., a big riverboat building and construction firm, then trust officer with Peoples-Pittsburgh Trust shortly before the war. Indicative of the new way of doing things, and the way in which business intertwines in the new civic movement, is an incident that occurred when a vacancy appeared recently on the committee for rebuilding Pittsburgh. Dick Mellon called Downie and said: "Bob, why don't you take the Vice Chairman's job?" Downie did. "We've got to cooperate," he says, and his reasons reflect the thinking of the new crop of executives. Not only is it impossible, he thinks, under present taxes, to pile up wealth by the "individualistic methods of our grandfathers," but to retain what wealth we have, it is absolutely imperative to pay attention to the wants of the mass of the people, because "if they don't get what they want under our system, they'll be fooled into believing they can get it under another."

A Postwar Crop of New Executives

For Pittsburgh, such views constitute a managerial revolution. And when the number of new men who have risen to top management since the war ended is totted up, it becomes easier to understand the change of climate in Pittsburgh and to credit the change with some permanence.

Westinghouse has a new President in the younger brackets. He is Gwilym A. Price, who left the presidency of Peoples-Pittsburgh Trust in 1943 to help Westinghouse on cancellation of war contracts, became Executive Vice President in 1945, and President in January, 1946. Like Bob Downie, who has now stepped into his old job, Price is a product of Pitt law school, and was with Peoples-Pittsburgh for seventeen years before he worked himself out at the top. Under him Westinghouse is planning a $50-million preferred-stock issue to add needed working capital and finance a two-year moving and expansion program to unscramble its war-choked plants and postwar lines.

Carnegie-Illinois Steel has a new President, Charles R. Cox, who comes from a U.S. Steel subsidiary, National Tube, to replace Carnegie's retired President, J. Lester Perry. Up from the ranks in Big Steel, Cox fits in well in the younger, aggressive management group built around U.S. Steel President Ben Fairless. New blood is also rising in the independents. Fifty-five-million-dollar Pittsburgh Steel Co. and $7-million Superior Steel Corp. have both taken on new Presidents, and $285-million Jones & Laughlin Steel, oldest and biggest of the independents in the Pittsburgh steel family, is rumored to be about to select a new President to succeed ailing H. E. Lewis. As for coal, foundation of the area, Pittsburgh Consolidation Coal's strapping young President, George H. Love, took over on the merger in November, 1945, having come up through Union Collieries and Consolidation with an aggressive program to modernize the mines and put real money into long-neglected research for new markets, particularly chemical and synthetic products. In ten years, he enthusiastically predicts, the Pittsburgh area can have a rebirth on the basis of new methods for burning coal close to the mine heads, cracking by-products such as synthetic oil and gasoline out of the gases, and then enriching the residue to be piped as a cheap fuel to homes and industries.

New Day Coming?

The tangible vehicle for this new civic consciousness is called the Allegheny Conference on Community Development—the citizens' committee of 1943 that has set out to remake the area. It is unique for Pittsburgh, and may be unique in the country. The original sponsoring committee came together under the chairmanship of Dr. Robert E. Doherty, head of Pittsburgh's Carnegie Institute of Technology. It included not only top representatives of the social agencies, city and state governments, and all local newspapers, but, as prime movers, such potent members of the business community as Richard K. Mellon, U.S. Steel's Ben Fairless, Westinghouse's Board Chairman Andrew Wells Robertson, Aluminum Co.'s Roy Hunt, H. J. Heinz Co.'s H. J. Heinz II, banker Arthur E. Braun, and Kaufmann Department Stores' Edgar J. Kaufmann. This committee adopted as its long-range program a complete inventory of the region, its people, labor force, industries, resources, transportation, housing, the needs and potentials for growth. Its purpose was to get the facts, then do something about them, step by step, within a unified plan for the region as a whole. It set about to work through existing agencies, recommending or commissioning them to carry out specific projects. If an agency dawdled, it was prepared to take over the work and see that it got done.

The first big project promoted was the complete rehabilitation of the Point—a historic thirty-odd acres at the tip of the Golden Triangle, where the Allegheny and Monongahela meet to form the Ohio River, now a dilapidated warren of decayed buildings, warehouses, parking lots, and ugly railroad trestles. Here late in the last century, the Pennsylvania Railroad balked Jay Gould's attempt to push another railroad west to Chicago by building a trestle and freight terminal directly in the path of its projected right-of-way. The remains of this battle have cluttered the Point for over half a century. Now a Point Park Committee is advising the state on plans for turning the area into a park, a project for which the state has allocated $4 million. In addition, an Urban Re-development Authority was set up last November to acquire and develop twenty-three blighted acres adjacent to the new park, with Mayor David Lawrence as chairman, and Carnegie-Illinois Steel's J. Lester Perry, Mellon-man Arthur B. Van Buskirk, Edgar J. Kaufmann, and former City Solicitor William A. Stewart as board members. On this plot there are already prospects of building new quarters for Alcoa, U.S. Steel, and Westinghouse, a new state office building, and a medium-range housing development.

The conference met its first big test of power on smoke abatement, a project almost first on the list. After pushing through legislation for smoke abatement, there was a knockdown battle over the date and order in which control should take effect. The coal interests were all for postponing it indefinitely. Pittsburgh-district coal is a high-volatile coal that produces smoke in heady quantities; smokeless stokers and other equipment for burning it more efficiently were in short supply; if enforcement were clamped down, Pittsburghers might switch to other fuels. It finally took a call from the top Mellon office to remove the obstruction. The effective date for commercial and industrial buildings was set for last fall, the date for home-furnace conversion was pushed up to October 1, 1947. But the battle isn't over. If equipment doesn't loosen up, the coal men will be back for a postponement. Industrial plants are last on the list for control, with no effective date set as yet. And the powerful railroads, heavy producers of smoke in the district, so far seem to have got themselves exempt from regulation.

Nevertheless, the conference is now pushing to extend the smoke-abatement legislation and a unified control authority over the whole county, the only effective way to control the smog that periodically rolls down the valleys into Pittsburgh. One conference member explains some of the business opposition that has been met like this: "Some of the men down the line—the older men—haven't gotten wise yet that the boys at the top really mean business on this."

Now under the chairmanship of Dr. Edward R. Weidlein, head of the Mellon Institute of Industrial Research, Allegheny Conference committees are churning forward on a dozen fronts. It is characteristic that the conference boasts no grandiose master plan, such as has been fatal to so many city-planning schemes, but is proceeding on a practical level, project by project, to get things done. Some of the works-in-progress give some idea of the conference's scope.

Highways.
Presented and promoted a highway program to relieve congestion

by building through parkways down the sides of the Golden Triangle to Point Park, linking with a $53-million Penn-Lincoln freeway under construction by the state from the east and a new airport nearly completed to the southwest. The county voted a $34-million bond issue for this last fall. Plans also include a crosstown highway along the base of the Triangle.

Flood control.
Through a hard-working chamber-of-commerce committee and the Mayor, construction is going forward on Connemaugh Dam, being built on federal funds by U.S. Army Engineers. This, along with other dams already completed, is expected to eliminate Pittsburgh's annual spring floods—of which Pittsburgh has had sixty-four since 1900, the historic 1936 flood alone doing $95 million in damage.

River pollution.
Pushed the creation of a County Sanitary Authority, under which ninety communities, with 90 per cent of the district's population, have agreed to be controlled. The authority bans dumping of raw sewage into rivers and streams, and is working out unified plans for disposal.

Traffic.
Has completed a parking survey and report that recommends creation of a city parking authority to build and operate parking garages for complete off-the-street parking. This is estimated to cost $34 million for the central business district alone. First stage in the program calls for garages in five locations to cost $10 million, for which a change in state law will be necessary to allow the authority to operate in competition with private parking lots.

Industrial development.
A new development corporation is being set up through the chamber of commerce to prepare plant and industrial sites, and go out on an aggressive campaign to attract the light and service industries in which Pittsburgh is deficient.

Housing.
Has delivered the first part of a giant housing survey, which finds that bad housing is not isolated in a few sore spots but spreads throughout the area and must, therefore, be attacked on the broad-

est scale possible. After a market analysis as the second part of the survey, long-range plans will be drawn.

Labor-management.
Admittedly the weakest part of the conference program. The chamber of commerce is supposed to be working on plans for bettering relations, but hasn't done much, apparently waiting to see what new labor legislation will do for it. Big names in labor are conspicuously absent from the conference's committees. If the chamber doesn't move soon, the conference will—probably attempting to set up a labor-management board along the lines of the Toledo Plan.

The Pittsburgh Pay-off
In the long run, the Allegheny Conference is likely to stand or fall on two projects alone—housing and industrial development—with the labor situation a critical background for the full realization of the whole program. Unless some of the aloofness that still hangs on in the upper stories of the Golden Triangle disappears, the whole design may come to nothing more than a downtown real-estate development. The hard stratification of the social order that has marked Pittsburgh, with no common point of communication between the various strata of society from labor to ironmaster, may prove recalcitrant ground for rebuilding a city.

The year 1946 was a running commentary on the power of labor and bad labor relations to disrupt even the best and most hopeful of prospects. In this first full year of peace, when peacetime production might have soared to record-breaking heights, Pittsburgh had about every type of labor disorder going. Even as the year waned peacefully for most of the nation, Pittsburgh was in the throes of a bloody jurisdictional battle between A.F. of L. truckmen and C.I.O. brewery workers over the control of C.I.O. beer-truck drivers—a strike in which drivers were roughed up, beer was dumped, bombs were tossed into dealer establishments, and taverns halted the sale of local beer for fear of reprisal. At the same time, Phil Murray and his C.I.O. high command were meeting in Pittsburgh to lay down strategy for another round of wage negotiations, which may or may not turn 1947 into a disjointed replica of 1946. Some Pittsburghers are inclined to write 1946 off to postwar fatigue and readjustment, and most top Pittsburghers now believe the worst is over. But beneath the carking weight of heavy industry in this area there is a heritage of illwill, a set of rasping living conditions, a sense of exploitation and non-community of interest, that will make labor unrest a recurring and increasingly violent pattern unless something is done to draw labor into a greater role of partnership in civic responsibility.

Housing is easily the most immediate and physical test of the conference's powers. In Pittsburgh the housing problem is not only dogged by high construction costs, cumulative depreciation, progressive blight, and all the usual array of housing frights, but it is saddled with a local tax structure that derives more than 80 per cent of its income from real estate. On these terms Pittsburgh real estate is a bad risk for even the riskiest capital. The only hope for new low-cost or even medium-range housing, in which Pittsburgh is far below the national level, is large-scale government condemnation and intervention. After making the usual statement that private investment is to be encouraged wherever possible, the conference is likely to go along on that. "We've *got* to develop low-cost housing," says one vehement conference member. "In my humble opinion you have to forget about encroaching on private rights. You have to sacrifice free competition. You *have* to get housing!" Probably the first move in this direction will be to tear out the notorious Hill District, a noisome slum of ancient shacks, beer taverns, and bawdy houses that straggles up a bluff directly behind the Golden Triangle and Pennsylvania Depot. How fast and how far this cleanup will go is not yet clear.

In the long pull, industrial redevelopment is basic. Pittsburgh has been losing industries, imperceptibly, over a long period. In the twenties, in its obsession with tonnage, it passed up its chance to get a share of the automobile-parts industry. When new developments in plate and safety glass came along, Pittsburgh plants remained on the older tonnage products while the new safety-glass mills went up in areas closer to the automobile market. In steel it has been the same story, with lighter steels largely going elsewhere. Since the war this tendency to decentralize and follow markets has become more pronounced. U.S. Steel is moving in heavily on the West Coast, and a newly developed continuous process for making seamless tubing will shortly cause National Tube to desert its old plant at Ellwood City for the Middle West, closer to the oil fields. Westinghouse, with operations now spread over twenty-five plants in different localities, is moving its motors division to Buffalo and its circuit-breaker division to nearby Beaver Valley. Alcoa, joining the exodus to the Middle West, is already moving its aluminum kitchenware and closure divisions from New Kensington. None of these moves leave Pittsburgh area plants with any current deficit in product or employment, but the new plants go elsewhere, the old remain—usually in the older and heavier durable-goods lines, vulnerable to every cyclical slump and technological change in the industrial weather.

Nothing so earth-shaking as the removal of any major part of Big Steel is in the offing. Steel has a $900-million investment in the area, and that figure is not lightly moved. But the massive, mechanized Irvin Works is probably the last great expansion for the foreseeable future. The days of endless expansion are over for Pittsburgh. It can hold its own, but all the conference surveys show a steady decline relative to U.S. growth, deepening over the next thirty years. The only way to halt this decline, or at least bring it to a viable equilibrium, is to bring in new light industries. The likeliest prospect is light-metal fabrication—for light metals, stainless, and alloy steels are about the only indices running counter to the Pittsburgh trend, growing ahead of the national average, showing none of the sharp peaks and valleys of heavy steel. Other prospects are chemicals, plastics, textiles, work clothes, light electrical equipment. To bring in these, Pittsburgh is in the position of having to juggle all its problems at once, making its city more livable to attract new industry to aid in remaking the city and reduce its heavy industrial tensions. It will take more than the usual chamber-of-commerce effort. It will take all the energy of the new generation. The determination of the younger Mellons to follow in the industry-building footsteps of their fathers is indication that this energy will be forthcoming.

Pittsburgh in its time has been a great generator of romantic prose and strong epithets. They range all the way from Dickens' horrified ejaculation on his American tour—"Hell with the lid lifted!"—to the contemporary Frank Lloyd Wright's terse, "It'd be cheaper to abandon it!" Pittsburgh is a city in which it is defensively easy for outsiders not to feel implicated. Yet much of the material greatness of the U.S. and the West had its birth here. And what is happening now in Pittsburgh is a foretaste of what is in store for other, younger industrial centers a little further along in time. Pittsburgh is the test of industrialism everywhere to renew itself, to rebuild upon the gritty ruins of the past a society more equitable, more spacious, more in the human scale.

David Lawrence: Boss of the Mellon Patch by Frank Hawkins

At some point in the Democratic party's proceedings in Chicago the amateurs, the favorite sons, and assorted dignitaries will step aside and the professionals will nominate a Presidential candidate.

When that occurs, those who know the party best will look expectantly to a few key figures. Senator Lyndon Johnson of Texas will be one. Chairman Jacob Arvey, of Cook County, Illinois, Harry S. Truman, and Carmine G. DeSapio, leader of New York's Tammany Hall, will be others. A fifth, and perhaps the shrewdest and most experienced of the lot, will be the least known—Pittsburgh's Mayor David Leo Lawrence.

Most durable of the Democratic party's big city bosses, Dave Lawrence is a veteran of more than fifty years in political life, most of them spent quietly and effectively pulling strings behind the scenes. He is also one of the nation's most successful municipal administrators, the principal governmental expediter of his city's $1,500,000,000 redevelopment program and an expert mediator of industrial strife.

It came as no surprise to his fellow citizens in May 1955 when the United States Conference of Mayors gave Lawrence its annual award for distinguished service. Chosen for "outstanding contribution" both in Pittsburgh and the nation, he became the first mayor so honored.

Nor will Pennsylvanians be surprised to see Lawrence play a leading role at the Democratic convention this summer. They have long

"Lawrence of Pittsburgh: Boss of the Mellon Patch," *Harper's Magazine*, 213 (August, 1956), pp. 55–61.

known him as a king-maker—most recently in the fall of 1954 when, under his tutelage, an obscure young chicken farmer was elected Governor of Pennsylvania and the Democrats were restored to state power after a forlorn interval of sixteen years. With that victory, Lawrence did more than return his party to control; he also completed a remarkable personal comeback from the brink of political ruin.

When the Democrats last ruled Pennsylvania, from 1934 to 1938, Lawrence was the power behind the throne. As Democratic State Chairman and Secretary of the Commonwealth, he ran the administration of playboy Governor George H. Earle. The Earle administration came down in disgrace. Lawrence and two other members of the cabinet were indicted for alleged malfeasance and one of them was convicted. Lawrence was cleared by Republican juries at sensational trials in 1939 and again in 1940, and he came back stronger than ever. Since 1940, he has been Democratic National Committeeman from Pennsylvania. In 1945, he was elected Mayor of Pittsburgh—an office to which he has been reelected twice to become the first third-term mayor in the city's 198 years. And in the ten years of his administration, a once grimy and obsolete industrial district has undergone a redevelopment program which has set the national pattern for municipal renovation.

Lawrence is the undisputed leader of the Democratic party in Pennsylvania. In February 1954, when party leaders met to shape a ticket for the spring primaries, it was he who advanced the name of State Senator George Leader, a thirty-seven-year-old York County poultryman. Leader had caught Lawrence's fancy in an unsuccessful race for State Treasurer in 1952. Nominated in the primary, Leader went on to score an upset victory in the face of a Republican registration lead of nearly a million.

Although Leader has since proved a disappointment to Lawrence on several scores, the 1954 victory put the Mayor at the height of his power in Pennsylvania and boosted his already considerable influence in the party's national affairs. He will be an even more potent force at the convention this year than in the past. He not only has the skill and prestige acquired during more than half a century in public life, but he will continue to control most if not all of Pennsylvania's seventy-four delegates in 1956 as he did in 1952, when he was one of Adlai Stevenson's most effective backers.

Mayor Lawrence and James Finnegan, then president of the Philadelphia City Council, and former Pennsylvania Senator Francis J. Myers were the first professionals to get behind the drive to nominate Stevenson. Lawrence had been won over to the Illinois Governor early in 1952. While recuperating from an eye operation, he heard Stevenson on a "Meet the Press" radio program. When it was over, Lawrence called his friend Jake Arvey and asked him to keep Stevenson from closing the door to the nomination. At Chicago, Lawrence declined to become Stevenson's floor manager, but Myers and Finnegan took over successfully.

Lawrence is still strong for Stevenson, whom he describes as "the best qualified man for the Presidency I've known"—an impressive tribute since he has attended every Democratic national convention in some official capacity since 1912, when as a page boy at the age of twenty-three he helped nominate Woodrow Wilson. He has been a delegate to every convention from 1924.

Over that period, he has shown remarkable political prescience. Beginning in 1928 he has backed the eventual nominee at every convention. In 1932, after supporting Al Smith at two conventions, Lawrence abandoned him in favor of Franklin D. Roosevelt, and—with the assistance of the late Senator Joseph F. Guffey—swung the majority to FDR, over the opposition of a faction which favored Smith because he was Catholic and more conservative.

Lawrence also helped send Harry Truman to the White House. At a crucial moment during the 1944 convention, when it looked as if Henry Wallace would be nominated for Vice President if the balloting began, Lawrence made a successful motion for adjournment. He also split the Pennsylvania delegation away from Wallace, who had heavy labor backing, and threw it to Truman. As the voting for Vice President got under way, Lawrence and the Missouri Senator were sitting together in offices under the convention floor. It was a tense moment for the Mayor but Truman was calm. He turned to Lawrence and demanded: "What are you chewing your nails for? I'm going to make it."

Truman again enjoyed Lawrence's support in 1948, when few of the professionals gave him any chance of winning. Arvey, the late Edward J. Flynn, boss of the Bronx, the late Frank Hague, boss of Jersey City, and others panicked and wanted to draft Dwight Eisenhower; but Lawrence and Frank Myers stood firmly behind Truman.

The Mayor had found an earlier opportunity to befriend the President in October 1947, when Margaret Truman made her concert debut in Pittsburgh's ornate Syria Mosque. "About a week before the concert," he recalls, "I had a call from Mrs. Strickler [Margaret A. Strickler, of Kansas City, Miss Truman's instructor and, at that time, manager]. She was worried because she didn't know how to get things organized and she asked to see me."

After huddling briefly with Mrs. Strickler and a local booking agent, the Mayor realized that virtually nothing had been done to sell the recital.

"Look," he said, "this is the President's daughter. We can't let this thing flop. How much are the cheapest tickets?"

"A dollar twenty," replied the agent.

"I'll take a thousand," said Lawrence.

He divided them equally among the public and parochial schools for distribution to pupils interested in music. Then he got women's organizations behind the recital and arranged a post-concert reception for Miss Truman at the Twentieth Century Club. Miss Truman sang to a full house of 4,000. When the Mayor visited in the White House soon after the concert, the President thanked him warmly.

"You turned a concert into a political rally," Truman said, "I'll always be grateful for what you did. You know, she's all I've got."

Lawrence likes to turn that over in his mind as a lapidarist might re-examine a precious stone for some new facet.

"Can you imagine," he asks, "a man sitting in the White House saying, 'she's all I've got'?"

Lovable Is Not the Word

To some Western Pennsylvanians, Lawrence is "Mr. Democrat." To others, he is known sarcastically as "David the King." Nearly all of them, however, recognize him as the complete political animal. He lives politics twenty-four hours a day, with little time for anything else.

At sixty-six, Lawrence is sturdy (five feet nine and a half inches: 180 pounds) with thinning white hair and astonishing energy. His ruddy face eases readily into a smile as he greets acquaintances on one of his frequent walks through Pittsburgh's Golden Triangle.

When bracing an offending ward worker, however, his manner is less genial. His blue eyes stare stonily from behind rimless glasses and he chews the offender out in language that might do credit to Harry Truman.

Lovable is hardly the word for Lawrence. He rules through respect and fear rather than affection. "He meets the model of the crack-the-whip type of politician who knows what he wants and walks over anybody who opposes him," according to a Pennsylvania Republican leader, "and that includes members of his own party."

Of Scotch-Irish ancestry, Lawrence makes a great show of being Irish. He tells Irish and Catholic stories as if he were fresh from County Mayo. But actually the Scotch predominates in his brusque personality. At noon on weekdays, Lawrence strides briskly to the downtown YMCA for a shower, a sunbath, and perhaps a workout on the Exercycle. At noon on Sundays he takes up collection at St. Mary of Mercy Catholic Church. He has little social life, except for taking bows at civic functions and proffering the city's keys to visiting celebrities. He doesn't smoke and for most of his life has been a teetotaler. Only in recent years has he begun to relax with an occasional whiskey sour or glass of wine before dinner. By and large, he leads an existence as lonely as is possible for a man surrounded by people driven to him by the exigencies of an insatiable political machine.

Lawrence has a strong sense of identity with the city in whose redevelopment he has played such an important role. He was born on June 18, 1889, in a modest home at what was then Greentree Alley and Penn Avenue. That is in the Golden Triangle, formed where the Allegheny and Monongahela Rivers converge to become the Ohio and provide a gateway to the West. Like a hardy weed, Lawrence took firm roots along the riverfront in the lower forty of the Mellon patch. He grew up to become the political boss of what has been described cynically as the world's biggest company town. (Four of the city's five tallest skyscrapers house interests of the vast Mellon family banking and industrial empire.) The site where Lawrence was born has at last been cleared of commercial blight to become part of a thirty-six-acre state project known as Point Park. This $12,000,000 park adjoins another twenty-three acres which were also cleared to permit construction of Gateway Center, one of the most spectacular urban redevelopments in America.

Pittsburgh's face-lifting program began about the time Lawrence took office as Mayor in January 1946. The extent to which he can be credited with the success of the program is always a subject of lively debate at election time. The Mayor's detractors argue with some justice that he just happened to take office at a time when the Pittsburgh district's civic planners and financial leaders were ready to make the city over. Without the initiative of the Mellon family and other big business interests, they contend, Pittsburgh would have accomplished little.

Nothing shakes the district's GOP leaders more than the hateful sight of a smiling Lawrence taking bows and making statesmanlike little bipartisan speeches at ceremonies marking improvements made with all that Republican money. They suffered *in extremis* one September day in 1953 when Richard K. Mellon, current head of the banking dynasty, figuratively draped an arm around the broad shoulders of the Mayor, then running for a third term, and praised him publicly at a ground-breaking ceremony. At that dreadful moment the Republican pulse in Allegheny County, long faint, became almost imperceptible.

But it can't be denied that state and local legislation was essential to most of the development projects. Nor can it be denied that Lawrence provided the leadership that produced the legislation both in City Hall and—with the cooperation of the Republican Martin, Duff, and Fine administrations—in the Statehouse.

In ridding Pittsburgh of smoke, in winning legislative permission to create an Urban Redevelopment Authority, and in other undertakings, Lawrence has had the whole-hearted cooperation of his traditional political rivals, the wealthy industrialists and financiers who support the Republican party. Lawrence and the city's business leaders faced a formidable task. Pittsburgh was a used-up city, unattractive physically and unpromising economically because of the trend toward industrial decentralization. The Golden Triangle, principal source of municipal revenue, was in a decline. Property valuations were falling.

Here, clearly, was a situation calling for concerted action of leaders in business, labor, and government. In the light of Pittsburgh's history of industrial strife and its rigid social stratification, this might well have seemed impossible. It was not at all odd in pre-1945 Pittsburgh—which still had medieval overtones—that its political boss, Lawrence, and its patrician banker and industrialist, Mellon, had never met until they had to join forces to save a city dear to both.

To this day a Democratic politician or labor leader is exceedingly reluctant to be seen entering the Duquesne Club, sanctuary of the district's rolling-mill aristocracy, lest he be suspected of selling out to the "interests." Political distrust has been subordinated, however, to civic rescue. To this common endeavor Mellon brought prestige and professional planning talent. Lawrence contributed the cooperation of a by-then firmly entrenched Democratic political machine and the confidence and support of organized labor. Between them, they accomplished what neither could have done alone.

Although Pittsburgh's business leaders are for the most part identified with the GOP and have been reluctant to speak well of a Democratic Mayor, there is no doubt that Lawrence is generally respected for his ability to get things done. His control of the nine-man City Council is such that if he makes a commitment he can deliver. He never backs down on pledges.

Lawrence's manipulation of the Council is, in fact, a vulnerable point at which the opposition never ceases to hammer. "There is no legislative representation at the local level," one of the County's few Republican officeholders complains. "Council is completely dominated. It could operate as well from Kokomo, Indiana."

In selecting Councilmen, the Mayor displays a sensitive regard for special group interests, if not for talent. Although Catholics on the Council outnumber Protestants five to four, Lawrence has seen to it that Negroes, Jews, Italians, and Irish are all represented. The same policy governs judgeships and other local offices. Thus the Pittsburgh pattern is, in microcosm, that of the political parties nationally.

Mayor Lawrence has a fine grasp of practical politics and public administration.

"He has an amazing facility," says a Pittsburgh business leader, "for quickly understanding your problem and arriving at a solution."

The Mayor is not a student, in the academic sense, and his formal schooling was limited, but he learns readily in daily contacts with people in all fields. He reads little except the newspapers, which he follows avidly.

However, aside from his role in the city's redevelopment—into which the city itself has put little money—Lawrence's record is not an unalloyed success. The public-health program and the parks and recreation department have been improved, it is true, but there are complaints about the quality of basic city services.

"The Mayor's great weakness," says a Republican critic, "is as a municipal housekeeper. The city's streets are full of potholes. Garbage collection is poor. The water system is worn out. The police are controlled by district inspectors who are purely political stooges. The budget is a phony, loaded with people who don't work but stand around on street corners and fix up traffic tags. Pittsburgh is like a shiny red apple that is rotten at the core."

Boy of All Chores

That extreme appraisal must be discounted somewhat by partisanship and the limitations of municipal finance in a period of inflation. Like most cities, Pittsburgh never has enough money. Consequently, some services suffer more from lack of funds than from negligence. In recent years, policing has been pretty good. The rackets, for example, are kept well under control. Nevertheless, Pittsburgh is probably the only city in the country where hoodlums can beat up cops and get away with it. There was the time a few years ago when an officer was thrown down a flight of stairs for nosing into a gambling establishment. Nothing was done about it. More recently, a police inspector was slapped around when he blundered into an earnest dispute among a party of numbers racketeers. When newspapers pointed out that the inspector had made no arrests in reprisal, he was suspended for fifteen days.

It is not as a municipal housekeeper, but as a governmental expediter and political strategist that Lawrence shows his real strength. In the latter role, his experience began, theoretically, as far back as Lawrence can remember. He was born into a home where politics was, like potatoes, a staple in the diet. His maternal grandfather had been a county assessor. His father, Charles B. Lawrence, was in the hauling business and later worked for the county as a warehouseman. At the age of fourteen, having completed a high-school commercial course, Davey's practical experience began when he became a stenographer in the office of William J. Brennan—lawyer, Pittsburgh Democratic Chairman, and prominent figure in the party nationally. In Brennan's office, Davey became a boy of all chores. He was so apt a pupil that in 1920, at the age of thirty-one, he succeeded the late Senator Guffey as Allegheny County Democratic Chairman. In the interim, he had served briefly as an enlisted man in the office of the Judge Advocate General in Washington. Defective vision, which has handicapped him most of his life, kept him out of the draft.

After the war, Lawrence returned to Pittsburgh and went into the insurance business. Today he receives a comfortable living from the Harris-Lawrence Company, a general agency of which he is president but whose operation is left to an associate. His salary of $20,000 a year as Mayor does little more than cover his political expenses. But Lawrence is far more interested in power than in dollars.

When Lawrence took the county chairmanship in 1920, the Democrats were a rather pitiful minority. For years Lawrence had to content himself with filling jobs that went to the minority party by statute. When Roosevelt made his first bid for the Presidency, however, Lawrence and Guffey conducted the campaign which reversed the political tide in Allegheny County. FDR carried the county, but not Pennsylvania, and Lawrence received his first political reward in 1934 when he was appointed a Collector of Internal Revenue. A year later he assumed the state leadership as party chairman, which he surrendered in 1940, when he became Democratic National Committeeman.

The Great Depression undoubtedly contributed most to Allegheny County's switch from Republican to Democratic. In 1933, some 300,000 of the county's 1,500,000 were on relief. The heavily industrial district eagerly embraced the New Deal's promises of recovery. Organized labor received much encouragement. And Lawrence was astute enough to take advantage of the New Deal trend and consolidate its gains locally under his own management.

After directing George Earle's successful campaign for Governor, he was appointed Secretary of the Commonwealth. In that post he literally ran Pennsylvania from behind the scenes. He was the unofficial "whip" who drove the "Little New Deal" legislation through the Legislature. And it was then that he made the major political mistake of his career—one which brought the Earle regime down in disgrace and himself to the verge of political destruction.

Trouble developed around the controversial figure of Charles J. Margiotti, a Pittsburgh criminal lawyer. Margiotti at that time was a Republican. He had run for the GOP gubernatorial nomination in the 1934 primary and, although defeated, had made an impressive showing. Now, against his better judgment, Lawrence assented to Margiotti's appointment as Attorney General, assuming that much of his following among Pennsylvanians of Italian extraction would be converted to Democratic ranks.

Margiotti's ambitions to become Governor were encouraged by the appointment. But when it became clear to him that he could not expect Lawrence's support for the Democratic nomination in 1938, he sought the nomination anyway in a primary campaign enlivened by his charges of scandal against various officials of the Earle administration, including Lawrence. The top law-enforcement officer of the Earle administration became its chief prosecutor. The upshot was a grand jury investigation which returned indictments against Lawrence and several others.

The next two years were the blackest in Lawrence's life, years in which he marked time between trials. On December 8, 1939, a Dauphin County jury, after deliberating six hours, acquitted him of three counts of conspiracy, one of statutory blackmail, and one of violating the election laws. The trial ran for twenty-three days, with a jury of nine Republicans, two Democrats, and one Independent.

The charges involved complaints that Lawrence had conspired with John J. Verona, a former Pittsburgh ward leader, to cheat and defraud the state by permitting substandard gravel to be bought by the state, to permit specifications to be drawn in favor of the Pioneer Materials Company, and to influence state officials for those purposes. The state also sought to show that Lawrence had extorted $5,000 from Spurgeon Bowser, head of the Pioneer Company, as a campaign contribution, and then in violation of the law had failed to turn the money over to the Democratic State Committee.

A cheering crowd met Lawrence at the train that brought him home from Harrisburg. But the following spring he had to stand trial again on a charge of conspiracy to extort money from the state payroll, an offense known in Pennsylvania as "macing." While macing, or forcing campaign contributions from payrollers, is a common practice of both parties, it is nonetheless illegal and thus affords an opportunity for the party out of power to make a great show of political morality just before elections. In any event, Lawrence stood trial for another seventeen days; an all-Republican jury deliberated four hours before acquitting him and seven other Democrats. In both trials, the juries put the costs upon the county.

Still Lawrence's sorrows were not over. Just two years after his second trial, in April 1942, his oldest sons, sixteen-year-old Brennan and thirteen-year-old David L., Jr., were killed when an automobile in which they were riding was wrecked on a highway near Middle Lancaster, thirty-nine miles north of Pittsburgh.

The Nightmare Year

After the death of his sons, Lawrence smothered his grief in renewed political activity. He tried in 1942 to regain control of the state, lost in the debacle of the Earle administration, but failed. Then he began to withdraw and concentrate his activities in Allegheny County, except for the 1944 Presidential campaign, in which he worked loyally for Roosevelt's fourth term.

Under Lawrence's management, the Democrats had in 1933 captured control of Pittsburgh's government for the first time in twenty-four years. As party boss, he installed the late William N. McNair, an eccentric single-taxer, in City Hall. But Mayor McNair, who sold apples in the lobby of City Hall and sawed soberly on his violin at night-club openings, refused to play ball. He defied Lawrence on patronage, taxation, and policy until the outraged Democratic leader threatened to have the legislature rip him from office. In 1936, McNair resigned and turned the city government over to Lawrence to control from that time, first through Mayor Cornelius D. Scully and later by his own administration.

By 1945 it was clear to Lawrence that the Scully administration, for all its progressive ideas about city government, somehow lacked ability to sell its program. He realized that if the Scully administration went down to defeat, his own battered prestige would suffer a perhaps fatal blow. In the course of deliberations over a successor to Scully, one morning in 1945 Lawrence met his late neighbor, James O'Toole, aged seventy-six, and the irascible O'Toole asked him if the party was going to nominate a certain judge for Mayor.

No, Lawrence replied, party leaders hadn't been able to agree on a candidate.

"What about me?" asked O'Toole.

"We could go farther and do worse," Lawrence conceded generously. Some hours later the newspapers announced that Lawrence had decided to take the nomination. Next morning, the neighbors met again.

"Well," said O'Toole, "I see they went farther and did worse."

Lawrence was elected by 14,000 votes in a Democratic sweep of City Hall. It was his first elective office; he had been defeated by 9,000 votes in a bid for county commissioner in 1931. As he looks back on it now, Lawrence realizes that from one point of view he could hardly have chosen a less propitious time to become Mayor of Pittsburgh. It was a year of great unrest as the nation made a turbulent economic transition from war to peace. Strikes were the order of the day, especially in the Pittsburgh district.

A little more than a month after he took office on January 7, 1946, the Mayor was confronted with the first in a series of industrial crises which were to make his first year in office a nightmare—a walkout in the Duquesne Light Company, which provides electric power for Allegheny and Beaver counties. Lawrence got the City Council to proclaim a state of emergency, unavailingly asked White House Assistant John Steelman for government seizure, and after nineteen and a half hours talked the union into returning to work while a three-man negotiating committee, including himself, sought to adjust wage differences.

In September, he obtained an injunction to halt another power strike, which was simply postponed until the following month, when the union walked out for 27 days. That same year Lawrence had to wrestle with a 26-day steel strike, two coal strikes, a 115-day walkout at Westinghouse, a 53-day hotel shutdown, several bus strikes, and an assortment of 81 other work stoppages.

"I fervently pray," he said toward the end of 1946, "that the other three years won't be like the first—if I last."

He has lasted much better than might be expected of an official caught in the middle of recurrent labor-management strife whose bitter roots can be traced at least as far back as the bloody Homestead riots of 1892. For more than ten years he has functioned as a mediator in labor disputes involving the public welfare. That is a delicate, if not dangerous, role for a politician and particularly in Pittsburgh, where a Democrat must have labor support or he isn't elected. The fact that Lawrence has somehow retained the confidence and respect of both labor and management is a tribute primarily to his courage. Inevitably he angers one side or the other but thus far he's gotten away with it.

Although much of his first year was devoted to labor crises, the Mayor also plunged into the cooperative attempt to halt the decline of Pittsburgh. Soon the results were visible everywhere. Skyscrapers rose in smokeless skies. When Pittsburgh had fog, it now was fog, not smog. A $150,000,000 Penn-Lincoln expressway crossed the city and the Monongahela River, linking east and west. By 1955, property valuations were up to $1,115,996,148 from $961,000,000 in 1947, when the decline had been reversed. The tax base had been broadened, and the burden on real estate had been eased.

Today the city has begun, with a stern mayoral warning to the "professional slum landlords," to enforce a new housing code aimed at upgrading residential areas and arresting blight. And this year the city, in cooperation with sixty-odd neighboring communities, began construction of an $87,000,000 sewage disposal system in compliance with the state's program to clean up the rivers.

End of the Bosses

Whatever Lawrence is denied in the way of political and financial support by the industrial barons is more than compensated for by his following among the rank and file. When he first ran for re-election in 1949, he received a record majority of 56,000 votes; in winning his third term in 1953, he received a 55,000 majority which, because of a lighter vote than in 1949, actually constituted a higher precentage of the total vote cast. This wide acceptance of his leadership sets him apart from the old-fashioned bosses in the tradition of Tweed, Curley, Hague, and Pendergast.

There is, in fact, unconscious humor in Lawrence's disparaging attitude toward political bossism. Like an actress who reads the lines in a rival's face as signs of age but thinks of her own in terms of character, the Mayor, as a senior member of the Democratic National Committee, observes with approval that most of the old bosses are no longer around.

"The new members of the committee are of a different caliber," he says. "They are progressive young people like Archibald Alexander of New Jersey."

Lawrence gives and demands loyalty within the party. A trustworthy and hard-working employee can expect nice promotions; the defaulting subordinate can count on a scathing tongue lashing if not dismissal. The Mayor is also quick to go to the defense of persons whom he feels are falsely accused. He went voluntarily before a special committee of the County Bar Association to defend an assistant district attorney who had been suspended because of alleged Communist associations. In like manner, he defended Roy Harris, composer and musician in residence at Chatham College, whose alleged Communist sympathies came under attack by a Democratic Pennsylvania Supreme Court Justice, Michael A. Musmanno.

Unawed by anyone in or out of public life, Lawrence will speak his mind bluntly on any issue. His enforcement of the smoke law and the injunction he obtained in a power strike are evidence that the Mayor dares to do the unpopular thing. In 1954, he did it again when he reversed his earlier position to impose a one per cent levy on wages—thus avoiding higher taxes on real estate. He has also given the back of his hand to some of the city's department-store operators for refusing his offer to mediate a strike that lasted for more than a year.

But if Lawrence is at times hostile to privileged groups, he is exceedingly diligent in the protection of more defenseless minorities. In a city in which Negroes make up about 13 per cent of the population, jammed mostly into Hill District slums, race relations have long been good. In 1946, the Mayor organized the Civic Unity Council, an agency devoted to improving race relations. In 1953, he pushed through a fair employment practices ordinance. In January 1954, Lawrence appointed Paul F. Jones as the first Negro to serve in City Council. And in the fall of that year he appointed a Negro reporter from the Pittsburgh *Courier,* Paul L. Jones, as his public-relations secretary.

For himself, Lawrence has no ambitions beyond those of Mayor. Before giving the nod to George Leader for the party's 1954 gubernatorial bid, he considered seeking the nomination himself; it was his for the acceptance. A hardheaded realist, however, he concluded that a Catholic could not be elected in Pennsylvania because of the heavy rural vote, which he believed would be attracted to a Lutheran farmer. Similarly, Lawrence passed up the Senatorial nomination this year in favor of former Mayor Joseph S. Clark of Philadelphia.

There is, in fact, only one development which could set the capstone on his career. In 1956 he would like to help put a Democrat—preferably Adlai Stevenson—into the White House. With Democrats in control of Pittsburgh, Allegheny County, Harrisburg, and Washington (an irreverent associate feels that this should also include the Papacy), Lawrence could ask little more of life. That, as he figures it, is about the way things should be. The opposition would be careless indeed if it underestimated his attempts to bring it off.

The Renaissance: A Catalogue of Projects
by Park H. Martin

Pittsburgh Background

The City of Pittsburgh is not only the center of Allegheny County but also the hub of the Pittsburgh industrial area. Within the corporate limits of the city are 54 sq. miles and 676,000 persons. The County of Allegheny, including Pittsburgh, contains 745 sq miles and a population of 1,515,000 according to the 1950 census.

Within the limits of the county are 129 separate municipal subdivisions. There is a County Planning Commission which has limited operations and also an effective Pittsburgh City Planning Commission which operates inside the city limits; some other municipalities have local planning commissions. The State Department of Highways and the County of Allegheny are responsible for the major highway routes and most secondary highways.

The Pittsburgh industrial area has long been known as an area of heavy industry. Because of this and because it was founded in part on the great bituminous coal fields in the region, Pittsburgh over the years had acquired a rather unsavory reputation for smoke and dirt. Its traffic problems were mounting, the parking problem had not been attacked, a new airport was greatly needed, assessed valuations in the city declined from a high of $1,211,867,000 in 1936 to a low of $961,000,000 in 1947, with the "Golden Triangle" showing a higher rate of decline. All this had become a matter of grave concern to its business and political leaders and, near the end of World War II, it was decided to do something constructive about the situation.

The Allegheny Conference on Community Development

It was agreed first to form a citizens' organization concerning itself

"Pittsburgh Comprehensive Improvement Program," American Society of Civil Engineers, *Transactions,* 121 (1956), pp. 885–892. Reprinted by permission of the American Society of Civil Engineers.

with the future of the region. Known as the Allegheny Conference on Community Development and now commonly called "The Allegheny Conference," its purpose was to stimulate and coordinate research and planning, having as its goal a unified community plan for the entire region. The Allegheny Conference was to secure, by educational means, public support of projects that were approved by the conference as parts of the over-all unified plan and to expedite the fulfillment of the plans. Where qualified agencies existed, the Allegheny Conference obtained from them research and planning assistance. In certain fields where no such qualified agency existed, the conference created its own staff to do the research and planning. Committees were formed to study various phases of the community's needs and to make recommendations in relation thereto.

Strong emphasis has been placed on the Golden Triangle. It is the business and commercial heart of the city and county, and its assessed valuation represents approximately one quarter of the assessed valuation of the entire city. The need for preserving and protecting the stability of the Golden Triangle was recognized and accepted, and the program deliberately placed great emphasis on this area. Although the county's suburban areas are growing both residentially and commercially it is believed that the central core must be preserved.

The emphasis on preserving the values in the Golden Triangle is further recognized in the highway program and mass-transit studies.

A Comprehensive Program
It is the feeling of the Allegheny Conference that a community improvement program must be broad and balanced. With that in mind, the conference has been concerned with smoke and flood control, highways, parking, airports, mass transit, sanitation and public health, recreation and conservation, zoning and urban redevelopment, libraries and other cultural institutions, and economic development.

The order in which these subjects are herein mentioned does not necessarily reflect their relative importance, except in the case of smoke and flood control. It is believed that had these two projects not been successful the entire program might have failed.

Smoke Abatement
Since the early 1900's, the people of Pittsburgh have been con-

cerned about smoke control. In 1911 the Pennsylvania Legislature passed laws permitting the City of Pittsburgh to control smoke from all sources, but powerful opposition and civic lethargy blocked all efforts to pass a city ordinance. However, in 1941 the City Council passsed an effective smoke-control ordinance. Because of World War II the effective date of the ordinance was not set. In 1946, with urging and support from the Allegheny Conference, the City Council fixed the effective date as October 1, 1946, requiring industries and railroads to burn solid fuels smokelessly or use other types of fuels. On October 1 of the following year, households within the city limits came under the provisions of the ordinance.

During the eight years that the ordinance has been in full effect (as of 1954) amazing results have been produced in this heart of the bituminous coal industry. Official figures of the Weather Bureau of the United States Department of Commerce show that Pittsburgh is now receiving 89% more sunshine than prior to smoke control. Soot and dustfall records reflect an average reduction of 20% for the period of 1938–1953, years of high industrial activity. In eight years—1949–1953—the hours of heavy smoke, as compiled by the Weather Bureau, have been reduced by 94.4%.

As a result of smoke control, building owners and managers in the Golden Triangle alone have spent more than $1,500,000 on exterior building cleaning, and other office building cleaning projects are planned.

The benefits of this smoke-abatement program have now been extended to all of Allegheny County. In 1949, the Board of County Commissioners enacted a county-wide ordinance which embodies the principal features of the Pittsburgh ordinance. To date, industry in Allegheny County has spent more than $200,000,000 in advancing smoke control. The installation of modern combustion equipment, dust collectors, new boiler plants, precipitators, and other modern devices are contributing greatly to the elimination, reduction, and control of smoke and other industrial pollutants.

Dieselization of the railroads has practically solved the problem of railroad smoke. Railroad operations throughout Allegheny County are now 81% dieselized and yard operations, 91%. Even the colorful, smoking, sternwheel river boats have largely been discarded for diesel power, and now these operations are 78% dieselized.

The result of the smoke-control program in Pittsburgh and Allegheny County is all the more remarkable because of the fact that this center of heavy industry consumes about 50,000,000 tons of coal annually.

Flood Control.

In 1936 a disastrous flood occurred at Pittsburgh and in the upper Ohio River valley. Flood crests from the Monongahela River and the Allegheny River converged at the "point," flooding the lower part of the Golden Triangle to a depth of about 10 ft. Property damage in the Pittsburgh district reached $94,000,000 and in the upper Ohio River valley, approximately $200,000,000.

Since 1936 the federal government, through the Corps of Engineers (United States Department of the Army), has constructed a $100,000,000 flood control system in this region. Eight major dams have been erected in the water-sheds of the Allegheny River and the Monongahela River and are all now in operation. If the dams had been in operation at the time of the 1936 flood, the Corps of Engineers estimates the flood level at the "point" would have been reduced 10.5 ft.

Stream Pollution Abatement.

Sixty municipalities in Allegheny County have entered into an agreement with the Allegheny County Sanitary Authority to design and construct a system of collector sewers and a disposal plant. At the present time nearly all the sanitary wastes of these communities are disposed of, untreated, in the rivers. Industrial wastes will also be treated. Construction work began during 1955.

Triangle Redevelopment.

The Allegheny River flowing down from the northeast joins with the Monongahela River flowing in from the southeast to form the Ohio River, near the geographic center of Pittsburgh. The area lying between these two rivers and extending about 1 mile east from their juncture is known as the Golden Triangle (Fig. 1). Comprising an area of approximately 330 acres of which 70 acres are occupied by streets, the Golden Triangle is the heart of the business and commercial life of Pittsburgh and Allegheny County as well as the hub of the highways and transportation systems serving them. It is also the regional and metropolitan center of a tri-state area of more than

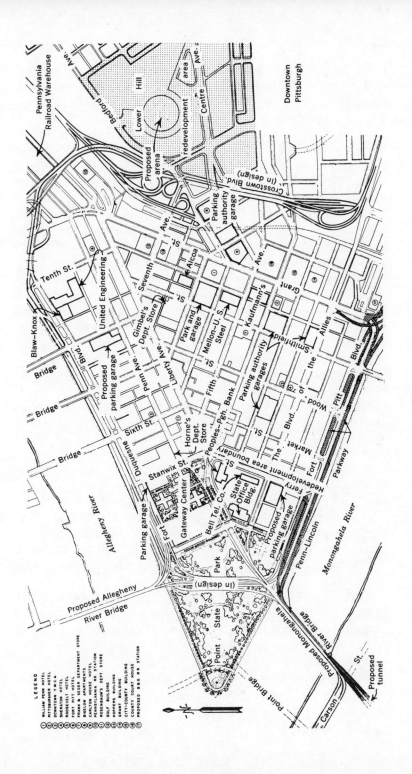

LEGEND
① WILLIAM PENN HOTEL
② PITTSBURGHER HOTEL
③ DOWNTOWN Y.M.C.A.
④ SHERATON HOTEL
⑤ ROOSEVELT HOTEL
⑥ FORT PITT HOTEL
⑦ FRANK & SEDER DEPARTMENT STORE
⑧ BIGELOW APARTMENTS
⑨ CARLTON HOUSE HOTEL
⑩ PENNSYLVANIA R.R. STATION
⑪ ROSENBAUM'S DEPT. STORE
⑫ BLOCK HOUSE
⑬ KOPPERS BUILDING
⑭ GRANT BUILDING
⑮ CITY-COUNTY BUILDING
⑯ COUNTY COURT HOUSE
⑰ PROPOSED B&O R.R. STATION

Pennsylvania Railroad Warehouse

Downtown Pittsburgh

Lower Hill redevelopment area

Centre Ave.

Bedford Ave.

Proposed arena

Crosstown Blvd. (in design)

Grant Ave.

Tenth St.

Alcoa

Seventh St.

United Engineering

Gimbel's Dept. Store

Park and garage

Parking authority garage

Mellon–U. S. Steel

Kaufmann's

Blaw-Knox Bridge

Proposed parking garage

Penn Ave.

Liberty Ave.

Fifth Ave.

Smithfield St.

Parking authority garages

Wood St.

Sixth St.

Horne's Dept. Store

Peoples–Pgh. Bank

of the Allies

Boulevard of the Allies

Duquesne

Stanwix St.

Bridge

Bridge

Bridge

Allegheny River

Parking garage

Gateway Center

Fort Duquesne Blvd.

Bell Tel. Co.

redevelopment area boundary

State Office Bldg.

Ferry St.

Market St.

Pitt Blvd.

Fort Pitt Blvd.

Parkway

Proposed parking garage

Penn-Lincoln Parkway

Monongahela River

Proposed Allegheny River Bridge

Point State Park (in design)

Point Bridge

Proposed Monongahela River Bridge

Carson St.

Proposed tunnel

4,000,000 people and is one of the most compact central business districts in the United States.

Point Park and Gateway Center Development.

The area at the juncture of the Allegheny and Monongahela rivers is known as "the point." This was the site of Fort Duquesne and Fort Pitt and it was here that the city was originally founded. To preserve the site of the two forts, the Commonwealth of Pennsylvania is constructing a historical park comprising 36 acres. Begun in 1945, this project is being financed entirely by the commonwealth and to date it has cost more than $7,500,000 in land acquisition alone. All the buildings in the area have been razed, and grading and landscaping is partly completed. A river wall around the park has been built together with riverbank slope paving.

In the park area an elaborate traffic interchange will be built which will connect Fort Pitt Boulevard along the Monongahela River and Fort Duquesne Boulevard along the Allegheny River with the street system in the lower triangle. Two double-deck bridges across the rivers will also be constructed by the commonwealth. Construction has begun on the bridge across the Monongahela River.

Early in this project the state requested the Allegheny Conference to represent it in the development of plans for the park and to coordinate local interest. This responsibility was accepted by the conference.

In addition to initiating studies on the park project, the conference studied the adjacent area as well. This area covering 23 acres was largely deteriorated as a result of floods, railroad yards, and old loft buildings. The Allegheny Conference evolved a plan for the redevelopment of the entire area. In July, 1946, conference representatives presented the plan to the Equitable Life Assurance Society of the United States with the request that that organization become the redeveloper.

It was apparent from the beginning of negotiations that, to acquire the land where so many different owners and relatively small parcels of land were involved, the power of eminent domain would be essential if the project were to succeed. At this time the City of Pittsburgh did not have an Urban Redevelopment Authority. The conference recommended to the City Council that such an agency of government with the power of eminent domain be created, and on November 18, 1946, the Urban Redevelopment Authority of Pittsburgh was established by action of the mayor and the City Council.

An essential step in the urban redevelopment process is the certification of an area as being subject to redevelopment by the City Planning Commission. After thorough studies the City Planning Commission certified the entire area of both the proposed 36-acre park and the 23-acre adjoining property as a redevelopment area. The Urban Redevelopment Authority acted as the land-assembler of the 23-acre tract and entered into an agreement with the Equitable Life Assurance Society to be the redeveloper. Called "Gateway Center," the plan provided for complete readjustment of the street pattern and the initial construction of three large office buildings with only 25% land coverage. Off-street loading and parking were required as part of the redevelopment plan.

Leading Pittsburgh corporations signed long-term leases with the Equitable Life Assurance Society to occupy space in the new buildings. These agreements were executed in February, 1950, by the Jones & Laughlin Steel Corporation, Mellon National Bank and Trust Company, National Supply Company, Peoples Natural Gas Company, Pittsburgh Plate Glass Company, Union Switch and Signal Company, Westinghouse Air Brake Company, and Westinghouse Electric Corporation. It is interesting to note that the agreements were negotiated before all the land had been acquired in Gateway Center and before the buildings were completely designed. At the present time (1954) two 20-story buildings and one 24-story building have been completed and are occupied. The Equitable Life Assurance Society's investment in Gateway Center to date is approximately $43,000,000. Occupancy began in the spring of 1952.

Construction of a fourth building (15 stories high) in Gateway Center will begin this fall (1954). It is being built, at an estimated cost of $6,000,000, by the commonwealth to house all of its departments now renting space in numerous buildings in the city. The Peoples First National Bank and Trust Company, in September, 1953, announced its intention of constructing a bank and office building in the area.

Gateway Center provides for open space around the buildings, creating, in effect, an extension of Point Park. The city has widened and relocated Liberty Avenue as part of the project, and certain other thoroughfares in the area will also be widened and relocated; others have been vacated.

The ultimate plan for Gateway Center provides for additional structures, including an open-deck parking garage. The existing Stanwix Garage in the area has already been enlarged by the addition of one story, providing a total capacity for 600 cars.

ACTION-Housing: The Building of
East Hills Park
   A.   Executive Director's Report, 1961
   B.   Chairman's Report, 1971
   C.   East Hills Park

A. Executive Director's Report, 1961
The first housing undertaking of the Pittsburgh Development Fund of ACTION-Housing, Inc.—East Hills Park—will comprise four complete neighborhoods, with a total of some 1200 to 1400 dwelling units, mainly two-story, single-family town (row) houses in groups of four to ten. Space has been reserved for multi-story apartment structures which will meet the anticipated demand for this type of housing.

After two years of intensive preparation and planning, construction work will start this November on the first 47 dwellings in Section I of Phase I. These 47 units will serve as a model group in Phase I which will comprise 210 one- to three-bedroom houses. Approximately 1200 more dwelling units will be built at East Hills Park in three additional Phases over the next three to five years.

East Hills Park has been a team effort involving ACTION-Housing, Inc., the developer, architects, lending institutions, the Federal

ACTION-Housing, *Executive Director's Report to the Board of Directors of ACTION-Housing,* September 21, 1961. Reprinted by permission of ACTION-Housing, Inc.

ACTION-Housing, *Chairman's Report to the Board of Directors,* February 5, 1971. Reprinted by permission of ACTION-Housing, Inc.

Beth Dunlop, "East Hills Park: A Mix of Problems and Potential," *The Pittsburgh Press,* July 11, 1973. Reprinted by permission.

Housing Administration, materials manufacturers, utility companies, the Building and Construction Trades Council of Pittsburgh and Vicinity, and a number of agencies of the City of Pittsburgh and the County of Allegheny.

Working together, we have constantly kept our sights fixed on the original objectives of the Pittsburgh Development Fund and East Hills Park:

1. Substantially increasing the supply of good sales and rental housing for moderate income families in the Pittsburgh area.

2. Achieving higher levels of urban livability through advances in community and housing design, and in the use of new building materials, techniques, production and financing methods.

3. Supplying the housing component of the Pittsburgh Renaissance, acclaimed nationally for its commercial, industrial and civic accomplishments.

The loan contract between ACTION-Housing, Inc., and the developer was executed in March 1961. This contract, unique in the history of home building, describes how ACTION-Housing, Inc., and the developer will work together to achieve the objectives of East Hills Park. . . .

Cluster Planning
East Hills Park will use cluster-type planning, which groups dwellings around court-like areas, in sharp contrast to the conventional method of placing the houses perpendicular to the street in a long row of 50- or 60-foot lots. Land saved through the cluster plan will be used in large plots of community open space, playgrounds, totlots, park and sitting areas, and large tracts preserved in a natural state. The cluster plan also leads to economies in road and utility construction, and means complete separation of automobile traffic from living areas.

The use of cluster planning will reduce by approximately 40% the average cost per dwelling unit for site work usually done by the builder, which includes installation of utilities, streets and rough grading. This savings permits the developer to include in the purchase price the fine grading, fully seeded lawns, shrubs and trees, walks, an enclosed patio and arbor for each group of houses, as well as driveways and off-street parking pads.

At East Hills Park, the purchaser will get a complete house with a finished yard in a totally developed neighborhood.

Planned Residential Unit Zoning

East Hills Park is the first development to be built under Pittsburgh's planned residential unit zoning, a pioneering concept which was added to the local zoning code last June by the City Council. The amended code made possible the use of site plan innovations at East Hills Park.

With planned residential unit zoning, an entire neighborhood can be planned as a coordinated unit. Unlike other zoning, it does not limit specific areas to a single use, i.e., one-family houses, apartment buildings, commercial establishments, or the like. Rather, it aims at creating an harmonious entity, with each building and land use properly interrelated.

Labor-Management Agreement

An unprecedented labor-management contract was signed on May 31, 1961, by the developer and the Building and Construction Trades Council. The major items are:

1. The builder or his sub-contractor is given the sole right to manage his business, including the right to decide the machines, tools, and equipment to be used, as well as construction methods, assembly processes, and the right to use factory-fabricated units.

2. The Building Trades Council and its affiliated unions fully agree to use improved methods, tools, equipment, and design changes determined by the builder or his sub-contractor.

3. The Council agrees that there shall be no work stoppages because of jurisdictional disputes. In the event of any jurisdictional disputes among the unions affiliated with the Council, the builder shall have the right to make work assignments to the trades, pending the settlement and adjustment of such jurisdictional disputes. This guarantees no work stoppages.

4. Unions affiliated with the Trades Council will have 72 hours in which to supply workmen as requested by the builder or his sub-contractor. If the unions are unable to comply, the builder or sub-contractor is authorized to hire labor wherever available.

5. If a full day's work is lost because of bad weather, that day may be made up the following Saturday at regular wage rates. No premium time rate will be paid for such Saturday work.

6. The wage scale for all trades and workmen will be 10% lower than the commercial wage scale. The reduced scale will apply to single- or double-family dwellings. Commercial wage rates will be paid on high-rise apartment buildings.

New Building Components

The design of the dwellings in Phase I of East Hills Park has served to focus the attention of major Pittsburgh corporations on the need for continued and extensive research in order to produce new building materials and components suitable for widespread use in housing built for moderate income families. East Hills Park has demonstrated that the research and development departments of those corporations must place more emphasis on this opportunity if they are interested in producing cost-saving innovations for the huge housing market for moderate income families.

Some new building materials and products will be used in Phase I of East Hills Park, while others not yet perfected may be used in Phase II. As still other innovations come on the market, they will be considered for use in the third and fourth Phases.

East Hills Park is both an opportunity and a challenge to industry to pioneer in the field of housing for moderate income families, not only in Pittsburgh, but also on a national scale.

B. Chairman's Report, 1971
Housing-Related Human Problems

Accompanying this increasing level of construction activity are a myriad of human or "social" problems that develop as these and previously completed units are occupied. Though ACTION-Housing has a proven record in accomplishing the difficult and frustrating task of putting together the "bricks and mortar" of housing construction, it is realistic to say that many of the roughest problems begin when occupancy occurs. However, we do not want anyone to have the impression that all, or even a large portion, of the blame should be placed upon tenants.

A strong commitment to the use of newly trained labor to rehabilitate the houses, the employment of neighborhood-based realtors to manage the developments and the use of newly trained work crews to maintain them—none of which we regret—has led to a variety of management problems. Rent delinquency has been high, partly as a result of these inherent problems, and steps are being taken to improve the quality of maintenance and tenant-management relationships.

We have learned many lessons over the past year and some were painful ones. For instance: We attempted to use the large open spaces encompassed by the back yards of many of the rehabilitation projects for community areas. This has proven impractical, and additional funds must be raised from private sources to fence in the individual yards. The residents want it this way in order to deal effectively with rubbish and to define other areas of family responsibility.

Security is a major concern of residents in both rehabilitated and new housing developments. The increase in drug traffic over the last few years in this city and across the nation has made the theft of goods easily sold a common occurrence. In one newly constructed housing development of ours there have been 41 such robberies in the last 5 months and in some 40 houses recently occupied and completely rehabilitated in Homewood there have been 10 robberies in the past two months.

But this problem is not just one for the police, it calls into question one of ACTION-Housing's basic tenets of producing housing of "good design" for low and moderate income families. Based on today's security problems, we have begun to re-think our definition of "good design" for multi-family housing developments, particularly where families of low and modest income are concerned. For example, in one of our new housing developments a sliding patio door designed to let in light and air, give a feeling of openness to the unit and invite outdoor living has become an entrance way for thieves though affording a recreational advantage for residents.

In Chicago, as reported in the January 1971 Journal of Property Management, some new in-city developments are being constructed with a raised walled plaza that provides open space as well as security for the residents of the development.

This is an expensive solution but with security needs becoming a primary and costly factor in providing housing of "good design," it becomes more and more difficult not to lean backward towards those institutional forms of housing that are safe even though forbidding in appearance.

Vandalism has also become a costly and worrisome concern to all our management operations. Glass replacement at the rate of approximately $350 per month in one new housing development, for example, eats into funds otherwise available for the operating expenses of the development.

A costly search had to be conducted for a non-breakable light fixture for the outdoor lights in this same development, and the replacement of vandalized fire extinguishers and hall mats is a continuous problem in the apartment units. Only a portion of this destruction and neglect can be ascribed to the residents in the development. Much of it relates to the drug problem and the lack of recreational facilities for the young people of the area.

Housing-Related Services

The need for services is great. New residents are in many cases unfamiliar with the operation of the appliances in their homes, and these families of low and moderate income need assistance in budgeting their limited resources so that they do not become delinquent in their rent payments. Social problems from vandalism and drugs to unemployment and family difficulties exist in these developments and must be dealt with.

There is a need for funds for community buildings and adequate recreational space, equipment and programming; for Homemaker Services and Day Care centers and for good, uncrowded schools. All these services are expensive and at the present time there is no financial or program commitment from the federal, state or local governments to move significantly on this vital area of the "housing problem."

Local agencies cannot look to the Community Chest or public funding sources for such monies at this time, but must turn to foundations, whose resources are limited, to assemble the funds to demonstrate both the need for, and the methods of, developing this necessary range of services.

If there is a bright spot in all this, what on occasion appears to be a sea of troubles, it is that more and more of the residents of these developments realize that they must share the responsibility with management for finding solutions to these problems. Constructive tenant councils are springing up and a dialogue with management, sponsor, police, the schools and other service agencies has developed which has already produced some beneficial results.

Over the years ACTION-Housing, Inc., has devoted a significant amount of its efforts towards developing and implementing programs that attempt to deal with the human problems of housing in the community and in the home itself. It has been and continues to be extremely difficult to raise necessary money for these programs, but the need becomes more urgent with each additional housing unit development we sponsor.

C. East Hills Park

Wracked by financial difficulties, East Hills Park is probably one of the most complex subsidized housing developments in the city.

It has problems that seem almost unconquerable and possibilities that, to many, are truly thrilling.

Right now, the 326-unit rental portion of the development, known as Second East Hills, is not paying its mortgage because there simply isn't enough money.

Owned by ACTION-Housing, the Section 221D-3 development's financial resources have been drained by vacancies, rent delinquencies, vandalism and security problems.

"The biggest problem there was security," said William Farkas, ACTION's executive director since December.

This security problem manifested itself in several ways—families moved out, or lived unhappily with fear. Kids—there are more than 800 of them there—loafed around or worse, pulled fire alarms almost nightly and constantly vandalized the entire development.

"At one point our bills for broken windows alone were $1,500 a month," Farkas said.

There were private security guards on duty, but until last February when ACTION set up a communications system, there was no way a resident could get in touch with them.

And according to Earl Chandler, a resident and chairman of the East Hills Community Council recreation committee, before January, the guards were primarily guarding Third East Hills, the final phase of the project which was then being completed and is just now being rented. That, he said, just didn't work.

Added Barbara Ramsey, another resident and former chairman of the council:

"The security makes a lot of difference. We had a lot of robberies up here, and a lot of the robberies weren't coming from outside.

"Now they [robbers] are not as active, now that they know you can get service in two or three seconds."

Rod Benner, a social work graduate student who worked in East Hills for a year, believed that solving the security problem was the key to making a dent in the other varied dilemmas East Hills was and still is facing.

"First you have to have a safe community," he said. "If people are afraid to come out at night, you really can't accomplish anything.

"Unless that problem is solved, you can't begin to do something creative."

The solution turned out to be relatively straightforward. With the advent of a stepped-up security force armed with communications equipment, crime dropped by two thirds in just a month and has been holding at that level ever since.

The financial problems, which were compounded by the security problems, are considerably more complicated.

The vacancy rate reached 12 per cent at one point and rent delinquencies plagued the development's budget. Added to that were soaring maintenance costs and rising utility rates, placing an additional drain on already-tight resources, Farkas said.

What it all meant was that ACTION-Housing, a Community Chest agency, simply could not meet the mortgage payments, and hasn't been able to since the beginning of the year.

The development is not officially in default, however. The U. S. Department of Housing and Urban Development (HUD) has given ACTION a grace period until the end of the year to see if the finances can be straightened out. If that works, this year's mortgage payments will be tacked on at the end of the 40 years.

But ACTION is trying to make the best of a pretty grim situation, and in conjunction with the Community Council, has embarked on an ambitious and exciting program which could prove to be the real turning point.

The program is a far-reaching one, ranging from beautification to recreation to community organization, economic development and adult education.

Beautification was the beginning.

At one point East Hills was a mess. Asked to describe the development at its worst, Mrs. Ramsey replied:

"Garbage is all over the driveway, cans are spilling over and rats are running around."

All that has changed. Garbage cans were replaced by ugly but effective dumpsters, and garbage is now picked up twice a week—a marked improvement over the previous once-a-week-or-less service.

That was the first step. Then this spring, thanks to contributions from the Pittsburgh Foundation, the Western Pennsylvania Conservancy and the Hillcrest Garden Club, ACTION and the Community Council planted hundreds of trees, shrubs and flowers.

"We gave away hundreds of rose bushes to residents," said ACTION's social services director Jon Zimmer. "The whole idea of beautification is that this community can get beautiful if they [the residents] put something in it."

Now saplings adorn hillsides and front yards, but it may be a few years before the landscaping effort matures enough to make a really visible difference.

"We gave away all those rose bushes and you still can hardly tell where they are," commented Gloria Chandler, Earl Chandler's wife and secretary of the Community Council.

Meanwhile, a unique demonstration parklet was completed by the Architects Workshop under another grant from the conservancy.

The main feature of the play area is an ingenious "jungle jim" which was constructed of old railroad ties, tires, wire spools and chains.

And there are always kids there, noted Mrs. Chandler. "They love it," she said.

An even more exciting endeavor funded by the conservancy is the creation of an adventure playground in undeveloped woodland within the East Hills boundaries.

Chandler explained that the playground will include a park shelter, tree houses and a natural zoo with wild animals now living in the area.

"There's a path carved out there now," said his wife. "You just can't believe that anything right here could look so much like the country."

On top of the physical improvements is a massive community program which the Chandlers are in the center of.

The recreation committee is running a drum and bugle corps,

with all the trappings, including 48 majorettes from the ages of two to 13, four little league teams and a day camp.

To help pay for equipment, the committee has set up a concession stand, which Chandler said is not "mostly a means of buying baseballs."

Shortly, too, the city should begin work on a large, long-promised playground, which will include tennis and basketball courts, a combined baseball-football field, a picnic area and a children's play area.

"It's more than just recreation," said Chandler of the program. "It's discipline. We have more than 500 kids in our programs. Before kids used to stand around on corners, throw things and pull fire alarms.

"Now we have benches. So now the kids don't stand on corners, they sit on corners—if they're not too tired out from our program."

In addition, the Chandlers are looking into some economic development programs—possibly turning an abandoned gas station into a training center for dropouts—and they have high hopes for an adult education program that is supposed to begin next fall.

"We had to build some kind of structure in terms of which way this place was going to go—was it going to go up or down," said Mrs. Ramsey.

"It could go either way, and we saw it going down for a while.

"Right now I think things are going to change, but that bad taste is still in people's mouths over how bad it had gotten. I think their concept of the place is going to change now," she said.

Her sentiments were echoed by Mrs. Chandler:

"Things are beginning to pick up."

ACTION has great hopes that the efforts of the recreation committee and the council will mark a turning point for East Hills.

"It's still tenuous whether we'll be able to solve the problems of rent delinquencies and vacancies," said Zimmer.

And there are other problems which are draining the finances.

Benner, the social work student, explained that the windows, including the glass sliding doors which open to small patios, were not designed to a standard size, which meant that all replacements must be special orders.

And, he said, the appliances were the ends of lots.

"When you need replacements, you have to send to Tennessee.

And you can't just replace a part, you have to replace the entire unit," he said, noting this applied to boilers, the heating system and plumbing too.

Farkas notes that when East Hills was built, maintenance costs were estimated at $6.64 a month for each unit. Today, the actual cost is $28.45—more than four times what was allotted.

And, he said, it is these hard economic facts which are draining six other ACTION-owned developments—all rehabilitated homes —which are also not paying their mortgages.

In Homewood, where there are five such troubled developments, the basic rents are $113 a month. Costs run between $135 and $140 a month.

For example, in 1969, the cost of gas was estimated at $6.76 per unit, and by 1973 that has jumped to $15.40 a month. Water has more than doubled—from $4.09 per unit in 1969 to $8.60 per unit now. Electricity has risen from $7.11 a month to $14.60.

Given in dollars, those costs may not seem so exorbitant. But multiply that by 12 months and more than 800 units of housing and it begins to look astronomical—almost $200,000 a year more than anticipated just in utilities.

So far, the seven ACTION developments—East Hills, five rehab projects in Homewood, and Clifton Park on the North Side—are the only 236 developments which are floundering financially here.

But, notes Farkas somewhat ominously, "We were the first. Maybe it's only a matter of time for the others."

Meanwhile, ACTION is applying as much energy and creativity as possible to rescue its ill-starred housing.

And perhaps most important, in places like East Hills there are residents who are committed to saving their community too.

"I moved here because I thought it was a good environment, and because no one had lived here before—it was new," said Mrs. Ramsey.

"I love it here in East Hills. I sincerely do."

Added Mrs. Chandler:

"People here will complain on one hand, but on the other hand they're not willing to move because it's the best place they've ever lived.

"And it will be a much better community when we get people involved and they begin to take pride in where they live," she said.

And this is happening:

"We're all trying to work together to make this a real flourishing community," said Chandler.

ACTION-Housing: Cora Street: An Experiment in Rehabilitation

Cora Street has not been an easy assignment. It lies in the very heart of the poorest area of Brushton, classified as a poverty neighborhood by the Mayor's Committee on Human Resources of the Federal Office of Economic Opportunity. However, Cora Street happens to be outside that portion of Homewood-Brushton designated an official urban renewal district by the city and federal governments after the publication of the "General Plan for Homewood-Brushton," a long-range planning study developed by City Planning, ACTION-Housing and the citizens themselves.

The Cora Street houses acquired for rehabilitation were 22 single-family, two-story row houses more than 60 years old, ten located on one side of the street, twelve directly opposite on the other side. Cora Street itself is short, level and runs between two through streets. Narrow and undistinguished, it follows a slight declivity in the terrain. The row dwellings are small and compact and the relative isolation and nondescript character of the street, together with its location in one of the poorest areas of the city, make it a difficult candidate for any kind of improvement. One realtor in the area said of it: "It is a sore spot, a cancerous spot; you name it and it takes place in that area."

This difficulty was one of the motivations for ACTION-Housing, however, when the executive director, Bernard E. Loshbough, began looking for an area in which to introduce rehabilitation work in 1965. The very impediments were the essence of the challenge. Slums are never pleasant or congenial places, and facing them realistically in the form of Cora Street made for a more widely applicable demonstration program. A typical, prototype area was needed if the results were to be transferable to other decaying neighborhoods. As Mr. Loshbough has observed: "If rehabilitation can be

ACTION-Housing, *Cora Street* (Pittsburgh, 1969), pp. 9, 51. Reprinted by permission of ACTION-Housing, Inc.

carried out successfully here, it can be done anywhere."

The 22 Cora Street brick row houses purchased by ACTION-Housing each contained a living room, two bedrooms, a kitchen, bathroom and basement. Their condition varied considerably. . . .

For twenty-two families Cora Street is a success. Twenty-two small houses that were dirty, deteriorating, cold and ill-equipped have become clean, snug, safe and modern. They are not luxurious, but they will meet anyone's standard for decent housing.

But what of the 40,000 other such units in Pittsburgh and the more than five million units across the country that are still in the deplorable condition that these 22 units were in a few months ago?

While Cora Street does not provide the whole solution to this program, it does define the obstacles that stand in the way of solving it. Out of the experiment comes that which was hoped for: the delineation of exactly what is needed to make the breakthrough to achieve massive rehabilitation in Pittsburgh and across the nation. . . .

The experience of the interviews of the prospective contractors and work with the contractor who was selected points up the lack of available contractors who are knowledgeable enough about rehabilitation and who are adequately financed and properly organized to handle the work. It would appear that the large contractors who have the financing are either inexperienced or not interested in rehabilitating while the small contractors who have some experience lack the financing and organization know-how.

We need not only a market demand for the services of a well-qualified, well-financed rehabilitation contracting industry; we must have a training program in the industry to provide the information and experience that these men require. Methods applied to new construction will not work on rehabilitation, and the contracting industry must research the problem and orient some of their members to this specialized work. The combined efforts of the private and public sectors are needed. Without them, rehabilitation cannot be carried out at all.

ACTION-Housing:
Neighborhood Urban Extension:
An Experiment in Citizen Participation

ACTION-Housing, as the Pittsburgh area's housing and renewal catalyst, has been concerned with plans and projects to vitalize urban life at all levels.

Pittsburgh is a metropolitan center of over two million persons. Since World War II, business and political leadership has been united in the world famous Renaissance effort to make Pittsburgh a modern and prosperous city. More than two billion dollars has been spent from public and private sources to redevelop downtown, clean the air, expand educational and cultural facilities, and carry out other large-scale improvements.

In 1957 ACTION-Housing was brought into being by Renaissance leadership to work for good housing in good neighborhoods. It is a broad-based, non-profit organization with strong business, labor, government, and civic support.

ACTION-Housing has evolved an overall program to bring Pittsburgh's housing and neighborhoods up to the high standards of Gateway Center, Mellon Square, and other achievements of the Pittsburgh Renaissance.

This program has moved forward in three areas: (1) increasing the supply of good new housing available to families of moderate income; (2) modernization of older housing and neighborhoods; and (3) developing a research base for future housing and urban renewal programs.

The neighborhood urban extension demonstration is the core of ACTION-Housing's program to modernize older neighborhoods. ACTION-Housing is already carrying on many activities essential to neighborhood urban extension, and is fully prepared to initiate the process in three Pittsburgh neighborhoods.

As in many older metropolitan areas, more than half of the people of Pittsburgh live in declining neighborhoods, most of which are possessed of considerable underutilized assets and great potential for modernization.

These neighborhoods have shabby housing, dirty and broken streets, abandoned cars, empty stores. But each also has thousands

ACTION-Housing, *A Plan of Operations for Neighborhood Urban Extension* (Pittsburgh, 1963), pp. 42–47. Reprinted by permission of ACTION-Housing, Inc.

of attractive homes, industrious people, and strong institutions.

All of these neighborhoods suffer from unemployment, violence in the streets, and family breakdown. But in each there are bright and eager children, dedicated teachers, and latent leadership.

The metropolitan area has 166,000 substandard homes; 10,000 more people move out of the area each year than move in; unemployment is double the national rate.

The City of Pittsburgh has lost 72,000 people in ten years—most of them members of younger families; the City in fact has 29% fewer persons 20–29 years old now than twelve years ago. Like most large central cities, Pittsburgh is in danger of becoming a reservoir of the old, the poor, the rich, and the minorities.

The ever expanding Renaissance effort—of which ACTION-Housing's program is very much a part—is aimed at ending deterioration, blight and unemployment, and at creating a vigorous urban center.

ACTION-Housing believes that alert citizens and vigorous officials, putting to work the resources of the Pittsburgh metropolitan center, can transform declining neighborhoods into living places that are orderly, attractive, and well-serviced, with a strong sense of community—and thus contribute substantially to the City's Renaissance.

Some of the available resources are: the departments of government; the Community Chest agencies; the colleges and universities; the public and parochial school systems; business and industry; communications media; law, health, architecture, and other professions; civic, veteran, social, ethnic, fraternal, and service organizations; libraries, planetaria, theatres, art galleries, symphony orchestras; churches, temples, religious institutions; and parks and playgrounds.

The Demonstration Defined
ACTION-Housing's neighborhood urban extension demonstration seeks to bring together the resources of the city and neighborhood people in a sustained effort of development at the neighborhood level—an effort that will make a substantial contribution to the creation of the new city.

The neighborhood is a piece of the city—it is the local community within the metropolitan community—the small place of human scale where government services most directly affect people. It is the center of family life, and especially of the child's education, and the level at which the citizen has strongest identity as an individual person.

Neighborhood urban extension will operate in the neighborhood as a dynamic, flexible, growing program, the basic objective of which is to develop good neighborhoods through the development of responsible people. In many ways, it is a prototype of a Domestic Peace Corps.

Through a neighborhood extension worker, the extension demonstration will seek to alert and equip citizens so that they are willing and able to take upon themselves *much* of the responsibility for developing their own neighborhoods.

In the words of an eminent educator, the chief aim of extension is to teach those who have a desire for information, and to create a desire for information in those who do not yet have the desire.[1]

Neighborhood urban extension will bring the universities, school systems, government departments, health and welfare agencies, and other resources of the City into a working relationship with neighborhood people.

Extension starts with a point of view about people. It is aimed at helping people help themselves. Extension in a neighborhood begins with the needs of the people, as they see them, or as they come to see them as education takes hold. Extension moves from the recognized problems, moving to a desire to do something about it, to an understanding of what caused the problem, to an understanding of what might be done to improve the condition, to a desire to take the necessary action, to their taking the action. Finally, having taken the necessary action and derived satisfaction from the new way of thinking and behaving, the new replace the old ways of thinking and doing.[2]

Neighborhood urban extension is an effective system for touching closely, motivating deeply, and educating constructively the mass of indifferent families. These are the families who do not come to meetings, who do not have an attitude of interest, but whose thousands of individual decisions day-by-day determine the life of a neighborhood.

Neighborhood urban extension is a flexible process to help vitalize urban neighborhoods of every kind, and to gain the responsible

1. Dr. Liberty Hyde Bailey, of Cornell University.
2. This paragraph paraphrases the words of Dr. Douglas Ensminger, the Ford Foundation's Representative in India.

participation of people from every level of society.

It is very much concerned with the transformation and involvement of the underutilized, the poor, the chronically unemployed, the discriminated against—"The Other America" of Michael Harrington.

As an important part of its program it will seek to help the underutilized help themselves to share fully the opportunities of the city.

Neighborhood urban extension, however, is not occupied exclusively with the underutilized.

It will enroll citizens rich, middle income, and poor, regardless of status. The talents of all are important to the building of the city. There are many citizens in every group in society who are cut off from the main stream, are alienated from decision making, and have potential that is not being used. It is concerned with gaining the participation of all of these.

Neighborhood Urban Extension Compared to Other Neighborhood Approaches

Most experienced urban affairs people are agreed that the neighborhood organization methods of past decades cannot do the job. There is a need for totally new approaches.

Every large city has its grey neighborhoods and in many cities attempts are being made to reverse decline and develop vital communities. Some of these approaches use methods that differ only in detail from traditional, ineffective methods. In addition to ACTION-Housing's extension approach, however, there are at least two other approaches which are employing imaginative new techniques, which have behind them substantial resources, and which stand out as worthy of attention. A comparison of these three approaches is helpful in understanding neighborhood urban extension.

There are both similarities and differences in the three approaches, all of which seek the same basic goal. ACTION-Housing believes all three should be given full opportunity to demonstrate their strengths and weaknesses, since neighborhood problems exist in endless variety and a variety of approaches probably are needed to solve them.

1. Industrial Areas Foundation Approach:
One of the three imaginative approaches is that of the Industrial Areas Foundation (IAF) now undergoing its severest test in the

Woodlawn Project in Chicago. IAF is a private, non-profit organization with headquarters in Chicago, receiving much of its financing from the Presbyterian and Roman Catholic churches.

Under the IAF approach, development of a neighborhood is initiated by a field worker from IAF who enters a neighborhood at the invitation of local groups, usually neighborhood churches.

The field worker uses frustration and injustice, crisis and conflict to rally neighborhood people against forces which are thought to impede their progress, forces which might be government, landlords, credit merchants, an expanding institution, and others.

IAF concentrates on the most deprived citizens to form a broad-based neighborhood organization with local leadership. The organization attacks the status quo and seeks to generate power to the point where it can control planning for the entire neighborhood, and demand and get what it wants from government.

It rejects many of the traditional concepts and methods of city planning and insists that neighborhood people work out their own destiny by hiring their own planners who do planning that is "an integral part of self-evident social and political reality, and must undertake the innovation of new techniques and procedures which directly address reality."[3]

IAF uses militant methods of neighborhood organization, adapting many of the techniques used in the civil rights struggle in the South, including the sit-in and mass picketing. As some observers point out, these methods were first used in militant labor and political protest movements.

The IAF philosophy is spelled out by its Executive Director:

> In the development of an organization for democratic citizen participation . . . resentments and dormant hostilities must be brought up to visible surface where they can become transformed into problems. . . .
> . . . A people do not break through their previous fatalism of submerged resentment and frustration into open problems which can be faced, and dealt with, until they have a mechanism, or a formula, for effectively coping with these problems. Since their only resource lies in their numbers, organization becomes the instrument for implementation of change and resolution of these problems.
> . . . There can be no darker or more devastating tragedy than the death of man's faith in himself, in his power to direct his future.[4]

3. Nicholas von Hoffman, Supervisor, Woodlawn Project of the Industrial Areas Foundation, Inc., Chicago, Illinois.
4. Saul Alinsky, Executive Director, Industrial Areas Foundation, Inc., Chicago, Illinois.

2. Community Agency Approach:

A second approach is that of a new kind of community agency, on whose boards both government and private agencies are represented; examples are: Action for Boston Community Development in Boston; Community Progress, Inc., in New Haven, Connecticut; Associated Agencies in Oakland, California, and Council for Community Advancement, Philadelphia.

These new agencies seek to have public and private resources and services better utilized and better coordinated at the neighborhood level; emphasis is placed on experimental activity which, when proven successful, can be permanently absorbed into governmental and private budgets and operations.

The Mayor of New Haven has described his city's program thus:

> New Haven is being renewed to promote social goals. Along with the rebuilding process, basic human needs are being tackled through relocation, homemaking, education, and housing programs. The time is now at hand to expand these efforts and to put into effect a comprehensive program which goes to the root of the city's social problems . . . . the people of our city will have the chance for much greater personal achievement. The great strength of the program is its focus on self-improvement. Services are but means to ends, and the ends are the ones people select for themselves.[5]

The Oakland program is described as follows in the city's proposal to the Ford Foundation:

> This proposal . . . is the outcome of an extensive process of community planning which was initiated and has been facilitated by the City Manager of Oakland. It represents what our community and its institutions consider to be promising approaches to problems—approaches which the agencies concerned are capable of carrying out and which the community will support. . . .
> The problems . . . are not structured as the agencies are structured. Agency operations must, therefore, be reshaped to fit the shape of problems; unilateral and uncoordinated actions by a variety of agencies are not only inefficient, they can be an active cause of disorganization. To achieve coherence in the community, administrative and policy coherence among the community's major institutions is essential.[6]

3. ACTION-Housing's Neighborhood Urban Extension Approach; A Comparison:

ACTION-Housing's extension approach is similar to Industrial

5. R. C. Lee, Mayor, City of New Haven, in "Opening Opportunities," booklet, April, 1962.
6. Proposal to The Ford Foundation for a Program of Community Development, Oakland, California, 1961.

Areas Foundation's in that it leaves largely to neighborhood people the determination of their own neighborhood goals, and decisions on what resources of the city can assist them in developing a revitalized community. It offers them no direct services to solve their problems—but only a process for identifying and utilizing services largely on their own.

ACTION-Housing's approach differs from that of the Industrial Areas Foundation in that it does not take a belligerent attitude toward government, but seeks to organize a joint effort involving neighborhood people, government, business, universities, public and private school systems, and all the other major interests of the urban community.

The approach of ACTION-Housing is similar to the approach of Action for Boston Community Development in Boston; Community Progress, Inc., in New Haven; Associated Agencies in Oakland, and Council for Community Advancement, Philadelphia, in this seeking to foster a cooperative effort of citizens and urban resources. The ACTION-Housing approach would seem to differ from these in that it offers neighborhood people a large planning and decision making role.

Civil Disorder, 1968

I. Preliminary Findings of the Task Force
—Like the racial disturbances in 113 other American cities, the disorders in Pittsburgh were triggered by the assassination of Dr. Martin Luther King on April 4. The first incident, according to police records, took place at 11:30 P.M., four hours after the news of the King murder was broadcast. It consisted of the fire-bombing of property in the 2400 block of Bedford Avenue in the Hill and was quickly followed by window smashing incidents on Watt Street and Centre Avenue in the Hill.

—The disturbances which followed resulted in the death of one Homewood woman, who died weeks after the disturbance from

City of Pittsburgh, Mayor's Special Task Force on Civil Disturbances, *Progress Report* (1968), pp. 2–6.

burns suffered after being struck by a fire bomb. Other consequences were:

—33 firemen and 12 policemen injured.

—505 fires throughout the City, but concentrated principally in
the Hill.

—926 arrests. This included 199 juveniles, 337 persons charged
with felonies and 589 persons charged with misdemeanors or
summary offenses.

—The Fire Bureau estimated property damage from fires at
$620,660. But the loss of goods through theft, the loss of trade
during the disturbance, the property abandoned in the critical
areas, the cost of police overtime, the cost of deploying State
Police and National Guard troops—easily boost the total cost
to the community in the millions of dollars.

—Most of the participants in the burning and rock-throwing stages
were youth. They were joined by older persons in the stage that followed the initial outbreaks, involving looting and further property
damage.

—While the task force has found no evidence to date that the Pittsburgh disturbances were part of a national "conspiracy," the task
force did note a similarity of events and reactions in all cities affected—prior to, during and following the disturbances. The severity of damage was not as great here as in some other cities.

—The task force did find that, at least initially, the burning and
looting were highly selective. Signs were quickly placed on "protected" establishments in the Hill and in Homewood. The printing
of placards, the making of fire bombs, the selectivity in establishments chosen for destruction—all of these point to some advance planning and preparation. The task force can only theorize
that Pittsburgh was a target city for some form of action during the
summer of 1968, but that the timetable was advanced by the tragic
King assassination.

—Also, there was evidence of growing unrest in some sections of the
City and sporadic incidents prior to the April disturbance. It is recognized that there are legitimate social and economic grievances in
these areas and much reason for despair. But some of the agitation
came from self-appointed leaders, opportunists, and the other types
of activists who single out existing institutions and democratic pro-

cesses as the targets for their venom and personal ambitions. Incidents of fire-bombing and looting have continued since the April disturbances and must not be tolerated.

—The behavior of police and firemen—their restraint and patience in what was a new experience for many of the men on the force—deserves special commendation. But, as the disturbance progressed, it became readily apparent the situation would get completely out of hand without a massive show of force, a curfew, a prohibition against the gathering of crowds, and restrictions on the sale of alcoholic beverages and firearms. There were no confirmed reports of sniping or the discharge of firearms by those causing the disturbances.

—Like the disturbances in scores of other cities—in 1968 and in years past—most of the witnesses interviewed by the task force stated that the seeds of discontent in ghetto areas encompass years of frustration born and bred in poverty, poor housing, deteriorated neighborhoods and continued discrimination in Pittsburgh and in the nation's other urban areas.

—None of the present governmental programs and governmental resources, or the business and social, educational and health programs, are geared to bring immediate and massive response to the chronic and overwhelming needs of ghetto residents, white and nonwhite. Nor is there any prolonged commitment of finances and talent to their problems. In the judgment of the task force, this void has created the climate for resentment, anger, despair, and has opened the door for the exploitation of the poor and the young and the black in the ghettos.

—Most of the governmental and non-governmental programs are underfunded, lack flexibility, involve a dissipation and duplication of existing efforts—and, for the most part, the agencies operating these programs are inadequately staffed.

—The task force recognizes the findings of sociologists and others that the Negro today is seeking identity, self-determination, and the opportunity to build pride and self-respect for the individual. But the Pittsburgh Negro community does not have the resources to do this task alone. According to a recent survey by the Business and Job Development Corporation, a private Pittsburgh agency created to promote business opportunities and business know-how for Negroes, the assets of the 39 largest Negro-owned and managed companies in Pittsburgh total $1,425,000. These firms employ a total of 268 men and women.

In the wake of the April disturbances in Pittsburgh:

—Many small businesses in the ghettos are at a loss to determine how and whether they can recover damages and whether they should permanently close their establishments.

—There are increasing reports that, in addition to prior cancellations, insurance policies will not be renewed in the ghetto areas, making the task of rebuilding and recovery that much more difficult.

—Some merchants and property owners have reported receiving threats of violence, have reported being coerced and, in some cases, confronted with extortion demands by those using the wake of the disturbances as a veil and screen for criminal activities.

—Police report that there has been an increase of crime within the City—principally burglaries, robberies, narcotics, and, in a few instances, the assault of persons.

—Racial tensions have increased, further widening the gap between those sympathetic to the plight of the poor and those willing and in a position to help.

—The disturbances have caused a number of business organizations, civic and church groups to offer their assistance; but, in the confusion that currently exists, no one can be sure help will be accepted or that it will have any meaningful effect in improving conditions or changing attitudes.

—Repeated incidents in various parts of the City and elsewhere in the nation have spread uncertainty and fear within and outside the ghetto areas.

II. Preliminary Conclusions of the Task Force

1. The highest priority of local government must be directed at the preservation of order and the protection of the innocent victims of disorder (and in the ghettos they are often in the vast majority). Full and prompt punishment should be meted out to those convicted of crimes, including acts of violence perpetuated during and following the April disorders.

It is the judgment of the task force that unless order is fully preserved, unless morale is lifted and confidence restored in the security and safety of the community, the turmoil will persist and no meaningful, orderly, and rational physical, economic or social progress can occur.

2. Concurrent with increased security measures, this City and this region must muster an effort—unprecedented in this City's history—to bring about immediate, visible, and tangible change which can be produced in a matter of months in three principal areas: the Hill District, Homewood Brushton, the Manchester District of the North Side. These interim steps will have to be financed locally—in large measure—and will require that the City and the State governments divert existing appropriations to assemble sites for housing low- and moderate-income families, to increase business and job opportunities for Negroes, and improve the environment through concentrated neighborhood development programs. In the process, communication must be strengthened with the inhabitants of these areas and with the agencies involved in these programs.

3. For the longer term—but starting now—a mechanism must be developed to bring together the many diverse groups and agencies for critical appraisal of their current activities and programs and for a reordering of their priorities and resources so that the maximum impact can be achieved from every public and private dollar spent to improve the lives of residents in the City's ghetto areas. This analysis in depth should cover all governmental agencies, the major corporate firms furnishing employment in the metropolitan area, foundations, civic contributors, educational, health and welfare groups. The results should be a long-term commitment of specific and unduplicated services.

Civil Disorder and Neighborhood Power
by James Cunningham

Why have Pittsburgh neighborhood people been so frustrated, so cut off from a legitimate part in making the decisions that affect their lives?

"The Need for Neighborhood Power" (Testimony, Mayor's Special Task Force on Civil Disorders), reprinted in *Pittsburgh Point*, June 20, 1968, p. 6.

It is necessary to look first at the Pittsburgh past to understand its present, and to begin to find an answer to the question of frustration. A community is a product of its history.

Beginning in the 17th Century settlers in this area complained of lack of representation in the state legislature, of discrimination in taxes, and of corrupt court officials. The result in the 1790's was a series of civil disorders in these parts known as the Whiskey Rebellion.

In the 19th Century the area became industrialized and from 1830 on attempts were made by workingmen to organize for a share in the flow of wealth and in the decisions to shape the growing city. Continually their efforts were beaten back, resulting in such well-known civil disorders as the Railroad Riot of 1877, and the Homestead Strike of 1892, when corporate power and government groups crushed the workingman and kept him crushed for decades.

The result of this lack of power in working people was that business leadership largely controlled the shaping of life in Pittsburgh. As historians have pointed out, this led by the early 20th Century to the mutilation and pollution of the physical environment, as factory development received a high priority, and housing, health and social welfare a low priority.

The famous Pittsburgh Survey of 1907–08, financed by the Russell Sage Foundation, found that no city in history had ever generated such industrial wealth, and used so little of it to give its people a good human life.

Neighborhood conditions worsened. Pittsburgh in the early part of this century had the highest death rate in the nation. In 1928, the Pittsburgh Housing Association reported many Pittsburgh neighborhoods marked by littered streets, wrecked houses, overflowing garbage cans, and general municipal neglect.

In the 1930's there was, at last, successful organization of the steelworkers and substantial improvement in wages and working conditions for a sizable number of citizens. This breakthrough, however, remained largely limited to economic wealth produced here. The spreading of decision making, however, matters for most people.

Rule by a limited business and government leadership continued unabated from the founding of the city in the mid-17th Century right up until the beginning of the Pittsburgh Renaissance in 1945.

When this great opportunity to improve living conditions finally came, there was only one way known to do it—by an elite.

The Renaissance has been a bold program, but it was conceived without any deep involvement of neighborhood people. It has been a repeat of past history. The highways, airport, factory sites needed by industry have been produced, but the neighborhoods have been little improved. The argument has been made that commercial, industrial, and institutional redevelopment results in jobs for workers and a strengthened tax base. This is the traditional trickle-down theory of economics. It is highly paternalistic. It is questionable economics. It leaves the people as powerless as ever.

History has momentum. It shapes the present. To test the legacy this history has left us, we need only examine the city's four main public decision making bodies as they stand today. These are the School Board, the Urban Redevelopment Authority, the Planning Commission, and City Council.

The School Board presently has 14 members. Four are professional men, five are businessmen, and four are housewives, mostly the wives of businessmen or professional men, and one is president of a union. It is an elite board. It is twice removed from the public. Its members are appointed, and the appointers are judges of the Common Pleas Court, many of whom run without opposition. Much of the mess our schools are now in probably could have been avoided if we had School Board members who are responsive and rooted in the neighborhoods.

The Urban Redevelopment Board presently has five members. One is the Mayor. One is a member of the City Council. One is a senior staff member from the Board of Education. One is a retired vice president of U.S. Steel, and one is a vice-president of the Mellon Bank. A solid elite group, all appointed.

The Planning Commission presently has nine members. Two are bankers. Two are architects. Two are public officials. Two are heads of major downtown corporations. And one is a university official. A solid elite group, all appointed.

City Council: This body is elected and does contain some neighborhood representatives. But, all its members are elected at large and none legally represents a district section of the city. All its members are from one party organization and there are no regular voices of dissent. Moreover, four of the last five new members joining the council came on by appointment—to fill vacancies. To run as an incumbent, of course, is of enormous advantage, and helps cut out possible opposition. The elective quality of council has deteriorated.

Another major barrier cutting neighborhood people out of power is the election practices in the city. Intimidation and irregularities are standard, traditional practices. Hundreds of volunteers who worked in campaign this past spring and a year ago found illegal and unethical practices so widespread as to render the democratic process inoperable in large sections of the city.

I make a modest proposal for two beginning steps toward ending the powerlessness of the neighborhoods of Pittsburgh, and thereby toward the removal of a major cause of civic unrest:

I. Divide the city into a number of neighborhood districts, with neighborhood people themselves doing the dividing. Each of these neighborhood districts to elect one member of the School Board, the Urban Redevelopment Authority, the Planning Commission and City Council, and other bodies to be determined. So that the city-wide view as well as the neighborhood view would be represented on these decision making bodies, each should retain its present number of at-large seats except the School Board which should be reduced to nine at-large seats to be filled by some democratic system.

II. Provide for open, fair and competitive elections by:
1. prohibiting all electioneering within polling places and within 100 feet of polling places.
2. requiring appointment by the courts from nominees proposed by neighborhood organizations of an able and objective citizen to oversee the voting in each polling place, such official to be unpaid, and not to be resident of the ward in which he serves. He should have full and final authority over conduct in and about the polling place, and be the only person authorized to assist handicapped voters in casting their ballots.

With neighborhood people given real power, that power can be harnessed to the constructive task of local decision making rather than to the violent struggle against oppression. With the gaining of local power, the neighborhood becomes responsible to itself. It can use the tool of authority—law—to advance its prosperity. We cannot have an orderly city when the main resources of neighborhood people are demonstrations, violence and civil disorders. We need to open up new orderly courses through the election process.

Ethnic Discontent

"What we want," said Paul Deac, "is justice."

"The white poor, specifically the ethnic poor, have been direly neglected by officialdom. They have been deliberately excluded from the benefits of the war on poverty. We intend to see that justice is done for these people too."

Deac, of Hungarian descent, is executive vice president and director of the National Confederation of American Ethnic Groups. He spoke from the Pittsburgh office of the organization, which consists of 67 groups with 18.6 million members. Despite its size, however, the group has never exerted much political influence.

All that, he says, is changing, and changing because of one fact. "There are," he said, "many, many more white poor than black poor. In the Pittsburgh area there are twice as many poor whites as blacks. The government and the foundations have forgotten the white poor. We intend to make them remember."

They intend to make them remember:

• The wrinkled old Slovak woman who spends much of her time cleaning and sweeping in her Southside home and caring for the geraniums in flower pots on the window sills. She lives on a $60 a month pension.

• The Croatian railroad laborer from the Northside who supports a family of six on an income of less than $5000 a year. His oldest children are nearing college age, but he cannot afford to pay for schooling out of his salary, and spiraling interest rates make it impossible for him to get a loan.

• The Polish youth who has just started to work in the mills. Like his cousin, he hopes to make enough money in half a year's work to attend a semester of college. That way, he can finish in eight years. A good high school student, he applied for a scholarship. "They told

Mike Brourman, "Ethnic Poor of City Organize to End Neglect," *Pittsburgh Post-Gazette,* September 15, 1969. Reprinted by Permission.

me that for this year I was the wrong color," he said bitterly.

These are not isolated instances. They are examples of what Deac, like President Nixon, calls "the forgotten American," and there are millions like them throughout the nation and many thousands right here in Pittsburgh.

Robert C. Wood, former under secretary of the Department of Housing and Urban Development (HUD), tried to define the "forgotten American" with statistics:

"He is a white, employed male . . . works regularly, steadily, dependably wearing a blue collar . . . lives in the gray area fringes of a central city or in a close-in or very far-out cheap suburban subdivision . . . 91 per cent have no education beyond high school."

Father Louis Hohos has been pastor of St. Matthew's Church, a Slovak parish on the Southside, for 21 years. He has his own definition:

"These people never make the headlines as far as crime is concerned. They are peace-loving, orderly, respectful and try to obey the laws. They have worked hard for what little they have and they don't want to see it destroyed. They are industrious, honest, good citizens. They are interested in their own welfare and want to see they get a fair shake. Above all they want the same consideration as any other minority."

Right now they don't believe they're getting that consideration.

According to statistics of Community Action Pittsburgh, the local anti-poverty agency, 69 per cent of the city's poor are white.

Many of them are second and third generation descendants of Eastern and Southern European immigrants—Polish, Slovak, Italian, Hungarian, Greek, Ukrainian, Croatian, Serbian, and others—groups which make up 65 per cent of the city's overall population.

They are openly bitter with the way the war on poverty is being fought:

"We get practically nothing," said J. L. Lesniewicz of the Ethnic Foundation. "Everything is going to the Negroes. I don't deny they need help, but so do we."

The theme of neglect is echoed everywhere, with most of the complaints centered on CAP and the local Model Cities program.

CAP, although not disputing the fact that 69 per cent of the city's poor are white, admits that 79 per cent of those receiving benefits from its more than 20 community programs (budgeted at nearly $6 million a year) are black.

Aside from a multi-service program for the aged in an integrated senior citizens' apartment building in East Liberty-Garfield, the only CAP program located in a primarily white area is Lawrenceville Youth Leadership.

It had the lowest budget of any CAP program for 1968–69, $8,374, of which $7,974 went for administrative costs and only $400 was allocated for services.

Robert Rapp, public information director of CAP, admits it is not a very impressive record. But he denies a deliberate program of exclusion. "Most white people exclude themselves from the program," he said.

Model Cities is currently functioning in one area where a majority of the citizens are white—Oakland. There the program has been riddled with dissension, as citizens have charged that their ideas went unheeded in the final Model Cities report, which they said was geared to the primarily black Hill District.

William Pendleton, a black, was director of the Oakland Model Cities area, although the population is overwhelmingly white (90 per cent in the 1960 census). He was fired last July, shortly after the dispute became public.

Model Cities Director Carl Payne said Pendleton was dismissed for insubordination and incompetence. Pendleton charges he was fired for standing up for the rights of the citizens of Oakland.

Another primarily white area, Polish Hill, withdrew entirely from Model Cities in the summer of 1968. A leader of the Polish Hill Civic Association said the move was taken because "the original Model Cities concept of community action was never put into practice. We were being subjugated to black power and militancy."

Particularly exasperating to community leaders was the fact that all four of their recommendations for the area's representative on the citizens' governing board were turned down by Model Cities leaders.

All were considered "educated and fully qualified" by the community. One was a high school teacher, two were graduates of Duquesne University, and the fourth was a real estate agent. All were Polish, as are the majority of residents of Polish Hill (hence the name).

For various reasons all were turned down. The real estate agent allegedly because his business might provide a conflict of interest. Model Cities then designated a representative—a woman real estate agent from outside Polish Hill. Her business apparently did not conflict.

"We were completely exasperated," said a community leader. On July 29, 1968, Polish Hill pulled out of Model Cities.

The community itself is perhaps typical of the poor white areas of Pittsburgh. Most of the residents earn less than $6,000 a year—that is, those who are working. The unemployment rate is high.

The young, when they can, leave. Only the old stay by choice. "It's sure death if we don't get help," said one leader.

"We want to get the community on its feet. We want better lighting, better streets and better garbage collection. We need recreation facilities, a library, a health center."

"We're striving hard. We're looking for help. So far we've mostly been groping—looking for someone who'll help."

The National Confederation of American Ethnic Groups, headed by Paul Deac, intends to see to it that areas like Polish Hill don't have to "grope" any more.

They intend to help.

Ethnicity and Voting
by Michael Margolis and George H. Foster

Ever since Al Smith's presidential candidacy in 1928, the Democratic party has been the home of "nonestablishment" ethnic minorities. Smith won over large segments of the Irish, Italian, Polish, and eastern European communities in urban areas in the East, areas which had previously voted Republican. Franklin D. Roosevelt consolidated Smith's white ethnic vote, and he won over the blacks, forming the so-called "Roosevelt coalition" of working-class minority peoples, a majority coalition that has maintained the Democratic party's numerically dominant position to this day.

To a large extent, Pittsburgh politics not only followed these national trends but exaggerated them. Between 1928 and 1936 party

"The Ethnic Vote in Pittsburgh," *Pitt* (Summer, 1973), pp. 25–29.

registration in Pittsburgh shifted from a massive Republican majority (fewer than 5 per cent registered Democratic in 1929) to a solid Democratic majority (56 per cent in 1936). Since 1932 not one Republican has been elected as mayor or to serve on council. And today Democratic registration has grown to 80 per cent of the voting population while Republican registration has shrunk to under 20 per cent.

Under David Lawrence's leadership the Democrats fashioned a political machine of textbook proportions. Built upon a solid base of city and county patronage coupled with influence over state and federal patronage, the machine provided jobs and services to thousands of Pittsburghers for whom the depressed private economy could provide none. As the economic situation improved, machine politics provided a means for members of ethnic minorities, who might be discriminated against in private industry, to achieve positions of responsibility and influence. Among other developments, a Nationalities Committee was formed to keep close contact with the various ethnic groups which generally voted Democratic. Through these contacts candidates were recruited for party and public office; funds were raised for electoral activities; and jobs, policy, and campaign information was distributed. The party also worked to protect the insurance programs of ethnic beneficial societies from encroachment by establishment-controlled insurance companies. Post-World War II, the party helped organize the anti-communist activities of eastern European ethnic organizations. The only major ethnic group that the Nationalities Committee did not deal with was the blacks. Contacts with the black community were maintained through the regular party ward organizations.

Times, however, have changed. Decreased immigration, increased affluence, mass education, mass-media communication, and mass transportation have all contributed to a decline in the importance of ethnic-group politics. Decreased immigration has meant a lessening of direct contact with citizens whose language, customs, and concerns derive directly from first-hand experience in the "old country." Increased affluence has down-graded the importance of political patronage jobs as major sources of income for minorities. Mass education coupled with affluence and mass communication have produced standardizations of language, dress, and everyday living habits, which make distinguishing all but racial characteristics increasingly difficult. Finally, mass transportation has tended to break up many ethnic neighborhoods, scattering erstwhile ghetto residents among the amorphous suburban masses. In 1970 the Census Bureau officially recognized the decline of ethnicity as a central concern when it reviewed the enumeration of ethnic background (excepting race) from the normal 100 per cent to only a sample count of 20 per cent.

Pittsburgh's Democratic party has reflected this trend. The Nationalities Committee ceased to function in the late 1960s. Ticket balancing—the fine art of maintaining a fair distribution of offices among ethnic groups on party-endorsed tickets—remains a major concern, but, increasingly, Democratic party endorsements have involved other considerations, such as party faction of the candidates. Prior to the recent spring primary, for instance, party factions could not agree upon an endorsement for the "Jewish seat" on City Council, from which Councilman Edgar Michaels is retiring. As a result, the endorsement went to former state representative William Coyne, an Irish Catholic. As well, when ethnicity has been considered, endorsements have sometimes been based on inaccurate information. As an illustration we can point to the experience of County Treasurer (and professor of political science) Edward Cooke. Cooke, an Irish Catholic, received his 1967 party endorsement for Treasurer in part because party leaders saw him as perfectly matched to popular conceptions of a fiscally responsible public executive—a solid, white, Anglo-Saxon Protestant!

Traditional ethnic politics may be declining, but the political importance of ethnicity has by no means disappeared. Political scientists such as Edgar Litt, Michael Parenti, and Raymond Wolfinger have argued that ethnic minorities have been "acculturated" but not "assimilated" into American society. Acculturation means the acceptance of the dominant norms and values of the society by minority groups into the social structure so that members of the groups are no longer distinguishable from other citizens. The above-mentioned political scientists point out that powerful ethnic organizations still remain viable; that social contacts within ethnic groups stretch beyond neighborhoods; that ethnic identity remains strong among most white ethnic minorities and is indeed growing stronger among blacks. Complete economic assimilation has not occurred. In comparison to their proportions in the population, members of America's ethnic minorities are greatly under-represented among the directorates of America's major corporations. America's ethnic minorities, these authors contend, have not succeeded in penetrating the white, Anglo-Saxon, Protestant elite. Some ethnic groups actively resist assimilation.

In the analysis that follows we shall look at some of the contemporary characteristics of ethnic politics in Pittsburgh. We will focus upon the extent to which the Democratic party continues to hold the primary allegiances of non-establishment ethnic minorities. The data we shall examine consist of survey samples of Pittsburgh voters and party officials collected by university students in the years 1970 through 1972, official election returns by district for the election of November 1972, and the 1970 census-tract data for the City of Pittsburgh.

The political parties elect a committeeman and a committeewoman in each of the 423 districts in the city. Table 1 presents the ethnic composition of these party officials according to country of origin, race, and religion. As can be clearly seen, the make-up of the two parties corresponds rather closely to the traditional expectations. Republicans draw most heavily from the "establishment" ethnic groups—British, Germans, and Protestants. The Democrats are more heavily composed of Italians, Poles, blacks, Catholics, and Jews than are the Republicans, and the Irish make up about equal proportions of each party.

When we turn to the composition of party supporters, however, the picture changes rather dramatically. The Democratic party no longer over-represents the newer immigrant groups. Every major white ethnic group, not just the British and the Germans, is found in the Republican party in numbers larger than its proportions in the general population. In contrast, only the blacks are found in the Democratic party in numbers considerably disproportionate to their number in the general population. Blacks, who comprise 21 per cent of the population, comprise 27 per cent of the Democratic party supporters, but only 4 per cent of the Republican supporters.

Glancing down at religion we find some related phenomena. To begin with, Catholics, who comprise most of the non-establishment white minorities, are now distributed in each party in proportions nearly equal to their numbers in the population. Although Protestants tend to be over-represented in the Republican party, the breakdown of Protestant denominations indicates that this distribution is by no means uniform. Presbyterians, a higher-status denomination, account for nearly all the over-representation of Protestants in the Republican party. On the other hand, Baptists, many of whom are black, are the only Protestant group which is over-represented among the Democrats.

TABLE 1—ETHNIC CHARACTERISTICS OF PITTSBURGH DISTRICT PARTY OFFICIALS 1971

Country or Race	by Percentage	
	Democrats	Republicans
Great Britain	5	13
Ireland	13	14
Germany	13	20
Italy	13	8
Poland	8	4
Black	24	19
Other	24	22
Total	100%	100%
	(N = 158)	(N = 140)

Religion	Democrats	Republicans
Catholic	51	45
Protestant	33	47
Jewish	8	3
Other, No Preference	8	5
	100%	100%
	(N = 158)	(N = 140)

The data in Table 2 must be interpreted with some caution. Even though blacks are the only large ethnic group which is found in disproportionately large numbers in the Democratic party, we need only percentage the table horizontally to affirm that a majority of every ethnic group examined (except Presbyterians) is to be found in the Democratic party. Nevertheless, the data are suggestive of a potential loss for the Democrats of traditional ethnic supporters like Italians and Irish; the data also suggest a developing white-versus-black polarization among the parties. An examination of the 1972 election return will amplify this point.

Table 3 presents the correlation coefficients between the percentage of the vote received by candidates George McGovern, Robert Casey, and Grace Sloan, and the percentage of various ethnic groups found in Pittsburgh's 423 voting districts in the November 1972 general election. The correlation coefficients comparing the votes of the candidates with one another's votes are also included.[1] Correlation coefficients range from a maximum of +1.00 to a minimum of −1.00.

The high positive correlations among candidates McGovern, Casey, and Sloan indicate that in large part their votes increased and decreased together, an apparent manifestation of party voting. The table also shows that the votes of all three candidates correlate positively with Democratic registration, although McGovern's vote shows the weakest relationship here.

As we continue down the table, however, we find a pattern of correlations analogous to the make-up of the party supporters found in Table 2. The votes of all three Democratic candidates are negatively correlated with the percentage of every white ethnic group. (The only exception is a slight positive correlation between Grace Sloan's vote and the percentage Polish in each district.) Furthermore, the magnitudes of the correlations correspond closely to the general degree to which whites are over-represented in the Republican party. The highest negative correlations, for example, occur between the candidates' votes and the percentages British and German, followed by negative correlations with the percentages Irish and Italian. Only the Poles show correlations that are near zero. In contrast, blacks are the only ethnic group whose percentages in the voting districts correlate positively with the votes received by all three Democratic candidates. Over-all, the Democratic percentage of the two-party vote decreases as the percentage of white ethnics increases; this same percentage increases only as the percentage of blacks in the districts increases.

Table 4 translates these correlation coefficients into percentages of the vote received.

The mean percentage of the two-party vote received by each candidate in the 211 districts with the greatest proportions of each ethnic group is compared with the mean percentage received in the 211 districts with the smallest proportions of each ethnic group. The figures clearly illustrate how Democratic candidates received their

1. Percentages of ethnic groups are calculated from the 1970 census, which counts only first- and second-generation white ethnics, approximately 25 per cent of the white population. Religion of citizens is not included in the census.

greatest shares of the two-party vote from blacks and their smallest shares from whites. It is also clear that McGovern received a smaller percentage of the vote than the other two candidates, and that his vote fluctuated the most, indicative of the stronger correlations between the McGovern vote and district ethnic composition. The figures also show a rear uniformity in the mean percentages of votes received from white ethnic groups by each candidate. The only real contrast is in the percentage received from blacks versus the percentage received from whites.

The data we have presented here accord with the impression that traditional ethnic politics is declining in Pittsburgh. The contrasts between white ethnic groups with regard to party support and party voting appear to be considerably smaller than the over-all contrast between blacks and whites regarding these phenomena. Before we can definitely state that these data indicate a trend in Pittsburgh politics, however, several questions must be answered.

First of all, the data we have examined thus far have revolved around partisan choice. It is reasonable to ask, therefore, what the effects of ethnicity might be once party labels have been removed.

For this question, the 1972 election provides some answers. The ballot included a non-partisan election of eleven members to the Pittsburgh Home Rule Commission, an election in which a diversified field of 42 candidates ran. Examination of the correlations between the percentage of the total vote cast for the candidates in each district with the percentage of the ethnic groups in the districts indicates that ethnicity played an important role only for those candidates who were otherwise unknown to the voters. Councilman Robert Rade Stone, for example, is very active among Serbian ethnic organizations. Nonetheless, he showed only minimum correlations (.16 or less) with eastern European ethnic groups. In fact, his largest correlation with any ethnic group was $-.31$ with blacks. Similarly, other well-known commission candidates, such as former police commissioners David Craig and John Bingler, also showed low correlations with every ethnic group examined.

Less well-known candidates, on the other hand, showed much higher correlations with ethnic groups. Votes for Edith Abdullah, a successful black candidate, correlated .63 with percentage black in each district. The vote for Edward T. Ignaski, unsuccessful candidate receiving only 11,800 votes, nonetheless correlated at .67 with the percentage Polish in each district. Similarly, the votes of two unsuccessful Jewish candidates, Joseph Lenchner and Philip David Marcus, correlated at .64 and .76 respectively with the percentage

TABLE 2—ETHNIC CHARACTERISTICS OF PITTSBURGHERS   1970–72[2]

Country or Race	Democrats	Independents	Republicans	Entire Population
	by Percentage			
Great Britain	7	15	14	9
Ireland	8	18	11	10
Germany	16	15	26	18
Italy	9	9	14	10
Poland	10	3	11	9
Black	27	15	4	21
Other	19	19	13	17
Not Ascertained	4	6	7	6
Total	100%	100%	100%	100%
	(N=294)	(N=34)	(N=85)	(N=413)

Religion	Democrats	Independents	Republicans	Entire Population
Catholic	46	50	46	47
Protestant	41	32	48	41
Presbyterian	4	6	20	7
Lutheran	6	9	7	7
Methodist	6	3	7	6
Baptist	15	3	4	12
Other Protestant	10	11	10	10
Jewish	8	11	2	7
Other, No Preference	5	6	4	5
Total	100%	100%	100%	100%
	(N=294)	(N=34)	(N=85)	(N=413)

2. The figures represent the 1970 and 1972 samples combined. The questions asked to distinguish party preferences were: (1) Generally speaking, do you think of yourself as a Democrat, a Republican, an Independent, or what? (2) (If Independent) Do you think of yourself as being closer to the Republican or Democratic party? Respondents were coded as Democrats or Republicans if they indicated partisanship in answering either question (1) or question (2).

TABLE 3—CORRELATIONS BETWEEN PER CENT DEMOCRATIC VOTE, PERCENTAGE DEMOCRATIC REGISTRATION, AND THE ETHNIC COMPOSITION OF PITTSBURGH'S 423 ELECTION DISTRICTS

	McGovern	Casey	Sloan	Percent Democratic Registration
McGovern	1.00	.94	.77	.62
Casey	.94	1.00	.87	.76
Sloan	.77	.87	1.00	.78
Foreign Stock	−.58	−.46	−.29	−.26
British	−.55	−.56	−.50	−.55
Irish	−.46	−.46	−.38	−.37
German	−.63	−.59	−.46	−.29
Italian	−.30	−.26	−.20	−.14
Polish	−.18	−.06	.08	.20
Black	.84	.75	.55	.47

TABLE 4—MEAN PERCENTAGE DEMOCRATIC VOTE AND DEMOCRATIC REGISTRATION VS. HIGH/LOW ETHNIC DISTRICTS

		McGovern	Casey	Sloan	Democratic Registration
Foreign Stock	H	50	68	67	79
	L	63	73	69	81
British	H	48	65	64	76
	L	66	77	73	85
Irish	H	49	66	64	77
	L	63	75	72	84
German	H	47	65	64	78
	L	67	77	73	83
Italian	H	49	66	65	77
	L	63	75	71	83
Polish	H	51	68	67	80
	L	63	74	69	81
Black	H	67	75	71	82
	L	47	66	65	78

Russian, the ethnic group containing the largest number of first- and second-generation American Jews. Similar, though less spectacular, patterns are found throughout the list of lesser candidates.

Another place where the effects of ethnicity may be measured without interference from partisan considerations is in the primary elections. While we have not as yet engaged in systematic study of recent primaries, Mayor Flaherty's impressive vote in Italian areas this spring, the rejection of the endorsed black councilman, George Shields, and the nomination of all four of the endorsed white councilmen, each receiving nearly equal numbers of votes, suggest that, except for race, ethnicity is unimportant in determining voting choice for well-known candidates.

Two other questions may be raised, however, which we must save for future analysts. All the above data examine only the bivariate relationships between each ethnic characteristic and the vote. It is reasonable to ask about the joint effects of several ethnic variables. For instance, do ethnics in mixed neighborhoods behave differently from those in neighborhoods where they comprise the dominant group? The answers to this sort of question must be sought through multivariate analysis techniques, such as multiple and partial correlation, which are technically beyond the scope of this article.

Finally, we should want to study a series of elections in order to explore whether the trends indicated by the 1972 election data are in fact corroborated by other election years. Unfortunately, Allegheny County began computerizing its district returns only in November 1971, a circumstance which makes research of past elections prohibitively expensive. Computerized results of future elections, however, promise to provide a rich source of data for research into trends in ethnic voting.

How Goes the Renaissance?

A popular way to describe Pittsburgh's Renaissance could be called the "flashback" device.

People will point out, for example, that a spot occupied today by a gleaming skyscraper was, in the 1940s, the site of a dreary, rusting warehouse. Or, they might say the Gateway Center area, which

Robert Voelker, "How Goes the Renaissance: Was It Business Before People?" *Pittsburgh Post-Gazette,* October 16, 1971. Reprinted by permission.

today employs 23,000 persons, provided jobs for only 4,000 in pre-Renaissance days.

Let's look at some other flashbacks.

Flashback one (1950s): A slum house is being torn down in the Lower Hill District. Among the occupants were three unmarried mothers having a total of 21 children.

Later scene (this year): Robert Pease, former official of the Urban Redevelopment Authority, recalls the incident and explains that housing was found for the three families. However, he added:

"But we could not find a way to provide the continuing social services that these kinds of families obviously needed. That was 20 years ago almost, and what's happened to those families and the children I have no idea.

"To that extent, we failed."

Flashback two (again in the 1950s): Workmen demolishing another slum house in the Lower Hill make a horrible discovery in the basement—an armless and legless alcoholic lying in his own excrement.

Later scene (1969): Former Mayor Joseph M. Barr, in his role as chairman of the Redevelopment Authority, signs a report saying:

"The public-private partnership which worked so well for Pittsburgh in the late 1940s has to be made to work as efficiently in behalf of deprived neighborhoods and the people in them. . . ."

Although they're isolated and extreme cases, the flashbacks and later scenes illustrate what some critics regard as serious shortcomings of the Renaissance. They say the main thrust was concentrated on economics at the expense of human development and the living conditions of large segments of the city's population.

Specifically, they charge that business, industrial and institutional interests were served first with the lion's share of resources while, trailing far behind, were housing, job training, work for the so-called hard-core unemployed, education, health and problems associated with poverty and race.

The critics would say the pitiful stump of a man found in the Hill District basement wasn't even in the Renaissance picture. He was just something they stumbled onto while clearing land for the Civic Arena.

And, they could regard as significant that as late in the game as 1969 Barr found it necessary to say the Renaissance "has to be made to work" for poor people.

Especially ignored by the Renaissance planners, some critics say, were problems of racial discrimination in employment and housing. Indeed, they say segregation patterns actually worsened because of the Renaissance.

In sum, they say the Renaissance's direct impact on poor people was either non-existent or detrimental; thus, those who needed the most got the least.

The criticism gained some support from a recent public study which declared that a startling 25 per cent of the residents in the six-county Pittsburgh region are existing below the poverty level.

The report issued by the Citizen's Advisory Committee of the Southwestern Pennsylvania Regional Planning Commission classified 161,000 families, or approximately 500,000 persons, as poverty-ridden. Nearly 23 per cent of all households in Allegheny County were adjudged to be poor. Of the six-county figure, two-thirds of the poor families live in Allegheny County.

The report said:

"The economically disadvantaged citizens of the region have not shared in the area's general progress and have not benefitted proportionately from public investments in new facilities. . . . They have not shared equally in the benefits of investments in highways, transit, utilities and open space."

Norman Howenstein, the commission's comprehensive planning director, praised the Renaissance for improving the city's tax base and making the city more attractive to investors, but said it followed an historical pattern here of deferring human programs and projects.

Although not a Renaissance critic as such, Howenstein made this observation:

"There's been a historic process of decay and neglect here. And there's been inordinate emphasis placed upon productivity and economic stability to the jeopardy of human conditions and environmental circumstances.

"I believe the Renaissance marked the first point in our history when something was actually done to begin to correct some of these deficiencies and I think that many of the human problems have yet to be tackled."

Using housing as one example, Howenstein said the city has built about 10,000 units of public housing since 1949, but said nearly 52,000 families are currently eligible for public housing under the accepted poverty criterion.

"Which means," he went on, "that for every five families there's only one unit available. Now, it gets worse if you look at Allegheny County. The ratio is 14 families for every unit."

Not even the most severe critic questions the premise that strenuous efforts had to be made in the 1940s and 1950s to rebuild the Downtown area. That was the way to keep the big corporations here; and from the corporations flowed vital paycheck dollars.

However, one of them, James V. Cunningham, argues that a better balance should have been struck between resources poured into economic-centered development and those allotted to human development. Also, he contends, large amounts of money were "going Downtown" while other city neighborhoods were neglected and became bleak and rundown.

Cunningham, author of two books, a Pitt professor and recent unsuccessful candidate for City Council, studied renewal efforts here and in three other cities. He pointed out that New Haven, Conn., split its resources about 50-50 and, as a result, succeeded much better than Pittsburgh in human areas.

As an example of the way things were done differently in New Haven, Cunningham said in an interview:

"They pioneered very early in employment programs and training programs and new kinds of community schools. Even their elementary schools were built like little campuses that were tied into the neighborhood with 24 hour use; and neighborhood recreation and health services as well as education were a part of those campuses."

However, renewal efforts here, he went on, followed the pattern of giving priority to jobs and corporations, adding:

"It seems to me [the late Mayor David L.]Lawrence accepted too readily the plans of business without being critical; without looking at alternatives and without seeing there was a better way to do it. He had the power to force it to be done differently."

Part of the decline of some city neighborhoods stemmed from the Renaissance itself, Cunningham said, explaining:

"The highways and other public works dislocated large numbers of people and accelerated the decay and the splitting up of many neighborhoods and cast a shadow over real estate in a lot of areas.

"One of the best examples of that is the East Street Valley. And, it's happening now in Hazelwood where they've been fiddling around with highway plans for ten or eleven years and Second Avenue is just falling to pieces because nobody wants to invest any money until they know just what the plans will be."

Cunningham and others say Renaissance leaders failed to deal with the problem of discrimination against blacks.

Moaned Byrd Brown, president of the local chapter of the National Association for the Advancement of Colored People: "The acquiring of property was the single most important factor in creating black ghettos. The Renaissance caused more segregated schools and more segregated communities, and as segregation developed the level of understanding (in the communities) tended to diminish."

Also noting the new racial patterns induced by the Renaissance, Bernard H. Jones, community activity adviser for the Allegheny Conference on Community Development, explained: "Whites had a place to go, but the blacks didn't have too many places to go so they were pushed into small areas."

As an example, he pointed out that Fifth Avenue High School was about half black and half white when he was graduated from there in 1949; and today it's virtually all black. With a snap of the finger, he added: "Westinghouse High turned from white to black just like that."

Pease, the former URA official who now is executive director of the Allegheny Conference, acknowledged that the Lower Hill renewal project worsened segregation elsewhere. He said: "The Lower Hill project removed 1,000 units which were occupied by black people. And, there was not in the city of Pittsburgh any additional new units earmarked for those people. So it caused a tightening of segregation in black neighborhoods and to that extent the renewal program contributed to segregation."

Pease remarked, however, that not even the sociologists were alert enough to spot the trend as it was developing. "We have to learn by doing," he said.

Although the tightening of segregation was a negative result, Pease said, studies made by Pitt and Chatham College showed that some 85 per cent of the families removed from the Lower Hill found new homes "far superior to the housing they formerly occupied."

Not only were blacks uprooted, said Brown, but some seeking new homes were victimized by private real estate interests, explaining: "Old houses in Homewood were selling at exorbitant prices, and rents were exorbitant. It would be interesting to compare what some houses were selling for in Homewood compared with houses selling in, say Green Tree, at the same time."

Cunningham deplored racial discrimination in Renaissance construction jobs, recalling: "Here were all these buildings going up, and out-of-town people were working in a lot of the jobs. The trades ran out of iron workers, and they ran out of electricians from this area. So they were drawing them in from other states. And, here were those unemployed blacks who couldn't even get to work on these Renaissance buildings."

Brown lamented the fact Renaissance planners failed to "build in some kind of arrangement that the great corporations would have become concerned with solving the problems of race and poverty," stating that only 16 per cent of Pittsburgh was black then and the problems were not overwhelming.

"It could have been a fantastically great thing," he declared.

Echoing Brown's remarks, John J. Grove, assistant director of the Allegheny Conference, said: "I think that perhaps here in Pittsburgh we were more complacent about it [plight of blacks] for too long because we did not have the in-migration from the South that affected Philadelphia, Cleveland and Chicago on the direct rail route to the north. We certainly should have taken steps much earlier to provide here an open society which now is being achieved."

Pease defends the Renaissance's high-level economic spearhead. However, he said the conference has been shifting gears in the last few years, undertaking programs to put "money in a man's pocket." Also, he said, the conference recognizes now that social, physical and economic programs must be interwoven.

As to his overall defense of the Renaissance, he declared flatly: "A significant number of families are living better than they lived before in housing and jobs." He went on: "If I were a citizen in one of the slum areas of Pittsburgh," he continued, "and I looked at the shiny new buildings Downtown and at my own surroundings, I would be apt to say, 'Oh look, the big shots are doing everything for themselves and nothing for me.' It's a very easy thing to say and a very popular thing to say from that context.

"On the other hand, if I were able to pull myself apart from the city and look at the whole city without being emotionally involved, and then if I can remember what Pittsburgh was 30 years ago, I would recognize that had it not been for the purification of the air, the improvements of the rivers, the new industrial expansion, the office building construction in Downtown Pittsburgh, we wouldn't have as many companies in Pittsburgh as we do now.

"And, I have to say there is a direct relationship between having viable, growing companies in a city like Pittsburgh and its social services that are essential. Without the companies and the profit they make, there can be no United Fund, no social agencies, no tax base, and therefore I think that it's absolutely imperative to say that we did this right and to continue on this same pattern."

As to the future, Pease said: "I suspect the conference will recognize that no program by itself really accomplishes anything. You can't have a housing program by itself. You can't have an employment program by itself. You can't have a social renaissance program by itself. All these have to move forward hand-in-hand if we're going to get good results.

"The one thing we've learned from the employment and economic development programs is that perhaps the programs that relate to action that results in money in a man's pocket are maybe more important than the old-fashioned social programs by themselves."

With this goal in mind, the conference currently is involved with two employment programs: one to place the long-term unemployed in jobs; the other to help minority group members, principally blacks, establish businesses.

In the job placement program, carried out in conjunction with the National Alliance of Businessmen, some 200 volunteers fan through a four-county area each year, asking some 2,500 companies to pledge 10 per cent of its new jobs to the long-termed unemployed.

Pease said more than 10,000 persons have been placed in jobs over a three-year period with a dropout rate (workers lasting on the job less than six months) of 41 per cent.

"This means our retention rate is 59 per cent, and in this program that happens to be the highest in the United States," Pease said. He added: "What the businessmen have found is that hiring the so-called hard-core unemployed has been no different than hiring anyone else. You find good people and bad people. You find good work habits and bad work habits."

The small business program is being carried out jointly by the conference, four local banks and the federal Small Business Administration. Grove said more than 300 black-owned businesses have received loans or commitments totaling $7,411,000 as of last June 30, and actual disbursements as of that date amounted to $3,550,000.

Noting the city's late entry into the human renaissance, Grove had this to say: "I think we had to wait until all this ferment came to a focal point, and it was really triggered by the assassination of Martin Luther King in April of 1968. We had begun to deal with this problem prior to that tragic assassination.

"You could look back, too, as far as the physical renaissance is concerned and some critics might say we should have started before the mid-1940s. But, the time wasn't ripe. The crisis hadn't deepened sufficiently, and I think that was true in the human field. The crisis was not that stark, and as soon as it became that deep and all-consuming, then we did get into it."

Also defending the way the Renaissance was carried out was John T. Mauro, city planning chief in the Barr administration, and now associate director of development for the Allegheny Conference.

Mauro said the only public expenditures in the Gateway project was about $600,000 for the widening and construction on Liberty Avenue and for some sewer and water lines.

"There's an incredible lack of knowledge about how these projects were funded," said Mauro. "To date there's been close to $200 million in private money invested in Gateway Center compared with $600,000 the city put into it.

"Actually, there's been very little public investment compared to the private investment that made the Downtown healthier than it's ever been in its life. It was a tremendous bargain."

APPENDIXES

Population Trends in Pittsburgh and
Allegheny County, 1840-1940
by Bertram J. Black and Aubrey Mallach

One hundred years ago the City of Pittsburgh consisted of the present Triangle and the land east of it to a line running roughly from where 11th Street now reaches the Allegheny River to the point where the Liberty Bridge crosses the Monongahela River. Almost every decade since 1840 saw the area of the city expand by the annexation of adjoining areas. The most recent of these annexations took place in 1930 and 1931 when small parts of Penn, Mifflin, Baldwin and Reserve Townships were incorporated into Pittsburgh.

To show the growth of population in Pittsburgh during the last century by a continuous line would therefore be quite misleading. The number of additional persons in the city, as shown by the decennial census, has obviously been far greater than the increase by birth and migration in any specific area defined either by the inclusion or exclusion of annexations.

The annexations since 1820 and the resulting population increases are shown in the accompanying map and chart. The boundaries of Allegheny County have remained unchanged since 1800. The figures showing population increases in the county as a whole are the result

Population Trends in Allegheny County (Federation of Social Agencies of Pittsburgh and Allegheny County (April 1944), pp. 1–2, 4, 7. Reprinted by permission of the Health & Welfare PLANNING Association.

of actual additions to the population by excess of births and in-migration over deaths and out-migration and not to the inclusion of persons not previously counted.

As may be seen from the following table, the century ending in 1940 saw the population of Allegheny County grow from 81,235 to 1,411,539, more than 17 times its earlier size. In the same century, the Pittsburgh population grew from 21,115 to 671,659, almost 32 times its size in 1840.

TABLE I—GROWTH OF POPULATION, ALLEGHENY COUNTY AND PITTSBURGH 1840–1940

Year	Allegheny County	Per cent Increase in Preceding Decade	City of Pittsburgh	Per cent Increase in Preceding Decade	Allegheny County Outside Pittsburgh	Per cent Increase in Preceding Decade	Per cent Allegheny County Population in Pgh.
1940	1,411,539	2.7	671,659	0.3	739,880	5.0	47.6
1930	1,374,410	15.9	699,817	13.8	704,593	17.9	48.6
1920	1,185,808	16.4	588,343	10.2	597,465	23.3	49.6
1910	1,018,463	31.4	533,905	66.0	484,558	6.9	52.5
1900	775,058	40.4	321,616	34.8	453,442	44.7	41.5
1890	551,959	55.1	238,617	52.6	313,342	59.5	43.3
1880	355,869	35.7	156,389	81.7	196,480	11.6	43.8
1870	262,204	46.6	86,076	74.9	176,128	35.9	32.9
1860	178,831	29.3	49,217	5.6	129,614	41.4	27.5
1850	138,290	70.2	46,601	120.7	91,689	52.5	33.7
1840	81,235	—	21,115	—	60,120	—	26.0

The more rapid growth of Pittsburgh in relation to the county, as a result of migration and births as well as of annexations, continued up to 1910. In 1840, the population of Pittsburgh constituted 26.0 per cent of the total population of Allegheny County; in 1910 it was 52.5 per cent of the county total.

Actually, the figure for 1910 indicates not the peak of the proportion that the population of Pittsburgh was of the total population, but the early part of a decline. The City of Allegheny was annexed to Pittsburgh in 1907. If its population in 1900 were added to the Pittsburgh population in that year, the total would be 451,512 or 58.3 per cent of the total county population. The decrease to 52.5 per cent in 1910 was the beginning of a trend of a decreasing rate of increase which has continued through 1940.

The overall trend of a diminishing rate of increase in the county as a whole has not necessarily been applicable to the various civil divisions of the county, whose individual trends will be discussed later. Nor does the overall trend apply to the various nativity groups. For instance, as is shown in Table II, there has been an actual decrease in the foreign-born population in the county since 1910, the greatest decrease taking place between 1930 and 1940.

TABLE II—POPULATION OF ALLEGHENY COUNTY BY RACE, NATIVITY AND AGE GROUPS   1900–1940

	1900	1910	1920	1930	1940
Total population[1]	775,058	1,018,463	1,185,808	1,374,410	1,411,539
Native white of native parentage	283,974	369,561	460,794	583,116)	
Native white of foreign parentage	271,915	342,932	422,387	478,739)	1,141,770
Foreign-born white	191,141	271,350	248,581	227,536	179,352
Negro	27,753	34,217	53,517	83,326	90,060
Under 15 years of age	—	310,992	378,374[2]	402,535	323,595
21 and over	—	591,756	689,950	814,726	926,113
21 to 44	—	—	471,060	523,346	550,716
45 and over	—	—	218,890	290,380	375,397

1. Including persons of "other races" and persons of "unknown age."
2. Taking half the group 14 to 15 years old, inclusive, to be 14 years of age.

PER CENT CHANGE

	1900 to 1910	1910 to 1920	1920 to 1930	1930 to 1940
Total population	31.4	16.4	15.9	2.7
Native white of native parentage	30.1	24.7	25.6)	7.5
Native white of foreign parentage	26.1	23.2	13.3)	
Foreign-born white	42.0	−8.4	−8.5	−21.2
Negro	23.3	56.4	55.7	8.1
Under 15 years of age	—	21.7	6.4	−19.6
21 and over	—	16.7	18.1	13.7
21 to 44	—	—	11.1	5.2
45 and over	—	—	32.7	29.3

Note: Per cent change is increase unless designated by minus sign.

The great increase in Negro population occurred between 1910 and 1930, over which period it more than doubled. This growth of Negro population, coinciding with the decrease in foreign-born, might have resulted from replacement of the foreign-born laborers in the steel industry by Negroes. The halt in immigration resulting from the first World War came at the same time as the demand for more labor in the steel mills as a result of that war. The southern Negro was the most available substitute for the Central European immigrant who no longer was available in adequate numbers.

The native white population increased in each decade. In the decade between 1920 and 1930, the rate of increase of the native population of foreign parentage fell considerably, reflecting probably the decrease in the number of foreign-born which took place in the previous decade. In the decade 1930–1940, the native white population of foreign or mixed parentage in Pittsburgh showed a decrease.

By the end of the century 1840–1940, the great changes in population, both in regard to total population and in regard to the various groups included in it, seem to have ended. Allegheny County entered the 1940's with a population comparatively stabilized in size.

CITY OF PITTSBURGH, POPULATION SIZE,
CHANGE AND DISTRIBUTION, 1930–1970

CITY OF PITTSBURGH

Year	Population	Change from Preceding Census	Percentage Change
1930	669,817	81,474	13.8
1940	671,659	1,842	0.3
1950	676,806	5,147	0.8
1960	604,332	−72,474	−10.7
1970	520,117	−84,215	−13.9

CITY OF PITTSBURGH, POPULATION CHANGES
1950–1960–1970, BY THE THREE MAJOR AREAS

	East of the Rivers	South of the Rivers	North of the Rivers	Total
1950 population	360,161	184,536	132,109	676,806
percentage of 1950 population	53.2	27.3	19.5	100.0
1960 population	311,318	183,874	109,140	604,332
percentage of 1960 population	51.5	30.4	18.1	100.0
1970 population	264,904	171,354	83,859	520,117
percentage of 1970 population	50.9	32.9	16.1	100.0
Change 1950–1960	−48,843	−662	−22,969	− 72,474
percent change	−13.6	− .4	−17.4	− 10.7
Change 1960–1970	−46,414	−12,520	−25,281	− 84,215
percent change	−14.9	− 6.8	−23.2	− 13.9
Change 1950–1970	−95,257	−13,182	−48,250	−156,689
percent change	−26.4	− 7.1	−36.5	− 23.2

Pittsburgh, Department of City Planning, *Population and Housing: 1970 U.S. Census.*

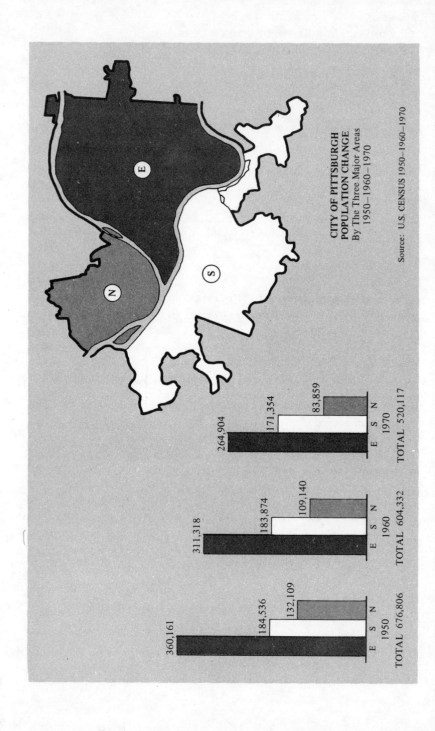

CITY OF PITTSBURGH
POPULATION CHANGE
By The Three Major Areas
1950–1960–1970

Source: U.S. CENSUS 1950–1960–1970

360,161

184,536

132,109

E   S   N
1950

TOTAL 676,806

311,318

183,874

109,140

E   S   N
1960

TOTAL 604,332

264,904

171,354

83,859

E   S   N
1970

TOTAL 520,117

CITY OF PITTSBURGH, ALLEGHENY COUNTY OUTSIDE OF THE CITY OF PITTSBURGH AND STANDARD METROPOLITAN STATISTICAL AREA (SMSA) OUTSIDE OF ALLEGHENY COUNTY, COMPARED 1960–1970

	SMSA	Percentage Change Over Preceding Census	Allegheny County	Percentage Change Over Preceding Census	City of Pittsburgh	Percentage Change Over Preceding Census	% of SMSA
1970	2,401,245	–0.2	1,605,016	–1.4	520,117	–13.9	21.7
1960	2,405,435	8.7	1,628,587	7.5	604,332	–10.7	25.1

	SMSA Outside of Allegheny County	Percentage Change Over Preceding Census	Allegheny County Outside of Pittsburgh	Percentage Change Over Preceding Census	City of Pittsburgh		% of Allegheny County
1970	796,229	2.5	1,084,899	5.9			32.4
1960	776,848	11.3	1,024,255	22.2			37.1

Pittsburgh, Department of City Planning, *Population and Housing: 1970 U.S. Census.*

CITY OF PITTSBURGH, GENERAL POPULATION CHARACTERISTICS, 1960–1970

Race	1960	1970	Change	Percent of Total 1960	Percent of Total 1970	Percentage Change
Total	604,332	520,117	−84,215	100.0	100.0	−13.9
White	502,593	412,280	−90,313	83.2	79.3	−18.0
Negro	100,692	104,904	4,212	16.7	20.2	4.2
Other	1,047	2,933	1,886	.1	.5	180.1
Age						
Male Total	289,318	242,343	−46,975	47.9	46.7	−16.2
Under 5	29,546	17,672	−11,874	4.9	3.4	−40.2
5−9	26,844	20,564	−6,280	4.4	4.0	−23.4
10−14	24,136	22,844	−1,292	4.0	4.4	−5.4
15−19	19,299	23,658	4,359	3.2	4.5	22.6
20−24	16,854	20,267	3,413	2.8	3.9	20.2
25−34	35,608	25,370	−10,238	5.9	4.9	−28.7
35−44	38,369	24,802	−13,567	6.3	4.8	−35.4
45−54	37,375	30,671	−6,704	6.2	5.9	−17.9
55−59	16,249	14,998	−1,251	2.7	2.9	−7.7
60−64	14,541	12,935	−1,606	2.4	2.5	−11.0
65−74	21,501	18,399	−3,102	3.6	3.5	−14.4
75+	8,996	10,163	1,167	1.5	2.0	13.0
Female Total	315,014	277,774	−37,240	52.2	53.3	−11.8
Under 5	28,555	17,054	−11,501	4.7	3.3	−40.2
5−9	26,293	19,966	−6,327	4.4	3.8	−24.1
10−14	23,899	22,451	−1,448	4.0	4.3	−6.1
15−19	22,211	25,183	2,972	3.7	4.8	13.3
20−24	20,377	24,971	4,594	3.4	4.8	22.5
25−34	37,274	27,490	−9,784	6.2	5.3	−26.2
35−44	43,661	28,561	−15,100	7.2	5.5	−34.6
45−54	41,593	36,532	−5,061	6.9	7.0	−12.2
55−59	18,022	17,878	−144	3.0	3.4	−.8
60−64	16,018	16,216	198	2.6	3.1	1.2
65−74	25,003	25,366	363	4.1	4.9	1.5
75+	12,108	16,106	3,998	2.0	3.1	33.0

Pittsburgh, Department of City Planning, *Population and Housing: 1970 U.S. Census*.

CITY OF PITTSBURGH GENERAL POPULATION CHARACTERISTICS, 1960–1970

Age	1960	1970[1]	Change	Percent of Total Nonwhite 1960	Percent of Total Nonwhite 1970[1]	Percentage Change
Male						
Nonwhite Total	49,277	48,788	−489	48.4	46.5	−1.0
Under 5	6,254	4,981	−1,273	6.1	4.7	−20.4
5–14	10,266	11,600	1,334	10.1	11.1	13.0
15–24	5,844	8,052	2,208	5.7	7.7	37.8
25–34	6,155	4,440	−1,715	6.0	4.2	−27.9
35–44	6,379	4,947	−1,432	6.3	4.7	−22.4
45–54	5,609	5,359	−250	5.5	5.1	−4.5
55–64	5,060	4,453	−607	5.0	4.2	−12.0
65+	3,710	4,956	1,246	3.6	4.7	33.6
Female						
Nonwhite Total	52,462	56,116	3,654	51.6	53.5	7.0
Under 5	6,223	4,813	−1,410	6.1	4.6	−22.7
5–14	10,282	11,827	1,545	10.1	11.3	15.0
15–24	7,140	9,406	2,266	7.0	9.0	31.7
25–34	7,413	6,193	−1,220	7.3	5.9	−16.5
35–44	7,408	6,731	−677	7.3	6.4	−9.1
45–54	5,948	6,509	561	5.8	6.2	9.4
55–64	4,582	5,094	512	4.5	4.9	11.2
65+	3,466	5,543	2,077	3.4	5.3	59.9

1. Excludes "Other Races."

**RACIAL CHARACTERISTICS OF THE POPULATION: TOTAL POPULA-
TION BY RACE, CITY OF PITTSBURGH, ALLEGHENY COUNTY OUT-
SIDE OF THE CITY OF PITTSBURGH AND SMSA OUTSIDE OF ALLE-
GHENY COUNTY, COMPARED 1960 AND 1970**

1960	City of Pittsburgh	Allegheny County Outside of the City of Pittsburgh	SMSA Outside of Allegheny County
Total population	604,332	1,024,255	776,848
White[1]	503,640	990,825	749,470
% of total population	83.3	96.7	96.5
Black	100,692	33,430	27,378
% of total population	16.7	3.3	3.5
1970			
Total population	520,117	1,084,899	796,229
White[1]	415,213	1,045,258	770,890
% of total population	79.8	96.4	96.8
Black	104,904	39,641	25,339
% of total population	20.2	3.6	3.2

1. Includes "Other Races."

Pittsburgh, Department of City Planning, *Population and Housing: 1970 U.S. Census*.

TOTAL EMPLOYMENT BY MAJOR INDUSTRY GROUP IN THE SOUTHWESTERN PENNSYLVANIA REGION, WITH PERCENTAGE DISTRIBUTION BY COUNTY, SELECTED YEARS, 1940–1960

Industry group	Year	Number of employees, The Region (in thousands)	Percent of regional total						
			Total	Allegheny County	Armstrong County	Beaver County	Butler County	Washington County	Westmoreland County
All industries, total	1940	711.5	100.0	66.0	3.2	6.9	3.7	8.9	12.2
	1950	865.9	100.0	66.5	3.0	7.5	3.6	8.3	12.1
	1958[a]	895.4	100.0	68.7	2.1	8.5	3.5	6.4	10.8
	1960	893.7	100.0	64.6	2.6	7.9	4.3	7.9	12.6
Agriculture, forestry and fisheries	1940	21.3	100.0	18.0	11.9	7.7	20.7	20.5	21.2
	1950	16.9	100.0	19.3	10.9	7.4	18.8	21.5	22.1
	1958[a]	10.3	100.0	13.8	10.2	7.6	20.5	21.0	26.8
	1960	10.8	100.0	21.7	11.6	5.7	17.1	20.1	23.8
Mining	1940	46.2	100.0	24.9	9.8	1.0	5.7	34.3	24.3
	1950	36.9	100.0	23.5	10.6	1.2	6.1	35.7	22.9
	1958[a]	14.9	100.0	27.2	10.6	1.2	7.2	38.5	15.2
	1960	13.5	100.0	30.8	9.3	1.9	6.4	35.4	16.2
Contract construction	1940	29.0	100.0	70.3	3.9	4.0	3.3	7.3	11.2
	1950	46.8	100.0	70.1	2.1	5.5	4.0	7.4	10.9
	1958[a]	41.5	100.0	73.7	2.8	5.2	4.2	4.3	9.8
	1960	45.9	100.0	64.2	2.9	5.7	5.4	8.8	13.0

TOTAL EMPLOYMENT BY MAJOR INDUSTRY GROUP IN THE SOUTHWESTERN PENNSYLVANIA REGION
WITH PERCENTAGE DISTRIBUTION BY COUNTY, SELECTED YEARS, 1940–1960 (Continued)

Industry group	Year	Number of employees, The Region (in thousands)	Total	Allegheny County	Armstrong County	Beaver County	Butler County	Washington County	Westmoreland County
								Percent of regional total	
Manufacturing	1940	261.3	100.0	63.5	2.8	10.7	3.1	6.7	13.3
	1950	326.5	100.0	62.2	3.0	11.3	3.0	6.8	13.7
	1958[a]	330.2	100.0	63.9	1.8	13.9	3.0	5.4	12.1
	1960	331.7	100.0	58.6	2.8	11.5	4.3	7.8	15.0
Transportation, communication, and utilities	1940	57.3	100.0	73.6	2.0	6.0	2.4	6.5	9.6
	1950	79.2	100.0	71.3	2.2	6.6	2.4	7.0	10.5
	1958[a]	71.2	100.0	72.0	2.4	5.7	2.7	6.0	11.2
	1960	68.2	100.0	68.0	2.5	7.0	3.5	7.2	11.8
Wholesale and retail trade	1940	120.0	100.0	74.1	2.2	5.2	3.0	6.6	8.9
	1950	159.7	100.0	72.5	2.2	5.5	3.3	6.6	9.9
	1958[a]	189.0	100.0	72.9	1.9	5.9	3.4	6.4	9.6
	1960	159.4	100.0	68.7	2.5	6.0	4.1	7.2	11.5
Finance, insurance, and real estate	1940	21.8	100.0	83.7	1.0	3.3	1.9	4.2	5.8
	1950	27.4	100.0	81.6	1.2	3.6	2.2	4.4	7.0
	1958[a]	38.8	100.0	83.8	1.0	3.5	2.4	3.6	5.7
	1960	33.9	100.0	78.1	1.3	4.6	2.9	5.0	8.1

Appendixes

277

TOTAL EMPLOYMENT BY MAJOR INDUSTRY GROUP IN THE SOUTHWESTERN PENNSYLVANIA REGION
WITH PERCENTAGE DISTRIBUTION BY COUNTY, SELECTED YEARS, 1940–1960 (Continued)

Industry group	Year	Number of employees, The Region (in thousands)	Total	Percent of regional total					
				Allegheny County	Armstrong County	Beaver County	Butler County	Washington County	Westmoreland County
Business, personal, and professional services	1940	122.9	100.0	72.0	2.2	5.1	3.3	7.1	10.4
	1950	136.1	100.0	71.3	2.1	5.4	4.0	7.0	10.2
	1958[a]	166.9	100.0	73.0	1.8	5.6	3.6	6.1	9.8
	1960	167.0	100.0	69.7	2.0	6.0	4.1	7.4	10.8
Public administration and public safety	1940	21.2	100.0	77.9	1.8	4.2	2.5	6.0	7.6
	1950	27.4	100.0	78.1	1.6	4.4	2.6	5.8	7.5
	1958[a]	32.6	100.0	75.6	1.9	4.9	2.9	6.3	8.3
	1960	31.5	100.0	76.4	1.6	5.0	3.0	6.1	7.9
Industry not reported	1940	10.6	100.0	67.5	2.2	5.3	3.0	6.8	15.2
	1950	9.0	100.0	66.9	4.8	5.8	3.4	9.3	9.8
	1958[a]	–	–	–	–	–	–	–	–
	1960	28.7	100.0	76.6	1.5	5.6	3.2	4.8	8.3

Note: Detail will not necessarily add exactly to totals because of rounding off.

a/ Estimates for 1958 by county of work place. All others are by county of residence.

Source: 1940, 1950, 1960, U.S. Census of Population; 1958, Regional Economic Study, Pittsburgh Regional Planning Association.

Regional Industrial Development Corporation of Southwestern Pennsylvania, *An Overall Program for the Development of Southwestern Pennsylvania: Counties of Allegheny, Armstrong, Beaver, Butler, Washington, Westmoreland* (Pittsburgh, 1963). Reprinted by permission of the Regional Industrial Development Corporation of Southwestern Pennsylvania.

**DOMINANT MANUFACTURING INDUSTRIES IN THE SOUTHWESTERN
PENNSYLVANIA REGION, BY COUNTY, 1960**

County	SIC code	Dominant industry group	Number of persons employed (in thousands)	Percent of county's total manufacturing employment
Allegheny	33	Primary metals [a]	63.7	37.2
Armstrong	32	Stone, clay and glass products [b]	2.6	45.2
Beaver	33	Primary metals [a]	29.5	66.0
Butler	33	Primary metals [a]	3.9	34.8
Washington	33	Primary metals [a]	7.2	39.8
Westmoreland	33	Primary metals [a]	14.2	35.9

a/   Includes blast furnaces, steelworks, and rolling and finishing mills; iron and
        steel foundries; and iron and steel forges.
b/   Includes the manufacture of flat glass, glass containers; pressed and blown
        glassware; and glass products made of purchased glass.
Source: *Pennsylvania Industrial Directory, 1962.*

**EMPLOYMENT IN SOUTHWESTERN PENNSYLVANIA REGION BY
COUNTY, MAJOR OCCUPATIONAL GROUPS, 1960**

	Percentage of Work Force in		
	Manufacturing Industries	White Collar[1]	Other
Allegheny County	33.7	46.3	20.0
Armstrong County	39.6	31.0	29.4
Beaver County	53.8	33.0	13.2
Butler County	37.2	35.0	27.8
Washington County	36.5	33.7	29.8
Westmoreland County	44.1	36.4	19.5

1. Professional, managerial, clerical and sales.
Source: 1960 *U.S. Census of Population.*

CONTRIBUTORS

Pittsburgh in 1802
François André Michaux was the son of André Michaux, the noted French botanist. His visit to Pittsburgh was part of a tour commissioned by the Minister of the Interior to acquire information on American forestry and agriculture.

Pittsburgh in 1821
George W. Ogden was a Quaker merchant from New Bedford, Massachusetts. He passed through Pittsburgh in connection with a two-year business trip to the West.

Pittsburgh in 1866
James Parton was the English-born biographer of Horace Greeley, Aaron Burr, Andrew Jackson, and Benjamin Franklin. His vivid, informative account of Pittsburgh was written shortly after the Civil War, which had greatly accelerated the industrial growth of the city.

PART ONE

The Great Furnace of America
Willard Glazier was an author, soldier, and explorer. His adventures included several escapes from Confederate prisons and a cross-country horseback trip.

The Homestead Strike
T. V. Powderly headed the Knights of Labor from 1879 to 1893. He aspired to the abolition of wage labor through the development of producer cooperatives. The Homestead strike, which he described in his essay, testified to the more practical class- and union-oriented values of Samuel Gompers and the A.F. of L.

Family and Milltown: Homestead
Margaret F. Byington, long affiliated with the Russell Sage Foundation, published extensively on social work and social problems. Her full-length study, *Homestead: The Households of a Mill Town* (New York, 1910), prepared in connection with the Pittsburgh Survey of 1907–08, still ranks as a landmark in social research and community analysis.

The Immigrant Worker
Peter Roberts was Secretary for Immigration, Industrial Department, International Committee of the YMCA. Following the Pittsburgh Survey, he investigated conditions in the anthracite coal communities of Pennsylvania. (The Pittsburgh region produced bituminous coal.)

The Negro Migrant
Abraham Epstein's study of the black worker originated as a master's thesis at the University of Pittsburgh. He became one of the nation's leading advocates of old-age pensions in the 1920s and the organizer of the American Association for Social Security.

Steel Industry and Steel Worker
John Andrews Fitch was an economist specializing in labor relations. He served as editor of the Industrial Department of the social work magazine *Survey,* 1911–19, and was a member of the faculty of the New York School of Social Work, 1917–46. His full-length account of working conditions in the steel industry, *The Steel Workers* (New York, 1911), was one of the six volumes of the Pittsburgh Survey.

The Smoky City
John T. Holdsworth was an economist and the author of several studies on money and banking. He was the principal investigator for the Economic Survey of Pittsburgh from which the selection on smoke control is drawn. The study had been sponsored by the city council as a means of identifying conditions affecting the city's economic and industrial prosperity.

Housing Problems
F. Elisabeth Crowell, a social worker, was secretary of the Tenement House Committee of the New York Charity Organization Society. The investigations of Pittsburgh's housing conditions by the Survey staff were made under the direction of Lawrence Veiller, the nation's leading housing authority.

Children's Play
Beulah Kennard was president of the Pittsburgh Playground Association, 1906–14, and an organizer and director of the Playground Association of America. The recreational reform movements of the early twentieth century were often conceived as instruments of social control—a means of socializing the children of the immigrant and working-class population.

Adult Play: Commercialized Vice
James Forbes was secretary, Mendicancy Committee, of the New York Charity Or-

ganization Society, 1900–09. During Seth Low's administration as mayor of New York, Forbes had led a drive against professional beggars.

PART TWO

The Economics of Maturity
Glenn E. McLaughlin and Ralph J. Watkins were members of the Economics Department of the University of Pittsburgh and were associated with its Bureau of Business Research. The Bureau sponsored numerous studies of economic conditions in the Pittsburgh region.

The Steel Strike of 1919: Intimidation
S. Adele Shaw was a social worker and journalist. A native Pittsburgher, she had been a member of the Survey staff in 1907–08. In his investigations of the steel worker at that time, John Fitch had also found evidence of intimidation.

Pittsburgh Newspapers and the Steel Strike of 1919
The Commission of Inquiry had been established by the Interchurch World Movement to examine problems of industrial unrest in general and the steel strike of 1919 in particular. The commission's chairman was Francis J. McConnell, bishop of the Methodist Episcopal Church.

The Immigrant Community and the Steel Strike of 1919
David J. Saposs, a labor historian and economist, later served as chief economist to the National Labor Relations Board and World War II Production Board.

The Ethnic Community
Philip Klein was on the faculty of the New York School of Social Work. He was the author of studies on unemployment, penology, and family social work. The social survey of Pittsburgh, which he directed in the 1930s, concentrated more on social welfare agencies and their administration than the Survey of 1907–08.

Is Pittsburgh Civilized?
R. L. Duffus was an author and member of the editorial staff of *The New York Times*, 1937–62. A similar critique of Pittsburgh in the 1930s was written by Dwight Macdonald ("Pittsburgh: What a City Shouldn't Be," *Forum*, 100 [1938]).

Planning in Pittsburgh
Frederick Bigger, an architect by profession, was long associated with the Pittsburgh City Planning Commission and served as its chairman from 1934 to 1954. He was instrumental in keeping the planning movement alive in Pittsburgh during the interwar years.

PART THREE

A New Civic Elite
This article in *Fortune Magazine* describes the dismal environmental and social condition of Pittsburgh following World War II and the catalytic role of Richard K. Mellon in launching the Renaissance.

David Lawrence: Boss of the Mellon Patch

Large-scale urban redevelopment in Pittsburgh depended upon the cooperation of the Democratic political machinery under the leadership of David Lawrence. Lawrence's political career, and the symbiotic relationship that he developed with the Republican corporate elite, are examined by Frank Hawkins, a former editor of *The Pittsburgh Press*.

The Renaissance: A Catalogue of Projects

Park H. Martin had been the Allegheny County planning engineer in the 1930s and played a pivotal role in the postwar Renaissance as executive director of the Allegheny Conference on Community Development. He describes the three most important features of the early Renaissance: smoke control, flood control, and redevelopment of the Golden Triangle (Central Business District).

ACTION-Housing: The Building of East Hills Park

ACTION-Housing's innovative experiments in the financing and design of moderate cost housing were embodied in East Hills Park. Inadvertently, East Hills would also demonstrate some of the difficult social and managerial problems involved in the provision of such housing.

ACTION-Housing: Cora Street: An Experiment in Rehabilitation

Disillusionment with the bulldozer approach to urban renewal stimulated interest in the 1970s in the alternative strategy of housing rehabilitation. As a result of ACTION-Housing's Cora Street experiment, the Allegheny Housing Rehabilitation Corporation was created in 1968.

ACTION-Housing: Neighborhood Urban Extension: An Experiment in Citizen Participation

ACTION-Housing's neighborhood urban extension program was a significant experiment in community organization aimed at devising techniques to encourage participation in neighborhood affairs.

Civil Disorder, 1968

Following the civil disorders of April 5–12, 1968, Mayor Joseph Barr appointed a special task force consisting of city agency heads and two councilmen to investigate the causes of the riots and to recommend remedial programs.

Civil Disorder and Neighborhood Power

James Cunningham, a member of the faculty of the School of Social Work, University of Pittsburgh, had been executive director of the Hyde Park-Kenwood Community Conference in the 1950s. He came to Pittsburgh as associate director of ACTION-Housing to aid in the development of its neighborhood programs. Cunningham consistently favored neighborhood revitalization as the basis for community organization in the urban setting.

Ethnic Discontent

The resentments of Pittsburgh's blue-collar and ethnic population in 1969 would find expression, three years later, in the elections of 1972.

Ethnicity and Voting

Although traditional patterns of ethnic voting were changing, ethnicity remained a significant factor in party composition and voting. The article by Michael Margolis and George H. Foster concentrates upon the Democratic party and ethnic allegiances. Margolis is a member of the political science faculty, University of Pittsburgh; Foster was a student in the department.

How Goes the Renaissance?

The Renaissance successfully restored the economic vitality of the Central Business District, but many social problems persisted in the 1970s: employment, housing, discrimination, poverty. These issues were discussed in an article in the *Pittsburgh Post-Gazette.*

INDEX